Also by the author

"No Heroes Welcome," Poem

in

Inspiration in Ink, by Charles J. Palmer & Jacqueline Palmer
Published by Creative Arts & Science Enterprises

"Spider on the Wall," Poem

in

Inspiration in Ink, by Charles J. Palmer & Jacqueline Palmer
Published by Creative Arts & Science Enterprises

"Weep Old Glory," Poem

in

Of Sunlight and Shadows, by Charles J.
Palmer & Jacqueline Palmer
Published by Creative Arts & Science Enterprises

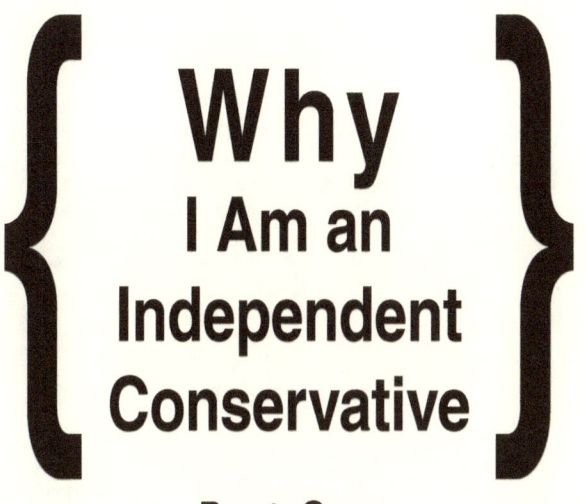

{ Why
I Am an
Independent
Conservative }

Part One

Karen Faith Jourden

iUniverse, Inc.
Bloomington

Why I Am an Independent Conservative

iUniverse books may be ordered through booksellers or by contacting:

iUniverse
1663 Liberty Drive
Bloomington, IN 47403
www.iuniverse.com
1-800-Authors (1-800-288-4677)

ISBN: 978-1-4697-3216-9 (sc)
ISBN: 978-1-4697-3217-6 (e)

Printed in the United States of America

iUniverse rev. date: 10/23/2012

Disclaimer

I am putting in this disclaimer because of the threat of lawsuits that could suppress freedom of speech.

Although every effort is made to assure the accuracy of the information contained in this book, neither Karen F. Jourden nor iUniverse assume any legal liability or responsibility for the accuracy, completeness, or usefulness of any information or process disclosed and are not responsible for the contents of any website pages referenced.

Also, I do not claim to represent anyone or any organization. Nor do I claim that these are the views of anyone other than myself. These are my views only, based on things I have seen, read, heard, observed, studied, and learned through the years.

In memory of my mother, who was always there for me in my struggles growing up. She served in the Navy during World War II. Also, to my husband, a retired veteran who is always supporting me.

Give me twenty-six lead soldiers
and I will conquer the world.

Benjamin Franklin

Contents

Weep Old Glory

Old Glory how you try and stand so tall,
While others try and make you fall.
You use to be the pride of state,
Now it seems all too late.
Can't they see that behind you is our strength?
That your principles are the link.
God was our beginning.
Liberalism will be our ending.
Socialism is their cry.
You only give them a sigh.
Old Glory weep for they wish to destroy you.
Is there nothing we can do?
Life use to be very precious.
Now like the Communist it's to their wishes.
For them right is wrong and wrong is right.
Disaster is clear in sight.
Weep for the country you stand for
As it is savagely being torn.
They deny the truth
And rape you of your roots.
It won't be long before the fall.
May God have mercy on us all.

Preface

I have neither words nor worth nor actions nor utterance nor the power of speech to stir men's blood: I only speak right on.
—Shakespeare

THE QUOTE YOU JUST READ is me. I decided to write this book because of a letter that was sent to the *San Jose Mercury News*. The letter was written by a lady from Santa Cruz, California. She asked if there were any conservative women out there who could explain why they would not get on the liberal bandwagon. Of course, those were not her exact words, but in essence, that was what she was saying. She couldn't understand why conservatives did not give their views.

First, I feel that the *Mercury News* is a very biased paper. Even my liberal friends have told me that they think it leans toward liberalism. Second, most liberals really do not want people to hear the other person's point of view if it is opposite theirs, because you might find out the truth. Therefore, you get only liberals' or moderate conservatives' ideas from the mainstream media. They have become more of a propaganda sheet than a newspaper. I do want to note that since the 1994 election, the *Mercury News* has put more responses from conservatives in their paper. I think this may be because some people were beginning to question why.

Most real conservatives want "just want the facts," as Jack Webb (Sergeant Friday) would say on *Dragnet*. They believe strongly in the Constitution and what our forefathers had in mind. They believe in researching the founding fathers' letters and diaries without taking them out of context, while Democrats and liberals laugh at them and scorn them for believing that. Why?

In this book, I will give a brief history of the Constitution and the Civil War. I feel the Constitution is very important because it is the foundation of our country; not only liberals but some conservatives have been chipping away at it. They have watered it down in our schools. The book will also show how the Bible was used to set up our government. The Civil War is important because liberals used it to create divisions in our country.

Abraham Lincoln said, "The people are the masters of both Congress and courts, not to overthrow the Constitution, but to overthrow the men who pervert it." As you will see, they have been perverting it for some time, and people today may not know it because they do not know the Constitution; our schools are not teaching it like they used to teach it. When a member of the news media read the Declaration of Independence in the streets, many people did not recognize it.[1]

No matter what the Democrats say, we have the right to stand up and express our disapproval of whatever Congress is doing. This does not make us Nazis or whatever those liberal Democrats call people to try and shut them up so they can do whatever they want. This is our constitutional right, and if anyone tries to suppress it, he or she needs to be voted out. This is one of the reasons we have elections, impeachments (which are hard if Congress is covering up), and recalls: to express our disapproval. This was not so in the time of our forefathers, before the Revolution. This book is my way to

---

1   Declaration of Independence, http://www.archives.gov/exhibits/
     charters/declaration_transcript.html

show my disapproval. There are many ways to do this without violence.

I will hit on a few hot topics. I want you to know that some things that happened were not bad, but when you get power-hungry people in government, they have the tendency to take it too far. Liberals of today are not like the liberals of the past. Socialism started to get a foothold in the late 1800s, after the ACLU got started. I will get into their roots later. Like Hippocrates, I say make your own observations. Use your common sense and logic with your research and do not take a paragraph or line out of context, like some people do to make themselves seem right or to discredit someone else. I hope this gets people to think for themselves and understand why we should study history.

I started working on this book in 1995. It was too large, so I split it into two volumes. I am not going to claim I know everything or represent everyone, like some people do to get people on their side. These are only my views, derived from what I've seen, read, heard, observed, and learned throughout my sixty years of life. If any information is wrong, then take it to the source that I got it from. I have taken great pains to make sure my information is correct.

"Train up a child in the way he should go: and when he is old, he will not depart from it"
Proverbs 22:6

Introduction

The moral law is written on the tablets of eternity. For every false word or unrighteous deed, for cruelty and oppression, for lust or vanity, the price has to be paid at last.
—J. A. Troude

I WILL TELL YOU A little about myself. I have been married to my husband for thirty two years since May of 2011. He had been in the Navy since he was seventeen years old. He has the same love for history as I do.

Spending four years in Japan, two weeks in the Philippines, and one day in Hong Kong helped me have a better understanding about people in other lands.

My mother was in the Navy. She entered in when she was sixteen. All of my Uncles on my mom's side were in the service. My dad had been in the Navy, also.

I will always remember my mom getting out the encyclopedia to look things up when she would hear something on TV. She would say, "I don't think that is right." She would have me look up things when I would ask questions. "Check it out." She would say.

First I want to say that I consider myself independent, because I do not vote for people based on whether they are liberal or conservative, male or female, or because of their race. I vote for them if I feel that they have this country's best interest in mind. I try to research as much as I can before I vote for anyone or anything.

When our forefathers came to America, not all of them were poor, of lower social standing, uncultured, and ignorant. Many were educated by their parents using the Bible. Some were educated in prominent European schools. Most came here for religious freedom.

My biggest pet peeve with liberals is when they change history and try to stamp out the important role Christianity and the Bible played in setting up our Constitution and government. They deliberately leave things out and control what is taught. The ACLU, news media, Democrats, and the entertainment industry are the biggest offenders of this. Nowadays, anyone who believes in God is depicted as some crazy nut. George Washington said, "It is impossible to rightly govern the world without God and the Bible."

In 1 Samuel 8, the people came to Samuel and said, "Behold, thou art old, and thy sons walk not in thy ways: now make us a king to judge us like all the nations."

Then the liberals said, "Behold, some of the people do not walk in the Christians' ways, so now it is our turn. We will go in the ways of those overseas."

"And the Lord said unto Samuel, Hearken unto the voice of the people in all that they say unto thee: for they have not rejected thee, but they have rejected me, that I should not reign over them.

"According to all the works which they have done since the day that I brought them up out of Egypt even unto this day, wherewith they have forsaken me, and served other gods, so do they also unto thee."

So the liberals have done just like the Jews did in those times, for they deny the roots of the United States. The Bible was used to help set up our government, and John Locke and Algernon Sydney depended on God to give them wisdom on how to govern our country. However, the liberals seem to say,

"Let's go unto other gods and lie about separation of church and state. Let's take God out of our country. Let's forget how God has blessed us because we followed his ways, for we are wiser than Him."

Jeremiah 6:16 says, "Thus saith the Lord, Stand ye in the ways, and see, and ask for the old paths, where is the good way, and walk therein, and ye shall find rest for your souls. But they said, We will not walk therein." As you can see, America has said, "We will not walk therein," and now we have more troubles with our youth and more crime than ever before. We elect presidents with no morals, who are selfish and pretend that they care. This goes for members of Congress, also.

Liberals have been slowly searing our children from the truth and have been guiding them into a liberal falsehood. Parents have been letting them control what our kids learn and think. Now we have no control because of the laziness of those parents who decided to let schools do the raising and teaching.

Communists always say that if they have a child for the first four to seven years of their lives, they would have them for life. Vladimir Ilyich Lenin said, "Give me four years to teach the children and the seed I have sown will never be uprooted."[2] He got that idea from Karl Marx.

Also, they say the way to destroy the United States is to destroy the family unit using the letters of the alphabet. It looks like they have succeeded. We now have people in Congress passing Socialist ideas. We have even had some claim that they admire dictators who committed mass murder of

---

2   AFRA Front Page News, http://afrafrontpagenews.blogspot. com/2011/04/liberty-quotes_14.html , BBC History, Vladimir Lenin (1870–1924), http://www.bbc.co.uk/history/historic_ figures/lenin_vladimir.shtm , *The Works of Karl Marx.*

people who did not agree with them (Mao).[3] They ignore what the Constitution really says and twist things around to what they want it to mean. We have Supreme Court justices who make laws instead of interpreting them.

Communists (mainly Nazis and Chinese) burned history, literature, and many other books that tied their people to the past and truth. Karl Marx said, "Take away the heritage of a people and they are easily persuaded."[4]

They especially wanted to keep God out of their countries. This is what the ACLU is doing by using the lie that our forefathers did not want God in our government. What our forefathers did *not* want is the government running the churches (the definition of a church is a called-out assembly of believers).

Also, anyone in a Communist country who talks against the government is shot or killed some other way. Sounds familiar: "Hush, Rush, Fox News isn't real news," even though the other news media has the same kind of format. They are now trying to pass a gag law so people are not allowed to speak against the government, which is totally against our Constitution. Instead of using guns to kill them, they use lies instead or make hateful remarks like "I hope someone will tighten the tie around their necks" or "I hope he dies of overcholesterol" (talking about Clarence Thomas).

By the way, have you ever wondered why they go after Republicans for something but not a Democrat who does the

---

3   Diane Watson, "Loves Castro?" http://gollygeeez.blogspot. com/2009/08/la-congresswoman-diane-watsonyou-will.html; Adrienne's Corner, http://adriennescatholiccorner.blogspot. com/2009/10/mao-tse-tung-killed-70-million-people.html ; Andrew Breitbart, Big Government; Dan Freeman, Lessons From Chairman Mao, http://biggovernment.com/dfreeman/2009/10/16/ lessons-from-chairman-mao/

4   *Works of Karl Marx: Scholar's Notebook*. Plymouth, Minnesota, Scholar the Owl, a.k.a. Matt Abe, America in your pocket, http:// mnedreform.blogspot.com/2005/04/america-in-your-pocket.html

same thing? That just shows me that it is not what they did they cared about, it is just because they have a different point of view. I know that Republicans go after Democrats but not to the extent that Democrats go after Republicans. People will not check things out. They just take their word for it.[5]

Other liberals have made remarks about Republicans that showed how they would like them to die. The media just shows what a few "conservatives" do but never play out what a "liberal" does. Look at what they said about the tea parties that have been going on around the country. How about when Democratic congresswomen surrounded Henry Hyde like a pack of wolves? That picture is still vivid to me to this day.

These are hateful remarks, and they have the gall to talk about others. These remarks show me violent tendencies and make me wonder why they want to get guns out of the hands of the citizens. Makes me wonder what kind of person they really are.[6]

In the January 14, 1995, *San Jose Mercury News,* there was an article entitled, "Educators accused of slanting history will reexamine work." It stated that "prominent conservatives" (they did not name them) claimed that the history lessons being taught in the classroom showed liberal bias, slighted well-known American figures, or marginalized Western civilization. Well, of course they do! I heard a liberal woman on TV say that now that they had control of the schools, they can do things their way. If they can tear down American heroes, they can replace them with their heroes, like Mao Zedong, Karl Marx, and others like that.

Gary B. Nash, ACLU member and history professor, said they would look into these accusations that were being made. Well, I am still waiting. I am not surprised that nothing came

5   http://www.freerepublic.com/focus/f-news/2479423/posts
6   The American Life League, Chapter 126. *The American Media: Pro-Abortion, and It Shows,* http://www.ewtn.com/library/PROLENC/ENCYC126.HTM ; Raymond Rivera, Abortion Violence, June 30, 2008, http://abortionviolence.com/0.HTM#SECT8B

of it. The ACLU has been trying to sever our Christian history ties for years. Don't worry, when I get to the ACLU's origin, you will be surprised.

Some schools threaten to ban good books like *Huckleberry Finn,* which merely depicts life during Mark Twain's time. These books are part of history and great literary works.

We should never forget history. We should show the good and the bad, lest we forget the good and repeat the bad. Twain's book does not put down blacks, but it tells it like it was during that time. Do you want history to repeat itself?

Socialism was tried in this country, and people practically started to eat each other. So why are they not teaching that anymore? This is just another way of trying to sever us from our history and put garbage books in, just like the Nazis. This is a way of brainwashing our kids. What was that song they were teaching our kids when President Obama won the election? "Mmm, mmm, mmm, Barack Hussein Obama … Hooray, Mr. President! You're number one!" This is all brainwashing.[7]

When I was in school, my mom claimed that the Democrats said we did not need to learn phonics. Well, that made things difficult for me when it came to the English language. Now they have gone back to teaching phonics after they messed up a few generations.

Liberals have tried to suppress freedom of speech by trying to force conservative talk shows off the air so all you hear is liberal views. I've heard this not only from tapes shown by Rush Limbaugh but also from the news. President Obama said that Fox was not a news station because it had talk shows. Well, the same goes for NBC, ABC, CBS, C-Span, and others, because they not only have talk shows but cooking shows and music shows, also. So isn't that the pot calling the kettle black?

I gave a speech at a Toastmasters meeting, and one of the

---

7   http://yesbuthowever.com/lyrics-to-school-childrens-song-to-
      obama-8136122/

questions I asked was this: "How many of you read the blue pamphlet that explains what laws or things you will be voting on?" Only two people raised their hands (and I was one of them). So don't think you can't be brainwashed. This is why we are in the state we are in.

They also label people they hate with names, knowing that a lot of people are too lazy to check anything out. The Nazis did this to get people to hate not only the Jews but also Gypsies and other groups. Then we ended up with the Holocaust. Liberals now do this with Christians. I want you to stop and push your hatred and bias aside. Listen to the people in Congress. Who does most of the name calling and the pointing of fingers?

I remember my mother saying that when a bully calls someone names, he is trying to hide his own inadequacies. Sometimes it is to hide what he is doing. So do Democrats feel inadequate? Is that why they do all that name calling and pointing of fingers? What are they hiding? Both parties try and pressure someone in their party to force them into voting the way they want and not how their people want them to vote. If they do not vote their way, they get them out by putting something in the news media that would upset the people and they get voted out. You really need to watch with an open mind to see what is really going on.

Now that I have done a long introduction, let's get into the main points of history that I feel need to be straightened out. When I get to the presidents, most of the material will be on the economy, since my major is business administration (heavy in accounting). Also we have a president who is out of control with spending, and no one is putting the brakes on.

Check things out! Do not take anyone's word for it! That includes what I say in this book! I want you to check it out!

History

*Tricks and treachery are the practice of fools, that
don't have brains enough to be honest.*
—Benjamin Franklin

Columbus Day is an area where liberals proceeded to do a character assassination on Christopher Columbus. They dragged it into the schools. I get so tired of liberals running to the schools, using our children for their political games. Then they got native American into this character assassination and to hold demonstrations. Now I am not saying that Columbus was a saint, but neither are they.

Columbus was an Italian sea captain who got Spanish backing to sail to the East Indies. Of course, we all know he ended up here and not the East Indies.

His philosophy was that the world was round and that he could go west to reach the East Indies. Columbus made a total of four voyages, in 1492, 1493, 1497, and 1502. He did not realize that he had found a new land. He called the natives Indians because he thought he was in the Indies.

Now let's set the record straight. In his first voyage, he landed in what is now San Salvador. He explored the Caribbean Islands before sailing back to Spain. His second voyage was in the same area. However, I found discrepancies about his third voyage. Some encyclopedias say he landed in South America, but others say he returned to the same islands. But nowhere in any of the history books or encyclopedias did it say that Columbus visited North America; no one has ever found proof to show that he came here.

Therefore, why would they claim that he was a tyrant to the North American natives? Why would native Americans go along with this farce? Why would the liberals try so hard to say that he had been to the Florida coastline? Could there be something behind this masquerade? Could this be to cause another division here in our country as well as severing our children from the truth? You know the old saying, "United we stand, divided we fall"? They seem to be trying very hard to divide us.

I say this because one of the demonstrators had said something to that affect. After that several people said the same thing to me. Now they just say American Indians but that can be miscued to include North American Indians.

Yes because he founded the area around us it brought in others but everyone talks about how the Spaniards enslaved the Indians but no one talks about how the Indian tribes treated their enemies.

I wish I could go into what the different tribes were doing to each other but I do not have the word count to do so.[8]

Another Italian, John Cabot, claimed North America for the British at the same time Columbus made his third voyage in 1497. So the influx of voyages started from other countries exploring North and South America. America was named after Amerigo Vespucci, who reached the coast of Brazil in 1499.

Since Haiti has been in the news lately, I will point out that it was the first permanent settlement of the Spanish in the New World. They also settled in Florida and California. Spain was primarily interested in gold and converting the natives to Catholicism, by force. The Spaniards enslaved the natives and also imported slaves from Africa. I would like to state here that

---

8   http://en.wikipedia.org/wiki/Columbus_Day

Africans sold Africans along with the pirates to the Spaniards. Later, the Spaniards sold them to the southern Europeans.[9]

Later Spain became weak, and Mexico won their independence. They took Texas and California from Spain. When Mexico started to become weak and the United States wanted to purchase these territories, Mexico refused.

The Mexican government would not allow any more Americans to settle in California because they feared losing Texas and California to the United States. A very understandable thing, since now we fear that Mexico is taking our jobs through illegal immigrants.

In 1848, the Mexican government asked for peace after about three years of war with the United States. The United States paid, let me repeat, the United States paid Mexico $15 million for Texas, California, and all the land in between. They do not teach that in the schools either.[10]

The reason I went into this part of history is because many Mexicans say the United States took California from Mexico. The United States negotiated with Mexico after the Mexican government realized the land could be taken from them. This way, they got paid for the land and the United States did not have to worry about some other country taking the land from Mexico. No other country would have done this but because the United States was founded on Biblical principles, they paid Mexico for the land.

Every year, Mexicans, not only in Mexico but here in the United States, celebrate the day they hope to take this land back from the United States. In some places, our government helps to fund this celebration. It is called *Cinco de Mayo*. Sound familiar? By the way, I am going on what some Mexicans who became US citizens said. Since I do not speak Spanish,

---

9   Columbus and Hattie, *Encyclopedia Britannica,* 1982, 15th edition
10   Treaty of Guadalupe Hidalgo, Answers.com, http://www. answers.com/topic/treaty-of-guadalupe-hidalgo http://www. americanhistory.com/history/ShortHistory/shorthistory11.html

it is hard to do real research, and I do not have the money to hire someone. However, every year during this celebration, a Mexican general crosses over our border with soldiers; it was in the papers. Therefore, I have no doubt that these people are telling the truth. It is something to think about. I bet they would not give that money back that we gave them for the land.

Jumping through history, I was listening to Rush Limbaugh around Thanksgiving some years back. He talked about how the Pilgrims tried Socialism, but they were starving. Then they changed to capitalism and had plenty to eat.

A woman called in and asked, "Wasn't it Jamestown?" Limbaugh did not really respond to the question but continued to tell her about the Pilgrims. This told me that he did not know. Well, I am here to set the record straight for those who are confused.

Many colonists tried Socialism and found themselves starving. The reason Jamestown and the Pilgrims are the most known is because they discovered the importance of owning land and producing for themselves (capitalism). The other colonists died out but they survived because they turned away from Socialism. Do you want to know why our economy is in bad shape? Is not our government stifling capitalism and putting more and more under government and wanting to "distribute the wealth"? The thing is that the government will get more and we will get less, like most Communist and dictatorship countries.

Let's start with Jamestown. Jamestown was settled for the sole purpose of the Virginia Company, a joint stock corporation between Spain and England chartered by the king of England.

Captain John Smith talked about the starving years at Jamestown. Only 60 out of the original 500 settlers survived. Some even went as far as cannibalism. It was even recorded that one man killed his wife and ate her before getting caught.

Smith said the survival of the colony came with the addition of 150 new settlers.

The reason for this was because when the new settlers came, the promoters decided to shift control to the company itself instead of the royal council. Then they established a governor for the colony, with dictatorial powers. The council had forced the colonists to grow what they wanted them to grow. It became a failure. However, the colonists themselves achieved economic success first by experimenting with tobacco plants in 1613, despite the Virginia Company trying to force them to produce a wide run of agricultural and industrial products. In 1616, communally managed land and stock became individually owned. In 1618, a more democratic form of organization was drafted in the colony. Then in 1619 came the beginning of a representative form of government in the colony.

Even though the Virginia Company went bankrupt and Jamestown fell into the hands of the crown, everything they had accomplished continued: private ownership of property, common law, and representative assembly. They became a pattern for all British colonies in North America. As our country has grown closer to Socialism, we have become weaker; we have more poor people than ever before (with the exclusion of the Great Depression).[11]

In 1620, a religious group headed for Jamestown but strayed north to Plymouth, Massachusetts. These missionaries had formed an agreement known as the Mayflower Compact.

---

11   *Encyclopedia Britannica*, 1982, 15th edition, Foundation for
      American Christian Education, America's Christian History, 1965,
      Iversen-Norman Associates, New York.

The Mayflower Compact

Some people think this agreement was written before the Pilgrims left for the New World. However, this is not true. It was written in Cape Cod and signed, "In witness wherof we have hereunder subscribed our names at Cap Codd." So what happened that they had to make this contract?

The reason was because a group of people who rode along with the Pilgrims declared that patents did not apply in the New World. They also claimed that there was no authority there to govern them and that they had their own liberty. Sounds like our liberals today and what they are teaching our children; you may have fallen for it: "No one can tell you what to do" and "I have my rights." It does not matter if you step all over someone else's rights as long as you get to do what you want, no matter what it is. Our forefathers set it up that your rights end when they infringe on someone else's, but liberals do not want to hear that. The Pilgrims knew this philosophy would cause chaos and crime, so they came up with the Mayflower Compact. They had everyone sign it.

In the contract, they declared this was an undertaking for the glory of God and the advancement of the Christian faith. Their idea was a government in church and state to permit and compel other men to walk in the right way (morally), not to do whatever they thought was right in their own eyes.[12]

On August 12, 1843, John Overton Choules wrote,

> "We should never forget that the prison, the scaffold, and the stake were stages in the march of civil and religious liberty which our forefathers had to travel, in order that we might attain our present liberty...
>
> Before our children remove their religious

---

12   William Bradford, *History of Plymouth Plantation*, also, http://www.ushistory.org/documents/mayflower.htm ; you can find other documents on this site.

connections…before they leave the old paths of God's Word…before they barter their birthright for a mess of pottage, let us place in their hands this chronicle of the glorious days of the suffering churches, and let them know that they are the sons of the men of whom the world was not worth; and whose sufferings for conscience sake are here monumentally recorded." (Neil 1844, reprint of *History of the Puritans*, 1731)

Yes, they had even thought of a falling away from the faith. The first start of this came when French Revolutionists, at home and abroad, brought a subversive doctrine (Jacobinism) to our shores. Noah Webster worked hard to dispel this doctrine. The Democrats held close to this doctrine, even today, and I bet today's Democrats don't even know it except those in the political realm. I'll get into this doctrine later and dispel Lyndon LaRouche's lies about this matter. Anyway, the Puritans' answer was to remind people that they had come from a line of ancestors who were persecuted and gave their lives for God and country.

After the Pilgrims arrived at Plymouth, everything they caught, hunted, or farmed was gathered and distributed equally among themselves. Half of the colony perished just like in Jamestown.

The Indians were stealing their tools. One day, an Indian named Samaset came to them, speaking broken English. He told them about another Indian, Squanto, who had been to England and spoke better English. He later returned with five others and brought back the tools that had been stolen.

They made peaceful terms with the Indians. Squanto showed them how to plant corn, set it, and dress and tend it. He showed them how to use fish as fertilizer and many other things.

New arrivals would come to the colony without provisions,

and this cut into their supplies. Food was being stolen day and night. Some colonists wouldn't tend the food like they should have. They were thinking, "No matter what I do, I will get my share."

Does it sound like welfare today? "I don't have to work. I'll get money from the government. I get more on welfare than if I work." I've heard them all. The liberals of today talk about your fair share. They are taking us back to those times of starvation. They take from us who work and give it to those who refuse to work because they can get their fair share. Illegal immigrants come in and get free medical care, free gas to go to work, jobs, and free housing; they tell US citizens that those jobs are not for them. I know what I am talking about, because clerks at Workforce told my husband that those jobs were not for him. Talk about discrimination! There is no job that Americans would not do! The government holds these jobs for immigrants!

Now there are those who use welfare just do so to get on their feet, but how many are really in that category? Because of this attitude, there was a food shortage in Plymouth. Today, we only get to keep about 47 percent of our pay. I do not mind helping people if their job does not support them that well or to get them on their feet, but why are we giving free everything to outsiders so they can be rich in their county and support their country and we do not take care of our own people?

The Pilgrims hung onto the Scriptures like Deuteronomy 8:3 and Genesis 42 and 43:1: "And he humbled thee, and suffered thee to hunger, and fed thee with manna, which thou knowest not, neither did thy fathers know; that he might make thee know man doth not live by bread only, but by every word that proceedeth out of the mouth of the Lord doth man live." Genesis dealt with famine in Jacob's time.

When more newcomers came, the planters complained because they knew the provisions they had brought wouldn't get them through the year, and they were right. The newcomers were also afraid because of the poor conditions they saw. Therefore, they set up a bargain or an exchange agreement.

Ships came in for furs and other trade goods. The colonists traded for everything they needed. It was written, "By this time harvest was come, and in stead of famine, now God gave them plente, and ye face of things was changed, to ye rejoysing of ye harts of many, for which they blessed God."
(History of Plymouth Plantation, William Bradford)

Seeing the effect of this agreement, they decided to give each settler their own property to grow their own provisions. This became very successful, and there was always plenty of food from that time on. It was written in the same manuscript, "These things premised, I shall now, prosecute ye proceedings and affairs here. And before I come to other things I must speak a word of their planting this year; they having found ye benifite of their last years harvest, and setting corne for their particular, having therby with a great deale of patience overcome hunger & famine. Which maks me remember a saing of Senccas, Epis:123. That a great parte of libertie is a well governed belly, and to be patients in all wants."

Our forefathers used this lesson to help set up our Constitution, our form of government, and our capitalist style of economy. The Constitution was a well-planned and constructed piece of work. It was not just thrown together to have something. They had taken all things into account, *including the future*!

Now all you people who think that our forefathers intended to keep God out of our government, look at Thanksgiving for a start. The first Thanksgiving proclamation was done by George Washington in 1789:

> Whereas it is the duty of all nations to acknowledge the providence of Almighty God, to obey His will, to be grateful for His protection, aid and favors ... Now, therefore, I do recommend and assign Thursday the 26th of November rest, to be

devoted by the people of these states to the service of that great and glorious Being, who is the Beneficent Author of all the good that was, that is, or that will be that we may then all unite in rendering unto Him our sincere and humble thanks for His kind care and protection of the people of this country, and for all the great and various favors which He has been pleased to confer upon us.[13]

So you see Thanksgiving was to be more than Pilgrims and Indians at a table being happy that they had food on the table. It was supposed to be a time when the nation came together and gave God thanks for the country's protection and the abundance that he gave us. Our country has a lot to be thankful for, even in this day and time, where liberals are throwing out what our forefathers had established. Also, in this we see that our forefathers believed that God's word was to influence our country and its leaders.

Before we get into the Constitution, I want you to look at the differences between forms of governments. Keep in mind that our forefathers set up a federal republic not a democracy or a simple republic. I get so tired of everyone saying this is a democracy. It is *not* a democracy! This is something the liberal Democrats started to get people to think in a different mode than what our forefathers set up. Also, I want to talk about political parties and the Declaration of Independence.

The parties before the Declaration of Independence were the Whigs and Tories. Afterward, the Whigs called themselves American Whigs and the Tories disappeared. Because of disagreements over the Constitution, they split into the Federalists and Anti-Federalists.

The Federalists wanted a national authority for the suppression of disorder. However, the Anti-Federalists feared a strong government because they were sure their liberties

---

13   Library of Congress.

would be destroyed. This is where I dispel LaRouche's claims in *The New Federalist* about the Jacobins and the Republicans. By the way, do not get them confused with the Federalists Papers written by Hamilton, Madison, and Jay, because their philosophies are as different as night and day.

The Anti-Federalists took up this Jacobin dogma[14] and became the Democratic-Republic, then just the Democrats as they later changed our country into a democracy, moving away from our Constitution.

The Federalists, on the other hand, became the Whigs and later the Republican party to show their dislike for the ideals of the French Revolution. They tried to hold on tight to the ideals our forefathers fought and died for.

Judith A. Best, a professor of political science at the State University of New York, stated, "We are not, never have been, and were not intended to be a simple democracy, because a simple democracy is a form of tyranny, a majority tyranny."

In our Constitution Article. IV Section. 4. It states "The United States shall guarantee to every State in this Union A Republican Form of Government, and shall protect them against invasion;…"

Let's see what Judith Best might have been trying to say.

Republic	Democracy	Monarchy
Representatives	Demagogues (a factious person or an orator with influence)	Tyrants (dictator)
Liberty	Licenses	Bondage
Justice	Anarchy (laws are not efficient)	Compulsion
Rights (God given)	Socialism	Rights Granted
Christian self-govern	Selfishness	Selfishness
Progress	Chaos	Reaction

---

14   A Jacobin was a radical leftist in the French Revolution.

You can see now that we are in between the middle and the last column today. We are getting into the government granting rights over others. Is that not what abortion is? How about bowing down to the EPA, animal rights activists, and others, even when they do not know what in the world they are talking about. It does not matter that our constitutional rights are violated as long as these groups can dictate our lives. They take property from people and so on. People are more selfish now than they have ever been, and we have chaos everywhere. We have to get a license for this, a permit for that, even when it is covered by the Constitution.

Fox News interviewed a teacher who said he was all for Socialism. I feel sorry for that teacher because he does not know what he is saying. Indirectly, he is saying it is okay for the government to take all of what he owns and distribute it to others, even if they did not work to contribute to the pot. This just makes people poorer, and you know that the government will get half to put in their pockets; they will not starve. Remember Jamestown and Plymouth Rock?

I have even heard Republicans call us a democracy, but we are not a democracy! The same thing happened in ancient Rome, and that became their downfall. I predict that before long, this country will no longer exist if it continues on this path!

Now the Democrats are trying to dictate what churches can say in the pulpit, which is unconstitutional, but they do not seem to care about our Constitution at all. They seem to only care about what they want, and that is power and money.

When our forefathers were putting the Constitution together, they kept in mind that each state was its own government in itself. Everything was set up where there was a dual citizenship. This is why we are called the United States of America. Even my liberal English teacher agreed to that and was surprised that I knew that. Well, in my day, the liberals did not get hold of history, so the truth was taught. A "state" means "a government." They united for protection, trade, and a few other things but not for the central government to take over the states as a dictatorship. They were not supposed to take over the schools or other things.

Felix Frankfurter,[15] a Supreme Court judge and a progressive, said, "We have enjoyed so much freedom for so long that we are perhaps in danger of forgetting how much blood it cost to establish the Bill of Rights."[16]

The thirteen states only surrendered their power to make war and peace, to enter into alliances with each other or with foreign nations, and to make treaties. The federal government was not supposed to get into all the domestic things that it has gotten itself into. Also, it has been done so cunningly.

Take this health care program. They were trying to make as many things a health care problem to get one sixth or more of this country under their dictatorship. This is Socialism! Now we have a socialized health care program that will cost not just us but our great-great-grandchildren. We will cut costs on Medicare or cut it out and force senior citizens into this health care program, where health care providers can refuse them care. Remember the movie Soylent Green where they were killing the old people and made food for the people? Well, we are heading that way, as I see it.

Liberals claim that our forefathers only had political rights in mind. I do not know who they are fooling, but even our Declaration of Independence and the Bill of Rights show that this is a lie. So why would they claim such a thing if it was not true? Something to think about, isn't it? You think about

---

15   [12] Lest We Forget, Teach Your Children about Freedom & Liberty http://www.homeschoolthroughhighschool.com/lest-we-forget-teach-your-children-about-freedom-liberty

16   Armstrong, Tad. How much freedom is in that Window? http://www.stltoday.com/news/opinion/article_591633ab-2ee2-5df8-ae89-a8795c712002.html , and quotes

these points as I get into the Declaration of Independence and the Constitution.

I had first thought about not talking about the Declaration of Independence. However, the more I kept thinking about people not knowing it when it was read to them, I changed my mind. This is why it is important to learn history and especially the documents that govern our country. Do not take the teachers' word or anyone's word! Do research! The reason people are getting fooled is because they are too lazy to do research!

Studying history keeps your eyes open and reduces the chance of being swayed in the wrong direction, but if you are greedy, you might find yourself in trouble. There is always a price to pay for being self-centered.

It is good to read the Declaration of Independence. It declares why the colonies broke away from Britain. The main thing was they were British citizens with no British rights. I am only going to concentrate on the first two paragraphs and the history of this document.

The clergies of New England were instrumental in teaching the colonists about government principles through the Scriptures. Yes, that is right, through the Bible. They were heavily involved in the political life of the United States. They were graduates of Harvard and Yale. Today a lot of our clergies are weak and afraid. Some go for the money. They do not want to claim the whole word of God because they are afraid of man more than God, or they want power and prestige. No John the Baptist they are, that is for sure. Some day they will have to give an account for it, just like I will have to account for my actions.

God said to beware. 2 Timothy 4:3, 4 says, "For the time will come when they will not endure sound doctrine; but after their own lusts shall they heap to themselves teachers, having itching ears; And they shall turn away their ears from the truth, and shall be turned unto fables." Also, in Titus 1:10, 11,

16, Paul says, "For there are many unruly and vain talkers and deceivers, specially they of the circumcision: Whose mouths must be stopped, who subvert whole houses, teaching things which they ought not, for filthy lucre's sake … They profess that they know God; but in works they deny Him, being abominable, and disobedient, and unto every good work reprobate."

Our forefathers talked about self-government using Hebrews 10: 16: "This is the covenant that I will make with them after those days, saith the Lord, I will put my laws into their hearts, and in their minds will I write them."

They taught that if one governed oneself, it would be outwardly expressed. Therefore, we are showing our ability to be good Christian citizens. Hugo Gallous in 1654 said it best: "He knows not how to rule a kingdom, that cannot manage a Province; nor can he wield a Province, that cannot order a City; nor he order a City, that knows not how to regulate a Village; nor he a Village, that cannot guide a Family; nor can that man Govern well a Family that knows not how to Govern himself; neither can any Govern himself unless his reason be Lord, Will and Appetite her Vassals; nor can Reason rule unless herself be ruled by God, and be obedient to Him."[(29)]

In 1 Timothy 3:5, Paul said, "For if a man know not how to rule his own house, how shall he take care of the church of God?" Other verses used included Proverbs 16: 32 and Romans 14: 11, 12.

Our forefathers learned about a better form of government, mostly from the Scriptures but also from John Locke and Algernon Sidney.[17] John Fiske said, "The mischievous doctrine of Rousseau had found few readers and fewer admirers among

---

17   Jon Roland, Algernon Sidney, http://www.constitution.org/as/foreword.htm , Sidney's speech upon his death, http://history.wisc.edu/sommerville/367/sidney%20speech.htm

the Americans. The Principles upon which their Revolution was conducted were those of Sidney and Locke."[18]

I learned that Rousseau attacked the rich just like the liberals, Socialists, and Communists. He claimed that the sciences and arts were the corrupting tools of the rich. I suggest you read Locke's and Sidney's[19] works along with the Scriptures, if you really want to know where our forefathers were coming from in their ideas. The judicial system came from the form that the Sanhedrin had during biblical times.

In the book *We Hold These Truths*, Mortimer Adler stated that Rome and Greece held the same kind of government as ours.[(70)] What he failed to say was Rome lacked the understanding of representation. Those who were assembled were nobles, not elected representatives. Rome's delegation of power was the government delegating to the generals to do their bidding. This is why it was easy for them to move from a democracy to a dictatorship.

Now Greece, on the other hand, combined federalism and self-government, but believed this form could not last long. They thought that absolute monarchy was a more stable form of government, but this is a fallacy, just like the liberals are teaching in our schools that Socialism is a better form of government.

If Socialism is such a great form of government, why is there more poverty under this form of government? Also, if these forms of government and these countries are so great, why do people from them flock to the United States for jobs, medical care, and so on?

I don't have room to get into the French Revolution and what started it. However, I will tell you this: there were certain people who were exempt from things like taxes. Sound

---

18   *Christian History.*
19   Sidney was a philosopher like Socrates. Locke believed in using reason to find the truth and not just accept the opinions of the people in charge (our politicians).

familiar? Members of Congress have exempted themselves from the health care bill they passed! Also, those in charge were partying and had plenty of food, while other people were struggling. How about all those "business trips" Obama and his family takes with our tax money? Why not stay home to help with the economy? By the way I heard that if he gets elected again he is not going to work on the economy but work on homosexual agendas like teaching our children homosexuality in the classroom and homosexual marriages.

In 1775, General John Peter Muhlenberg, a Virginia clergyman, ended a sermon with a quote from Ecclesiastes 3:1: "To everything there is a season, and a time to every purpose under the heaven." Then he said, "A time to preach and a time to pray."[20] He then declared that that time was gone, and it was time to fight. That day, about three hundred men enlisted in the Continental Army under him.

I think that if our clergies had said something back when the liberals started putting the cult religion of humanism in our schools and when we began to no longer cherish human life, about forty years ago or more, we would not be in the mess we are in today. We might not be killing one million unborn children a year today if they had all spoken up instead of repeating the liberal lie that we ought to be tolerant.

Christ was not tolerant. He turned over the moneychangers' tables because they were cheating people on temple grounds. He believed in self-defense when he asked his disciples if they had swords. The reason was to defend themselves against thieves on the road. That would be the only reason for him to ask them to buy swords. His disciples said they had two and he said it was enough. You say you do not think Jesus asked this look at Luck 22:35-38. When you tolerate sin, it consumes you and destroys society.

---

20   John Peter Gabriel Muhlenberg (1746–1807), Penn Biographies, http://www.archives.upenn.edu/people/1700s/muhlenberg_johnpg.html

Now we have the courts saying it is okay to lie.[21] When you lie to gain something, it is fraud! "Fraud" is defined as "deceit; deception; trick; artifice by which the right or interest of another is injured; to obtain some undue advantage; an attempt to gain or the obtaining of an advantage over another by imposition or immoral means." What was Rick Strandlof (aka Rick Duncan, aka Rick Gold) to gain? A job and money under a false pretense of being something he was not! He lied to obtain an advantage over his competitor for a position. Our country is making wrong things right and what is right is now wrong. Lying is not freedom of speech!

Mr. Stranlof claimed to have gotten the Purple Heart to climb the political ladder. He used it to get into the graces of the Veterans and to get political clout. When he claimed he was working for Sen. Mark Udall that is when things started to fall apart for him. He raised money for different things one being for a charity event and made off with $25,000. He appeared for Democrat ads for candidate Hal Bidlack. Something he would not have gotten if they knew he was not what he claimed to be. If he got paid for this it became fraud. This is just the tip of the ice berg and the courts let him go.

On the first day of Congress in 1776, John Witherspoon, a clergyman who signed the Declaration of Independence, said:

> Upon the whole, I beseech you to make a wise improvement of the present threatening aspect of public affairs and to remember that your duty to God, to your country, to your families, and to yourselves is the same. True religion is nothing wise but an inward temper and outward conduct suited to your state conformity to Him, adds to

---

21   Judge says Constitution protects right to lie About Purple Heart, http://www.wired.com/threatlevel/2010/07/stolen-valor-act/; http://www.ericjrosenberg.com/2011/08/rick-saga/ , http://www. moonbattery.com/archives/2009/05/phony_soldier_w.html

the sweetness of created comforts while we possess them, so in times of difficulty and trial, it is in the man of piety and inward principle that we may expect to find the uncorrupted patriot, the useful citizen, and the invincible soldier, God grant that in America true religion and civil liberty may be inseparable, and the unjust attempts to destroy the one, may in the issue tend to the support and establishment of both.[22]

So you see, God was not to be taken out of government. The separation that Jefferson was talking about is happening today when Pelosi told clergies to lie to their congregation about the Democratic programs being good, that if they did that, they could get grants and loans with low interest rates.[23] The government is telling churches what to say and preach. They have crossed the line of their own separation of church and state.

The first paragraph of the Declaration of Independence reads like this: "When in the course of human Events, it becomes necessary for one People to dissolve the Political Bonds which have connected them with another, and to assume among the Powers of the Earth, the separate and equal Station to which the Laws of Nature and of Nature's God entitled them, a decent Respect to the Opinions of Mankind requires that they should declare the causes which impel them to the Separation."

I found this paragraph very interesting. What did they mean by "Powers of the Earth" and "equal Station to which the Laws of Nature and of Nature's God entitled them"? Well, we know that "Nature's God" is Jesus Christ (John 1:1–3), because he created all things, including us. Our founding fathers were saying what Christ had entitled us.

---

22   *Christian History*, Library of Congress.
23   Fox News.

However, what are the "Powers of the Earth"? The only thing I could come up with was other nations. They had declared a separate station among the other nations and said that they should be considered equal among them. They declared that the Laws of Nature and Christ entitled them to do this for certain reasons, and they named those reasons.

The second paragraph in the Declaration of Independence states, "We hold these Truths to be self-evident, that all men are created equal, that they are endowed by their Creator with certain unalienable Rights, that among those are Life, Liberty, and the Pursuit of Happiness, That to secure these Rights, Governments are instituted among men."

Let's stop at this point and take this apart before we go on. The first section says, "We hold these Truths to be self-evident."

"Hold" is defined as "to maintain, as an opinion; to be true; not to fail; to stand, as fact or truth."[24]

"Self-evident" is something that produces certainty or clear conviction upon a bare presentation to the mind.

"Evidence" is defined as "apparent; clear to the mental eye."

Therefore, we could change the sentence to "We stand on these facts of reality to be apparent."

What facts were obvious to them? To find out, let's continue: "That all men are created equal, that they are endowed by their Creator with certain unalienable Rights." Our forefathers knew that God had created man, and through the Bible He had shown man that mankind was given certain orders and rights to be able to do His will. Men and women were given certain roles.

Let's look at the word "endowed." Endowed means

---

24   All of my definitions are from *Webster's Dictionary* (1828 reprint) unless otherwise stated because we should go by the definitions of our founding fathers, not what we have changed words to today. This way we know what exactly they were saying.

"furnished with a portion of estate." Therefore, God furnished man with certain unalienable rights, which mankind always tries to take away because of greed and wanting power over others.

"Unalienable" means "cannot be alienated (or taken from); may not be transferred." So now let's go through the whole thing: "We cling to these facts of reality to be apparent, that all men are formed equally, that they are furnished by God with certain rights that cannot be taken or transferred, among those rights are life, liberty, and the pursuit of happiness, and the governments are instituted (established) among men to secure these rights."

The government is to secure these rights for every citizen of the United States. I repeat, to every *citizen* of the United States. A noncitizen is given more consideration, not only by Democrats but now by Republicans as well. If you are of a certain group, you are allowed to step all over someone else's rights. This should not be! That is one of the reasons why there was a revolution. The government is not supposed to take these rights away, it is supposed to protect them!

Most conservatives believe everyone should be treated equal. This means you get the same opportunity as everyone else, not to get preference over another because of your race but because you can do the job. We do not need affirmative action any more. We have laws against discrimination, and I know that those with different skin color are not afraid to use them to their benefit. It is wrong to discriminate against someone, and that includes Caucasians!

The Democrats use laws to step all over our God-given rights, and people are too ignorant to realize it (if they knew, they would not let them stay in office and definitely would have not elected Obama).

My husband and I warned people about Obama before the election, but no one listened. The majority of the time when we tried to tell someone something, we were treated like we were stupid when about 96 percent of the time we were right.

People's rights are controlled by other people, and this is not supposed to be so. Liberals take them away with phrases like, "It's for the good of the whole, for the environment, for our economy," or "it's my right." One's rights, liberty, and property are subject to the majority's rule. Your rights end when they infringe on someone else's rights.

Our forefathers said that one's property was not to be taken for public use without compensation (Amendment V). It is not supposed to be taken at all for anything else, which includes private businesses, animals, plants, and all those other things liberals think of to take. However, local and federal governments (this includes Republicans also) have been taking homes to save trees, plants, and animals that are not really endangered. They take property for private businesses, and this is *not* public use! The majority are not compensated, and those who are, are lucky if they get half what their property is worth.

Now I realize some refuse to sell, but can you blame them? Today we are seeing more and more of this. This is just another way of taking our rights and putting everything under the government. If you can see the movie *Dr. Zhivago* again, do it. That is where we are headed if people do not wake up.

Last night Fox News showed that some of our politicians are saying, "Let's distribute the wealth among the nations." What wealth? Talk about stepping all over people's rights. Democrats do not seem to care about your constitutional rights or liberty. They are taking from you and from your kids' future to give to the world while we have a hard time making a living. Let them give their own money! We need to be paying our debt!

They use lies and scare tactics to get the people to help them step all over other people and suppress their God-given rights and liberty. I say actions speak louder than words!

Read the Federalist Papers and know the truth! It meant what it said for a reason! We had a military and navy during this time! What a farce! When are we going to wake up and see the truth?

Our forefathers died for these rights, which the liberals have taken away from us slowly, and now they are showing their arrogance by forcing us into things we do not want. They believe that they are above the laws that they make. They are supposed to put themselves under those laws because this is a safety thing to keep them from making grievous laws to suppress the people, but they have broken that rule also. They do not care about what is right and wrong. They are doing the very thing that the king of England was doing to the colonists. Why do you think the original tea party was formed? Do you think it was just because of taxes on tea? No! Read and learn.

Further on in the Declaration of Independence, it said that if the government becomes destructive, the people have the right to alter or abolish it. This goes into why I quoted Lincoln in my Introduction: "not to overthrow the Constitution but to overthrow the men who pervert it." The Constitution is not the problem, it is the people in the government. They talk about the rich but they are the rich! They no longer represent the people.

The colonies wanted an orderly government in 1775. However, the Continental Congress advised the colonists to set up temporary governments until the trouble with Great Britain was over, and they did.

They believed in the "Compact theory of the State."[25] The states originated through an agreement. This agreement was like one between king and nobles, between king and people, or among the people themselves. They quoted 2 Samuel 5:3: "So all the elders of Israel came to the king to Hebron; and King

25   American Creation, Compact Theory, Interposition & Nullification, http://americancreation.blogspot.com/2011/02/compact-theory-interposition.html ; American Christian History

David made a league with them in Hebron before the Lord; and they anointed David King over Israel."

To show how strong the colonists felt about this very thing, let's go to the 1688 English Revolution. Parliament adopted this resolution: "That King James the Second, having endeavored to subvert the Constitution of the Kingdom by breaking the original contract between King and people ... the throne is hereby vacant."[26]

They believed that if the government broke the contract to defend and keep the Constitution, they should be thrown out. It was each individual who voted for the Constitution and not each state.

Isn't that what they are doing when they lie about separation of church and state? Then they turn around and start telling clergies what to say in their pulpits and tell them that if they do not do what they say, they will make sure they do not get good rates on their building loans.[27] As my ancestors would say, liberals "speak with forked tongues." The Republicans are beginning to be no better.

Our forefathers set up a way to get rid of people who would turn this country away from the form of government they had intended. There is impeachment (if you can get Congress to do it), recalls, and of course, our votes. However, if you are ignorant about what our forefathers intended and the true history, then you will not know they are perverting the Constitution. Then they will continue until one day, without you realizing it, you will have let all your liberty and freedom be taken away. You are then under a dictatorship, whether it is within or under an organization like the United Nations.

The states only wanted people in office who believed in God and had good morals. The reason for this was because they were afraid of persecution and immorality later on if an

---

26   John Miller, *Cambridge Journals*, http://journals.cambridge.org/
     action/displayAbstract?fromPage=online&aid=3289600

27   CNN, Fox News.

atheist was to get in office. They knew that a nation without God's guidance would soon become a nation bases on greed and self-edification. This would breed a government that would become power hungry and not care about the people's liberty and freedoms. Then the people would become the slaves of the government instead of the government working for the people (so much for their separation of church and state).

Is this not what is happening with health care? They said we do not care what the people want, we are giving them what we want, and it does not matter if it hurts anyone. They have become self-righteous and think they are better than we, "the little people," are (well, that is how they see us). This is shown by the arrogance of the liberals in office. They have several times said they do not care what the people want, they are going to do what they want.

They think we are too stupid to know what is right and good for us, so they have to force us into what they think is good and right for us.

We are nothing but a bunch of babies. It is beyond my comprehension why anyone would continue to vote someone in office who has openly admitted they do not care about what you think, that you are too stupid to know the issues.

Daniel Webster made a speech in the Senate in response to Robert Y. Hayne, who wanted to nullify the Constitution; Webster said, "The people have preserved this, their own chosen Constitution, for forty years and have seen their happiness, prosperity, and renown grow with its growth, and strengthen with its strength. They are now, generally, strongly attached to it."[28]

Ever since people in Washington changed our Constitution, we are no longer prospering and our lives are being trampled on. Our rights are being taken away; this brings fear except for those who are too ignorant to see what is going on.

---

28   The Hayne-Webster Debate, Hal Morris, http://www.constitution. org/hwdebate/hwdebate.htm

When the colonies had a common enemy, they made an effort to unite. The New England Confederation of 1643 fought against the Indians and against the Dutch and French. The Albany Congress of 1754 dealt with the struggle against the French and Indians. The Stamp Act Congress of 1765, the Committees of Correspondence, and the Continental Congress were united efforts that led to the final breach with Great Britain.

The Continental Congress appointed one committee to draw up a Declaration of Independence and another to prepare articles of union. A month after the Declaration of Independence was adopted, John Dickinson, chairman of the second committee, presented the Articles of Confederation.

Let's talk about the Articles of Confederation. This was an agreement between the states listing certain articles and forming a Union. It was a quick Constitution that formed a union between sovereign states. Each state had one vote regardless of its size. Also, their representatives could not stay in office more than three years or be paid a salary. It stated that freedom of speech in Congress could not be impeached or questioned in the courts. The reason for the short term was to stop what is going on today in Congress, forming buddies or political elites and get all these benefits they give themselves.

States could not enter into a treaty without the consent of Congress, nor could they levy duties or commit to treaties with other countries. They could not make war. Those were the duties of Congress.[29]

The Articles of Confederation was a modification of Benjamin Franklin's Albany plan.[30] Congress was forced to act as if the Confederation had been formed and was duly empowered.

Later they tried to amend the Articles of Confederation,

---

29   Original Articles of Confederation; http://www.earlyamerica.com/ earlyamerica/milestones/articles/1.html

30   http://www.usconstitution.net/albany.html

but James Madison came up with the Virginia Plan. George Mason and James Madison were the primary authors of the Virginia Declaration of Rights, which was passed on June 12, 1776. It later became a model for the Bill of Rights.[31]

Thomas Jefferson said, "A Bill of Rights is what the people are entitled to against every government, and what no just government should refuse, or rest on inference."[32]

The reason I keep referring to Jefferson and his letters is because the Supreme Court used one of them to get separation of Church and State. It is to show that what they claim is not what he believed. This particular letter to James Madison was before the Bill of Rights. It is referring to Mr. Wilson saying that the Bill of Rights were not necessary. In this letter Jefferson clarifies why and what the Bill of Rights are.

So did you get that? It is what the people are entitled to, not what the government is entitled to! The Bill of Rights means exactly what it says, not what some liberal wants it to mean so they can squash us like a bug! If you put Jefferson's letter in context, he was commending the Virginians for what they had put in the Bill of Rights. That means the letter was written after the Bill of Rights, not before! He was out of the country at the time. Like everything else, the liberals take a phrase out of context and make it say what they want it to say! The wall he was talking about was the government not setting up a one state religion and not to interfere with the churches! This is what the churches feared!

Fighting broke out, and the debate lasted over six months, but Congress finally adopted it at the end of 1777. However, the people of each state did not ratify the Articles until March 1781.

I looked heavily into the *Encyclopedia Britannica* (1982)

---

31   Jefferson's letter, http://www.loc.gov/loc/lcib/9806/danpre.html ; U.S. Constitution Online, The Virginia Declaration of Rights, http://www.usconstitution.net/vdeclar.html

32   Thomas Jefferson to James Madison, 20 Dec. 1787, http://press-pubs.uchicago.edu/founders/documents/v1ch14s30.html

and other sources and could not find anywhere that they had canceled the Articles of Confederation. They just wanted the government to be able to collect taxes to pay for the $60,000,000 debt they owed for the Revolution and to enforce the Constitution (a more perfect union).

On August 13, 1800, Thomas Jefferson wrote a letter to Gideon Granger of Connecticut and stated, "The true theory of our Constitution is surely the wisest and best, that the states are independent as to everything within themselves, and united as to everything respecting foreign nations. Let the general government be reduced to foreign concerns only, and let our affairs be disentangled from those of all other nations, except as to commerce, which the merchants will manage the better the more they are left free to manage for themselves, and our general government may be reduced to a very simple organization, and a very inexpensive one."[33]

Since we are here in the Revolution, I want to bring up Patrick Henry. You know, the man who said, "Give me liberty, or give me death." That is all the schools tell you. I would like to give you a little more of that speech.

Patrick Henry was addressing the Virginia convention on March 20, 1775. He said:

> If we wish to be free, we must fight! I repeat sir, we must fight! An appeal to arms and to the God of Hosts is all that is left us! They tell me that we are weak; but shall we gather strength by irresolution? We are not weak. Three millions of people, armed in the holy cause of liberty, and in such a country, are invincible by any force which our enemy can send against us. We shall not fight alone. A just God presides over the destinies of nations ... There is no retreat, but in submission

---

33 *Encyclopedia Britannica*, http://www.britannica.com/presidents/article-9116899 : We Hold These Truths, Reprints of the Federalist and Anti-Federalist Papers.

and slavery … Is life so dear, or peace so sweet, as to be purchased at the price of chains and slavery? Forbid it, Almighty God! I know not what course others may take; but as for me, give me liberty, or give me death![34]

As you see, Patrick Henry claimed that God had control over the destinies of the nations, so he made an appeal to God in making it possible for them to separate from Great Britain so they could have liberty and not be slaves. Therefore, you who are willing to give up your guns for the false security that the liberals are promising, remember that many Communists have promised the same thing only to enslave their people and put them into poverty. May I add here that the Democrats are the ones who did not want to get rid of slavery, so now that they could not keep the blacks in slavery, it seems like they are trying to put the whole United States into slavery?

Northwest Ordinance

I find this topic[35] very interesting because it attacks the idea that liberals have been saying about taking God out of the school system using the concept of separation of church and state. Therefore, I feel I should give some background about it.

In 1784, Thomas Jefferson wrote a draft of this ordinance. However, by 1785, he had retired as chairman when the ordinance was adopted by Congress. Thomas Hutchins, a geographer, and William Grayson are given the most credit for the final draft. However, in my research, I could not find these men except under the subject of the Northwest Ordinance. So

---

34   Library of Congress.
35   Northwest Ordinance, http://www.ourdocuments.gov/doc.php?flas h=true&doc=8&page=transcript

I know nothing about them at all. Therefore, it is hard for me to believe this statement.

Thomas Jefferson was born on the frontier. His father was of the middle class, and his mother was a Randolph. He entered William and Mary College at the age of eighteen. He was a student in the law office of George Wythe and a friend of Patrick Henry.

Jefferson drafted the Declaration of Independence. Then he resigned from Congress to help organize Virginia's government. For two years, he served in the Virginia Assembly. He repealed the law of entailment (restricted inheritance of land to a particular heir or line of heirs), abolished primogeniture (the right of the eldest of inheritance), fought for the recognition of freedom of conscience, and was a big encourager of education. He served as governor of Virginia for two years and then returned to Congress in 1783. He helped persuade Congress to have a national system of coinage. Jefferson started the Democratic-Republic party. Little did he know that they would take on the whole dogma of democracy and step on people's constitutional rights. That party wanted to keep slavery so badly that there was a Civil War. He is probably turning over in his grave as he sees our politicians turning this country into a dictatorship.

Jefferson's draft was never put into practice. Some reasons were that he put the abolition of slavery in the new states after 1800. He also recommended that no state should be admitted unless its population was equal to the original states. He felt that there might be no new states if the original states should increase in population, and I can see his point.[36]

The main reason for it not going into action was that even though it fixed limits within the local governments, it left the creation of the governments to the future.

In July 1787, Congress brought up the matter of the ordinance and within one week adopted what we now know as

---

36 *Encyclopedia Britannica.*

the Northwest Ordinance. It dealt with the territories, dividing it, stipulations on becoming a state (you had to teach morals and God in the schools), slavery in those territories, and so on.

When it became so successful, everyone claimed authorship. Does it sound like Clinton in his campaign about welfare? It was the Republicans in 1994 who pushed that welfare bill. Why is it that people try to get credit where credit is not due? Why don't they just get off their seats of laziness and do something they know will work and then take credit, instead of taking it away from the ones who did all the work? Jefferson's Ordinance of 1784 formed much of this great ordinance. I wish Democrats would quit passing things that do not work and blaming it on the Republicans. I wish people would quit believing everything they hear and do research.

Webster's thoughts about the Ordinance of 1787's importance was stated in his debate with Hayne. He said, "We are accustomed … to praise the lawgivers of antiquity; we help to perpetuate the fame of Solon and Lycurgus; but I doubt whether one single law of any lawgiver, ancient or modern, has produced effects of more distinct, marked, and lasting character than the Ordinance of 1787."

Constitution of the United States

Ah, yes the Constitution, the one document that they changed and we did not get to ratify like we are supposed to. That is the one thing that they did not have the authority to do, but in their arrogance they felt it was okay. They ignored the law and did things they were not supposed to do, but then they took control of our schools and kept people ignorant so they can do whatever they want.

The preamble reads, "We the people of the United States, in order to form a more perfect union, establish justice, insure domestic tranquility, provide for the common defense, promote the general welfare, and secure the blessings of liberty to ourselves and our posterity, do ordain and establish this Constitution for the United States of America."

They first started the Constitution out with, "We, the people of the states of New Hampshire, Massachusetts, and Rhode Island," but then they changed it to, "We the people of the United States."

The reason for this is because these were individual states uniting for certain reasons, and I went over this. This is why a state can make laws as long as it does not go against the Constitution of the United States. This document was ratified by the people in each state; they agreed to it. The federal government is not to interfere with the states unless the laws they pass go against the Constitution. The Arizona law on immigration[37] is not unconstitutional! It is the state's responsibility to protect its citizens, not only their lives, but their liberties and the pursuit of happiness; that means you do not take their jobs away and give them to illegal immigrants! That is why our forefathers said that each state has its own military the National Guard! That is why it is called the Louisiana National Guard the Colorado National Guard and so on. They are not part of the federal government and it is not their job to go overseas! They are to protect the boarders of their state!

When the federal government refuses to do their job expressly the Executive branch to enforce the laws of the land it is left for the states to do. That is the Executive Branches job!

The officials must have probable cause to check for papers to show they are legally here in the US. They are required to respect the Federal laws on immigration and illegal aliens. They are to hand illegal aliens to the federal agency that handle this problem. Of course the federal agency has been letting them go back into the US. Look at the law.

When my husband and I went to Texas from Arizona we

---

37   http://www.azleg.gov/legtext/49leg/2r/bills/sb1070s.pdf

were asked where we were born and drivers license. We saw nothing wrong with that and it did not bother us at all.

Oh and how do you like this? Obama brought Mexico's president in to criticize Arizona's law on immigration and border safety, when he not only sends illegal immigrants back but imprisons them, also! The Democrats just applauded him like mad. What a bunch of hypocrites!

Other countries shoot illegal immigrants, imprison them, or even charge them as spies. We, however, give them jobs, welfare, free medical care, free housing, Social Security, and so on. What is wrong with this picture?

Now remember that the Federalists (Republicans) were for the Constitution, and the Anti-Federalists (Democrats) were against the Constitution because they were afraid of government interference in their lives. I find it quite ironic that neither party is like they were when they started, don't you? The Anti-Federalists started with more of a Republic view but now have democratic and socialist views. However, the Federalists leaned on the Anti-Federalists view, trying hard to keep the country a Republic as it was intended.

Even though Jefferson was not there for the final draft, he fought so hard to have the Bill of Rights put into the Constitution to insure our liberty and was happy to find out that they had included a Bill of Rights. Yet the politicians of today are trying so hard to get rid of them. What a shame Democrats do not follow the ideals and beliefs of the man who started the party.

James Madison opposed Congress setting up their own wages. It was to be left for the states to take care of their Congressmen. This was so they would work for the states that had elected them. Wouldn't it be nice if we could set our own wages like they do? However, I think the bosses would not go for it. I say since we are supposed to be the bosses of Congress, their wages should be left up to us, and if they play games like they did with balancing the budget to where the government had to shut down, they should not get paid until they pass a budget. Everyone else did not get paid, why should they? I bet they would stop all this politicking if we had control of their paychecks.

The first legislation defining the president's constitutional power to make war was the War Powers Act,[38] which Congress (remember Democrats had control) passed in 1973 over President Richard M. Nixon's veto. We now are seeing why our forefathers gave Congress the power over the military, and Nixon agreed with our forefathers that this power could become abusive; Bill Clinton showed this when he started firing missiles on other countries.

I believe that this constitutes a declaration of war. I imagine 9/11 came about because of this act. That is right; I feel that Clinton may be the reason why we are where we are now. Didn't Japan declare war when they bombed Pearl Harbor, so we declared war back at them? The act says that the president can only declare war if the United States is attacked!

Look at what Obama is doing today with this power.

Our forefathers did not want one man to have power over the military because it could be abused and used against the citizens, also. This was done by Great Britain, Hitler, and Clinton's people at Waco. I personally believe Waco was a test to see how far they could go, and no one caught it that I know of.

The Supreme Court is "a continuing Constitution Convention," it is not supposed to make the laws. It is called to order by "God save the United States and this honorable Court." This liberal court ruled that the Constitution declared separation of church and state. Therefore, to be able to get rid of any religious or should I say Christian symbols and get God

---

38   The War Powers Act; http://www.thecre.com/fedlaw/legal22/warpow.htm ; War Powers, http://www.loc.gov/law/help/war-powers.php

out of the schools is to brainwash our kids into humanism.[39] They declared separation of church and state.

Obama told the schools what to say about him and that they were to make them listen to his speech. You cannot tell me that is not brainwashing when you teach kids what Obama wants them to hear! They are not letting them think for themselves. If you cannot see liberals heading us to a dictatorship, then you might be blind.[40]

There used to be a religious test to get into office because they were afraid of this very thing. In article 6, section c of the Constitution, it stated the oath of office and no religious test: "The Senators and Representatives before mentioned and the members of the several State legislatures, and all executive and judicial officers, both of the United States and of the several States, shall be bound by oath or affirmation, to support this Constitution; but no religious test shall ever be required as a qualification to any office or public trust under the United States. However, they are to be of good morals" (I guess that leaves a lot of people out today).

Citizen requirements seem to have been changed somehow, and I am not sure where. There are several things that make a "natural born citizen," and it is not some alien that comes over and has a child born in the States. There are two tests that have to be fulfilled: They have to be born of US parents (not parent but parents). The reason for this was that if the president did not have two US citizens for parents, his loyalties would be not toward the United States but toward the country of his other parent.[41] What happened to the case *Minor vs.*

---

39   Put man in place of God, http://dictionary.reference.com/browse/humanism

40   Children Forced to Replace Jesus' Name with Barak Obama's in Song, http://www.youtube.com/watch?v=rOwXrI6v4uk&NR=1 ; http://www.youtube.com/watch?v=AGK8ZFKZZUk&feature=related

41   Vattel's Influence on the term a Natural Born Citizen, http://www.birthers.org/USC/Vattel.html

Happersett where the Supreme Court used the word "parents" and not "parent"?[42]

I read a comment from someone who was born in Venezuela to an American mother and a Venezuelan father. He said that he was told that even if he had been born in the United States, he would not be considered a "natural born" Citizen.[43]

They have to be born on US soil or equivalent (trust territories, US bases in foreign countries)[44]; to be president, you must have these and be at least thirty-five years old and have lived in the United States for fourteen years.

Now let's look at Obama. He was supposedly born in Hawaii if you can believe one of the birth certificates out there. He refused to let anyone see his birth certificate, and now all of a sudden one turns up, which usually means a person is hiding something. He was born to one parent who was a US citizen (his mother) and one who never became a US citizen (his father).

Obama's father is from Kenya. His loyalties are for that country. I believe this has an effect on the president and his decisions.[45]

What about the fact that when he was born, Hawaii was not a state but only a trust territory? Senator Orrin Hatch of Utah says that constitutes citizenship.

I have to put this last thing in. Obama is not the son of slaves! His father is a Muslim from Kenya, and his mother is

---

42   Natural Born Citizen, http://naturalborncitizen.wordpress.com/

43   *The Post & Email*, September 8, http://www.thepostemail.com/2011/04/10/when-did-the-definition-of-natural-born-citizen-change/

44   http://puzo1.blogspot.com/2010/04/founder-and-historian-david-ramsay.html

45   P.A. Madison on Nov. 18, 2008, Defining Natural Born, *The Federalist Blog*, http://federalistblog.us/2008/11/natural-born_citizen_defined/ ; When Did the Definition of natural born Citizen Change? Part II http://www.thepostemail.com/2011/04/28/when-did-the-definition-of-natural-born-citizen-change-part-ii/

white! Obama attended the Muslim temple and accidentally admitted his Muslim faith.[46] So all you liberals who are saying that he was the son of slaves need to stop lying to the American people!

He won the election on that lie. Therefore, you put two and two together. None of that was true.[47]

Nowadays if you are a Christian (for example, a strong Baptist who adheres to the King James Version of the Bible like our forefathers did), they take you out of public service because you do not believe what they believe: humanism.[48]

The First Amendment states that the government will not make any laws to establish (set up) a religion. In other words, they could not say everyone had to be Catholic, or Baptist, or Methodist, like England did. There is nowhere in our Constitution that actually speaks of separation of church and state. It only says that there is not supposed to be a religious test given and the government is not supposed to set up a church.

However, even though the government was not to interfere with the churches, our forefathers did expect God to be the center of the government, and if the government started to fall away, they expected the clergies to say something about it. You have seen this in some of the quotes I have already given you. They clung to 2 Corinthians 3:17: "Now the Lord is that Spirit: and where the Spirit of the Lord is, there is liberty." They knew liberty came from God and not through man for man is corrupt and greedy for power over others as we see today. "As it is written, There is none righteous, no, not one" (Romans 3:10).

As you can see there is no separation of church and state! This is just another way of trying to get God out of our country by the liberals. They twisted things around to get it to mean

---

46   http://www.youtube.com/watch?v=tCAffMSWSzY

47   Barack Obama Biography, http://www.biography.com/articles/ barack-obama-12782369

48   Thoughts to Ponder, http://www.behindthebadge.net/articles/a26. html

what they wanted it to mean! The liberals are like the people on the Mayflower that claimed they can do whatever they wanted to do because there is no law. They have to take God out and pretend He does not exist because everyone has to answer to Him. They do not want to be responsible for their actions. So they made a lie and changed our Constitution. Pelosi violated the Constitution by telling churches that if they do not go along with them and tell their people that Democrat programs are good they will not get good loan rates.[49]

The rest of the First Amendment reads like this: "or prohibiting the free exercise thereof; or abridging the freedom of speech, or of the press; or the right of the people peaceably to assemble, and to petition the government for a redress of grievances."

What does "abridging" mean? It means "shortening; lessening; depriving; debarring." Therefore, the government is not to shorten or take away these rights, but they do. Is not that what they are doing when they threaten you with RICO laws for protesting against abortion? No one called these liberals racketeers when they blocked entrances of places they protested when they were young.

This was pure mean spiritedness on Senator Ted Kennedy's part and the courts. Protesting is not the definition of racketeering. Now in some places you have to get a permit! Your permit is the Constitution! This is shortening the rights of certain people because of their beliefs.

Ted Kennedy wanted those that were protesting abortion clinics charged with racketeering, mainly those that did violence. However, even the peaceful demonstrators were being charged with racketeering.

What is racketeering? It is, "a person who obtains money

---

49   Fox News, http://nation.foxnews.com/nancy-pelosi/2010/05/10/ pelosi-tells-catholic-church-preach-amnesty ; YouTube; www. youtube.com/watch?v=BGvZAtOW1eU, Glen Beck ; http://www. foxnews.com/story/0,2933,593123,00.html

illegally, as by bootlegging, fraud, or extortion."(New World Dictionary) Is this what these people doing? No! If they do violence they need to be charged for the destruction. If they killed someone they need to be charged accordingly. Protesting you have that right and therefore they should not be charged with anything.

By the way it would be interesting to know how many of these Congressmen and women had protested things when they were young. That includes our Supreme Justices. How many of them were arrested for violence when protesting?

Also, what about those doing violence against pro-life people? Shouldn't they be charged also? No one talks about that! I will get into all that in my next book. Again I do not advocate violence but all this is interesting don't you think?

When the case NOW vs. Scheidler went to the seventh circuit court they declared that it was not racketeering because there was no economic motivation on his part. The Supreme Court did uphold that decision. There were other cases; United States v. Anderson, United States v. Turkette, United States v. Bagaric, and United States v. Ferguson.

What about Justice Kennedy that said that the First Amendment does not demand reading an economic motivation into RICO? Of course not because RICO did not even exist when our Constitution was formed![50]

The Second Amendment: This is one of the most controversial amendments, almost as controversial as the battle against separation of church and state. This is something the Democrats have been lying so much about and are trying to get rid of. It states, "A well-regulated militia, being necessary to the security of a free State, the right of the people to keep and bear arms, shall not be infringed." The liberals try to get you

---

50   Abortion-Increased Violence Changes The Debate, http://law. jrank.org/pages/3913/Abortion-Increased-Violence-Changes-Debate.html , ACLU Backs Free Speech for All-Except Pro-lifers, Robyn E. Blumner, The Wall Street Journal, February 10, 1999, http://www.forerunner.com/fyi/news/wsj021099.htm ,

to believe that this was until they got a regular military. Well, as I told you before, they had a military. Remember some of these men were in the British army and navy.

In 1788, at the ratification convention, George Mason said that the militia was the whole people because it kept them from being enslaved by their government. Giving up your Constitutional right to bear arms is giving yourself over to slavery.

Richard Henry Lee wrote, "A militia when properly formed are in fact the people themselves ... and include all men capable of bearing arms ... To preserve liberty it is essential that the whole body of people always possess arms."

Each state is to keep a well-formed military. Today, this is the National Guard. This group is to be under the control of each state, not the federal government. States have the right to protect their borders from illegal immigrants coming in. This is a form of invasion. Illegal immigrants have taken a hill here in the United States. They have killed and are bringing in illegal drugs.

Article III of the Articles of Confederation states, "The said States hereby severally enter into a firm league of friendship with each other, for their common defense, the security of their liberties, and their mutual and general welfare, binding themselves to assist each other, against all force offered to, or attacks made upon them, or any of them, on account of religion, sovereignty, trade, or any other pretence whatever."[51] Obama does not understand our Constitution and therefore should not even be President. How can one enforce the law if he doesn't even understand it or knows it? By the way executive orders are unconstitutional. It becomes a dictatorship!

Some Democrats have been successful in deceiving the people into thinking guns are a horrible thing. This is another scare tactic. They talk about Republicans using scare tactics. Let's see, they have global warming, they put every species

---

51   http://www.usconstitution.net/articles.html

they can think of on the endangered list (even if they are not endangered), and they claim the Republicans did this or that when it has been them that did it. It seems that they think that if something does not work, they tell themselves we will just blame the Republicans because no one checks things out anyway.

Karl Marx said that you can get people to do what you want them to do during a crisis, and everywhere you look there is another crisis, according to Democrats. It makes you wonder what the real reason is they want to get rid of guns.

Our forefathers knew that people fall under a dictatorship the minute they give up their weapons. They allow people to defend themselves from others or from an ambitious government that wants to control their lives and make them slaves.

On April 11, 1942, Adolf Hitler said, "The most foolish mistake we could possibly make would be to permit the conquered Eastern people have arms. History teaches that all conquerors who have allowed their subject races to carry arms have prepared their own downfall by doing so. Indeed I would go so far as to say that the underdog is a sine qua non for the overthrow of any sovereignty. So let's not have any native militia or police. German troops alone will bear the sole responsibility for the maintenance of law and order."[52]

Hitler knew history teaches you things! This is why it is so important to learn history! In my day, kids would ask, "Why do I need to learn this stuff?" This is why!

I will give one example. I read about one man saying he was willing to give up the Second Amendment for safety. How ignorant he is to believe that he would have safety!

Red China proved how much safety people have when they give up their liberty to the government. Our forefathers knew this, and this is why they gave us this safety net.

---

52   "Hitler's Table-Talk at the Fuehrer's Headquarters 1941-1942.," Dr. Henry Picker, ed. (Athenaeum Verlag, Bonn, 1951).

"Government is not reason; it is not eloquence; it is force! Like fire, it is a dangerous servant and a fearful master." This is attributed to George Washington.

Look at the incident in Indiana where the Supreme Court said that police officers can come into your home without a warrant, that they can enter your home for no reason at all. They are not upholding the law of the land. This was one of the reasons our forefathers declared independence from Britain! What is going on here in the United States? The government is giving permission for the police to come into someone's home and do whatever they want! That's what they are going to do, especially if there is no reason to do so![53]

However, the police in Indiana had a reason in this particular case. A husband and wife were arguing and went inside their home, and the police wanted to go into the house. Even though they did not say why they wanted to go in, it was to make sure the woman had not been physically assaulted. But they could just drive by and say, "Hey, let's go into this person's home and harass them because we do not like them. Our word will be taken above theirs because we are police officers."

Do not tell me I do not know what I am talking about. I used to live in East Palo Alto. I have been told things have changed, but I lived there when things like that happened!

East Palo Alto, California was declared the murder capital of the world because they would have at least one murder a day. Drug dealers would come into this small two mile radius town because about half of the police force was not straight. There was a group named UMAD that we helped in the 1980s. We would gather together and preach against drugs and that there was a better life than what they were living. We talked about God and what he had done. Because of this we started getting harassed by these particular police.

---

53   Dan Carden, Court: No right to resist illegal cop entry into home, Nwi.com, http://www.nwitimes.com/news/local/govt-and-politics/article_ec169697-a19e-525f-a532-81b3df229697.html

My husband talked to one police officer who was Muslim and asked him about guns that was being confiscated showing back up on the streets. Later this officer told my husband that he was quitting the force. My husband asked him why. He told him because he was right that the guns in the evidence locker were missing and there is nothing to show a sign out to destroy those guns.

There was a guy who harassed a lady that had testified against him. But somehow he always managed to be gone by the time the police arrived. Before we moved the Police Chief quit and some of the other police left when we got a new Police Chief. According to my best friend things are a lot better now. So you cannot depend on every police officer to be honest and people trust them to be telling the truth but if they are crooked you are the one to get in trouble.

What about here where I live now? Some years back the police knock at an twenty one year old's house. She opened the door not wide and it was the police. They asked her to step outside. Just as she begun to open the screen door they jerked her out and went inside. They gave everyone a sobriety test. Some that were in the house were underage and the police did not even contact their parents before giving them the sobriety test.

When it came before the judge the police said they saw a beer can on the table. They did not see the other people until they entered the house. The judge said they had entered into the house illegally. They did not have probable cause. I'll say they did not have probable cause. What you cannot drink in your own home!

So you see they will do this if we continue saying the police can do whatever they want. Yes she was wrong in that she had underage children but there are reasons for the laws we have.

They are to protect us from abuse. The reference I give

the law firm agreed that a police have done things without probable cause or search warrants. Know your rights.[54]

Benjamin Franklin said, "They that give up essential liberty to obtain a little temporary safety deserve neither liberty nor safety."

Our forefathers had a reason for everything they put into our Constitution; do not let any liberal tell you they did not think about the future, because they did, as well as the repetition of history and man's greed for power and domination over others (which today's Democrats want). Why do you think they are using excuses to take over companies and our health care?

George Mason said, "I ask, sir, what is the militia? It is the whole person … To disarm the people is the best way and most effectual way to enslave them." This dispels the liberal lie that our forefathers only wanted weapons in the hands of the citizens until they had a military.

What about James Madison, who wrote the draft of the Bill of Rights? On January 29, 1788, Madison wrote in the Federalist Paper 46:

> Besides the advantage of being armed, which the Americans possess over the people of almost every other nation, the existence of subordinate governments, to which the people are attached, and by which the militia officers are appointed, forms a barrier against the enterprises of ambition, more insurmountable than any which a simple government of any form can admit of. Notwithstanding the military establishments in the several kingdoms of Europe, which are carried as far as the public resources will bear, the governments are afraid to trust the people with arms. And it is

---

54   Wisconsin Criminal Defense Attorneys, Search & Seizure Legal & Illegal, http://www.vanwagnerwood.com/CM/Custom/Search-Seizure.asp

not certain, that with this aid alone they would not be able to shake off their yokes. But were the people to possess the additional advantages of local governments chosen by themselves, who could collect the national will and direct the national force, and of officers appointed out of the militia, by these governments, and attached both to them and to the militia, it may be affirmed with the greatest assurance, that the throne of every tyranny in Europe would be speedily overturned in spite of the legions which surround it.

Alexander Hamilton said in the Federalist Paper 184, "The best we can hope for concerning the people at large is that they be properly armed."

On August 20, 1789, Samuel Adams said in Philadelphia, "That the said Constitution shall never be construed to authorize Congress to infringe the just liberty of the press or the rights of conscience; or to prevent the people of the United States who are peaceable citizens from keeping their own arms."

Thomas Jefferson said, "No free man shall ever be debarred the use of firearms."[55] He also claimed, "The Strongest reason for the people to retain the right to keep and bear arms is, as a last resort, to protect themselves."

Today, there are about 309,250,515 citizens in the United States. According to Ben Best's website:

> In 2006, homicide was the second leading cause of death for infants in the United States. Homicide with a firearm was the second leading cause of death for persons between the ages of 10 and 24, the third leading cause of death for persons between ages 25 and 34, and the fourth leading

---

55   The Obvious Intent of the Second Amendment to the Constitution of the United States, http://www.kc3.com/editorial/quotes.htm

cause of death for persons between ages 5 and 9 or between ages 35 and 44. For persons between ages 45 and 64, homicide with a firearm was the seventh leading cause of death. Homicide with a firearm or by any means was not among the top ten causes of death for persons aged 65 or older, whereas there were at least two forms of homicide among the top ten causes of death for all persons under age 44...

In a Memphis, Tennessee, study, 85% of murderers and 75% of murder victims were intoxicated during the murder. A review of 331 American medical examiner (coroner) studies published between 1975 and 1995 found that victims tested positive for alcohol in 29% of suicides, 38.5% of unintentional injury deaths, 39.7% of motor vehicle deaths and 47.1% of homicides. Half of those murdered by drowning were intoxicated at the time, but only 16% of those murdered by strangling or suffocation were intoxicated. This could mean that it pays to be able to put up a fight! However, the vast majority of murder victims were killed by gunshot or stabbing/cutting of which 30.6% and 43.0% of the victims were intoxicated, respectively. The higher rate of intoxication for stabbings may indicate a greater impulsiveness for crimes committed with this kind of weapon (grabbing for a handy knife or pair of scissors in a moment of drunken rage).[56]

So to me, the real culprit is alcohol and drugs, but no one wants to touch this. We are making drugs legal just like alcohol, and we have already seen the effects of alcohol. They found that places where people can carry concealed guns had

---

56   http://www.benbest.com/lifeext/murder.html#circumstance

fewer murders. Murders are done by objects as well as guns. So are we going to take away our kitchen knives and tools to fix the house? If one wants to commit a murder it will not matter whether it is a gun, knife, rock, hand, or any other object. What is the real reason liberals are trying to get rid of guns? In 1994, US Senator Howard Metzenbaum (D-OH), said, "I don't care about crime, I just want to get the guns." Being a Jew himself, it is a shame that he forgot what happened to the Jews with Hitler's way of thinking.[57]

Now we have a Congress that is handing us over to the United Nations. Obama said that the UN takes precedence over our Constitution, even though he took an oath to defend the Constitution. This is another reason he should be taken out of office.[58] A lame duck law, H.R. 2159,[59] allows the attorney general to revoke the Second Amendment rights of any citizen he suspects is a terrorist, whether there is proof or not.[60] And a Republican introduced it! No proof, just suspicion!

Those who have been in the military are on the list of possible terrorists, and they get searched every time they take a flight. Many of them do not even know why, but my husband learned why. We no longer fly because of this, unless we absolutely have to. We travel everywhere by car.

The Assault Weapons Ban is a law to permanently get rid

---

57 Spirit Caller, The Right to Bear Arms, http://www.spiritcaller. net/quotes/guns.htm ; http://thefiringline.com/library/quotes/ antifreedom.xml ; Transcript of Written Testimony by Tanya K. Metaksa, House Judiciary Committee, April 25, 1994, http:// www.firearmsandliberty.com/metaksa.testimony.html

58 Alec Jones, The DMonline, Barry's constitutional blunders, April 27, 2011, http://www.thedmonline.com/article/ barry%E2%80%99s-constitutional-blunders , http://wtpotus. wordpress.com/2011/03/06/obama-chrysler-fiat-and-gaddafi/

59 Gun Owner Blacklist Bill Introduced in U.S. House, http://www. nraila.org/Issues/FactSheets/Read.aspx?id=253&issue=010

60 NRA, http://www.nraila.org/Issues/FactSheets/Read. aspx?id=253&issue=010, Bill H.R. 2159 , http://www.govtrack.us/ congress/billtext.xpd?bill=h111-2159

of automatic rifles and shotguns. H.R. 45[61] creates a national gun registry, requires a two-day waiting period, raises taxes on gun sales, bans all private firearms sales, and forces you to take a written exam to prove you can own a gun. I do not see that anywhere in the Constitution!

The Small Arms Treaty allows the United Nations to come into your home and confiscate your guns and destroy all "unauthorized" civilian firearms. Hillary Clinton said, "The United States is committed to actively pursuing a strong and robust [Small Arms] treaty."[62]

This is totally illegal. You want to tell me that the Democrats are not trying to hand our country over? One of the reasons for the Revolution was because British soldiers could go into people's homes without cause. Now the Democrats want foreign countries to come into your home! Who are they for? Not you!

They are into squashing our freedom of speech. They are trying to pass an act to silence any political organization that refuses to submit to their unconstitutional regulations and fights for its members' right to privacy.

If there needs to be any fear going on, it is fear of the Democratic Party for ignoring our Constitution and getting rid of our liberty.

I want you to give this some thought. Some Democrats who want to get rid of your guns actually have permits to carry their own guns. Doesn't that sound strange to you? Who are the real hypocrites?[63]

When it came time to ratify the Constitution, the debates got even hotter. I found it hilarious that when the Philadelphia Assembly called for a ratifying convention, the Anti-Federalists

---

61   H.R. 45, http://thomas.loc.gov/cgi-bin/query/z?c111:H.R.45
62   http://www.nagr.org/1dpetition.aspx?pid=1&r=
63   NRA: Marc Chamot, *SF Conservative Examiner*, April 16, 2011,
      http://www.examiner.com/conservative-in-san-francisco/ca-
      assembly-democrats-want-gun-carry-permits-but-don-t-want-you-
      to-have-one

absented themselves, leaving the Assembly two short of a quorum. The next morning, a crowd gathered and dragged two of the absentees into the State House and held them firmly in place until roll call was over and a quorum was reached.

We probably should have done that when the Brady Bill was being passed, because there was only one Democrat present. This is a shame on the Republicans' part as far as I am concerned. They did not care enough for our constitutional rights.

Anyway, a ratifying convention was ordered. Pennsylvania was the first state to call for a convention.

In Delaware, the convention was held, and on December 7, the Constitution was ratified by unanimous vote.

In Philadelphia, there was three weeks of discussion, and on December 12, it passed by a forty-six-to-twenty-three vote.

In New Jersey, there was one week of discussion, and it passed unanimously on December 18.

In Connecticut, there were five days of discussion, and on January 9, it was passed by a vote of three to one.

In Massachusetts, they would not ratify it until amendments were guaranteed in the Constitution. On February 6, John Adams promised that amendments would be allowed. After the guarantee, they voted it in by 187 to 168.

Jefferson wrote to Alexander Donald from Paris, "I wish with all my soul that the nine first conventions may accept the new Constitution to secure to us the good it contain; but I equally wish that the four latest, whichever they be, may refuse to accede to it till a declaration of rights be annexed."[64]

So you see that Jefferson was not against the Constitution but wanted to make sure that certain rights were not infringed upon, which the government has been doing for the past forty years. This also shows that it was well thought of by our

---

64   A Strategy on Ratification, http://www.let.rug.nl/usa/P/tj3/ writings/brf/jefl67.htm

forefathers and dispels the lies that they did not think of the future.

Maryland ratified the Constitution on April 26 by a vote of sixty-three to eleven. I had to laugh when I read that Luther Martin told Daniel of St. Thomas Jenifer, "I'll be hanged if ever the people of Maryland agree to it!" His colleague replied, "I advise you to stay in Philadelphia, lest you should be hanged." This shows how hot the debates were over the Constitution.

On May 28, South Carolina ratified the Constitution by a vote of two to one. This state, along with Virginia, was important in determining public opinion. New Hampshire was slow in making their decision. They met in February and then adjourned until June, mainly to see how the other states felt about this new Constitution. After eight states ratified it, New Hampshire ratified it on June 21 by a vote of fifty-seven to forty-six.

The people in Virginia had many heated debates over the same issues the people of Massachusetts had. Tempers were high and the contest was bitter, in spite of the support of Washington and Madison. Part of the reason was that Patrick Henry and George Mason opposed it to the very end. They finally decided to ratify, "Under the conviction that what so ever imperfections may exist in the Constitution ought rather to be examined in the mode prescribed therein, than to bring the Union into danger by delay, with a hope of obtaining amendments previous to the ratification." So again you see that there was careful consideration when it came to the amendments. So when a Democrat knocks down the amendments, they are knocking down their own party, for they insisted on having amendments (for which I'm glad).

New York began its convention on June 17. New York was more Anti-Federalist than Federalist. However, even with those odds, the people of New York ratified the Constitution.

It is felt that most of the credit for this should go to Alexander Hamilton. He published a series of essays in *The*

Independent Gazetteer known as the Federalist Papers. When Newt Gingrich suggested that people should read them, the Democrats objected and said they would not put them in the school curriculum.

First of all, it is not up to the federal government but the individual states to decide what should be put in their school's curriculum. Remember the twenty-six lead soldiers that one can conquer the world with? Well, Karl Marx said something similar. Why do you think that Hitler and Mao destroyed books and took over the education of the children?

Does not Obama keep having the schools teach songs about him, lifting him up and making him look good in the children's eyes so that when they grow up, they will think he is great? In the meantime, he is destroying our economy. This is brainwashing; shame on the teachers who do it.

Second, is the reason they discourage people from reading the Federalist Papers because they will find out the truth about the Constitution and show how liberals have been changing it?

Third, could it be that it might show why things are not working in our government, because they have gone so far from what our forefathers intended, hmm?

Karl Marx said, "Take away the heritage of a people and they are easily persuaded."

Hamilton wrote fifty of these essays. Madison wrote about thirty, and John Jay wrote five. Hamilton's personal influence was a strong force in New York. He met every objection that came at him. Finally, on July 26, with the same stipulation over amendments, New York voted thirty to twenty-seven to ratify the Constitution. (70)

Stephen Hopkins wrote to Jefferson in April 1788, "You will be surprised when I tell you that our public papers have announced General Washington to be a fool influenced and led by that knave Dr. Franklin, who is a public Defaulter for Millions of Dollars, that Mr. Morris had defrauded the public out of as many Millions as you please and that they are to cover their frauds by this new Government."[65]

They made false statements against them to get rid of the Constitution. This sounds like a typical liberal of today, when they do not want people to look at an issue in depth. I see name calling and cutting someone's character has not changed.

Those who came out to vote were a small percentage of the population, and mostly upper class.

The new government was already in operation before the people of North Carolina and Rhode Island ratified the Constitution. The new government passed a revenue act, levying duties upon foreign goods, specifically toward imports from Rhode Island and North Carolina. So on November 21, 1789, the people of North Carolina ratified the Constitution. However, the people of Rhode Island held out until a bill was taken up to grant the president authority to stop all commercial trade with them and demand payment of its share of the federal debt. The bill stopped at the Senate. The people of Rode Island finally gave in and ratified the Constitution on May 20.[70]

Now I'm going to skip all the way to the Civil War, where people like Theodore Parker, Harriet Tubman, Hoh Greenleaf, Frederick Douglass, and the Republicans wanted to get rid of slavery.[66] The liberals are not going to like me shedding some light here, and neither are some of our citizens with African ancestors.

Now I want you to hear this and think about it I will not call anyone African American, Japanese American, Mexican American, and so forth! The reason is, you are either a US citizen or not. This is just another way of splitting the country. This is just another way to focus on race under the falsehood of political correctness and supposed sensitivity.

---

65   *Documentary History of the Constitution*, vol. IV, p. 563.

66   Abolitionists, http://www.saylor.org/site/wp-content/uploads/2011/05/Abolitionism.pdf ; Carleton Mabee, *Black Freedom*, 1970.

When I was working at Ford Aerospace, I knew a woman whose parents and uncles were naturalized citizens from Mexico. I mentioned what I just stated, that you were either a US citizen or not. Not this Mexican American and so on. This is indirectly saying you are only half a citizen. She asked me to explain what I meant. I guess I had upset her and she had fallen for this junk.

When she told her uncle what I had said, he said that I was right. I know I am right! This is a way for liberals to separate Americans! This creates division in the country, and you have to have division to set up control over people. You know the old saying, "United we stand, divided we fall." This is so true; liberals want to create this division. You find unity by finding what you have in common: we are United States citizens!

I think another big cover-up in teaching US history involves the Civil War. Democrats do not want people to know that the battle against slavery was really Republicans against Democrats, not the North against the South. The southern states were well known as Democratic states.

My grandmother would go to the polls and just pull the Democratic lever without even checking out the candidates. There are many people like that on both sides of the fence. Look at what we have today with Obama.

Spain brought the Africans over and made them slaves with the help of other Africans. The Spaniards also made the Indians slaves.

Because England had serfs (white slaves) and brought over indentured servants (supposedly five to seven years), it was easy for them to transfer over to mostly blacks in the South and Indians in the West.

The Spaniards called the Africans "Negros" ("e" has a long "a" sound), which in the Spanish language is "black," nothing else! I am tired of people trying to lie and keep the race card going! These people were so dark skinned that they called them black, because they were almost black color. Just look at some who have not intermarried![67] Believe me, if "Negro" meant anything else, they would not have given the United Negro College Fund that name! I took basic Spanish in high school. "Negro" means "black"!

Now I know that a lot of people are not going to like what I say next, but both blacks and whites owned slaves. That is right, blacks owned slaves, also. This was mentioned in the TV show *A Different World*. One of the characters found out that her ancestors had once bought slaves. A teacher replied that they could have bought their relatives. I think that these people need to face reality. They are not so clean in their background either.

The United States had indentured servants. "Indentured" means "a worker for a set of time"; some servants agreed to work (usually three to seven years) in exchange for passage to the United States, food, and clothing. After their servitude was over, then they were freed. One black indentured servant, Anthony Johnson, gained his freedom and bought land and his own black indentured servant. Now I knew that blacks had slaves, but Glen Beck on Fox News taught me who the first slave owner was. I looked it up and it was true. It was not a white person who started slavery here in the United States. It was a black man. Surprise! Surprise!

Three servants ran away: two whites and one black. The two whites had extended time put on their servitude, and the black was ordered to work for life under Johnson. It was probably someone from an enemy tribe. Who knows?

Natives in Africa sold their enemies into slavery; do not give me this garbage that they treated their slaves differently. That is not true. These were their enemies. They hated them!

Do I believe in slavery? Emphatically, *no*! This is why I am bringing up this subject. If we keep going toward liberalism, which leads to Socialism, which is a step toward Communism, we will all be slaves to the government, and the only ones who

---

67   Dictionary.com, http://dictionary.reference.com/browse/negro

will be able to live decently will be our dictators. It will start with all these illegal immigrants.

If we do not open our eyes, we will repeat history. Then it will be the people called Christians and Jews. Mankind loves to have power over other people. Why do you think there are bullies?

There is slavery even today. Oprah Winfrey demonstrated this when she bought one and showed it on a documentary. Many women are kidnapped and put into slavery overseas.

How about the Mexicans who come over here illegally? People exploit them because they can hold it over their heads that they are over here illegally, and that includes some of our self-righteous politicians. Sweatshops in this country as well as other countries are in the news. It all boils down to this: man, no matter what race, likes to dominate others.

I think what irritates me the most is some men of color think they have a patent on oppression. There is not a race that has not been oppressed. I can tell them how the Indians were treated. They were here before the Spanish, before the English, before the French, and so on. By the way, the French were the only ones who treated the Indians decently (for the most part). They intermarried with them and respected the land.

Because the Indians' ways were strange, they were considered barbarians. When they tried to defend their homes and families (as we would), they were called savages. The media depicted them as horrible creatures, just like the media today depicts anyone who believes in family values, God, and country like our forefathers intended, people who have morals, do not go for Socialism, are against killing babies just because they are not outside the womb, and a lot more I could name. Are you beginning to see the parallel?

The Indians were marched onto reservations. Their women were raped, their babies were ripped from their bellies, and their breasts were cut off. Of course, this would not really bother liberals; after all, those were not really babies in the women's bellies, they were just blobs of cells, so it does not matter. However, you do not read about this in the history books.

It has only been since the 1970s that they have really been able to pass the boundary lines. Oh sure, some went to war for us, but it was back to the reservation after the war.

What about the Jews? They have been in bondage to different races for thousands of years. Hitler did all he could to annihilate them, and what about the Egyptians, who put them into slavery? The Muslims want to get rid of them, also.

What about all the lies that have been spread about the Christians? They have been killed in other countries because of their beliefs. Liberals today are trying the same tactics that Hitler did with the Jews. They use fear to make people dislike Christians. People of every race are Christians.

I remember very vividly when my husband and I moved to East Palo Alto. We ran into such bigotry from people of color there. The thing was they were going by skin color and did not know that there was black in Don's family background.

You cannot judge someone by his or her color; you must decide what kind of person they are inside. Remember, it was whites who wanted to end slavery! I will get into how white Christians helped bring about the end of slavery. I put down anyone who teaches our children prejudices of any kind. I do not care what race you are.

Another incident occurred when we moved to Costilla County in Colorado. Now I want you know that Don has black in his background and I have Mohawk in my background. My dad was French and Indian. The prejudices that ran there in Costilla were high also, against whites.

I talked to one lady about people's attitude, and she said, "Well, now you know how it feels." Excuse me? Now I know how it feels when I have never shown any prejudice against anyone! I have not judged someone by race, so why should it be okay for someone to judge me when they do not even know me? I have had attitudes against me just because of my faith. I have even had noses put up just because I am a woman. How about when I go job hunting and I am looked upon with reproach because of my age?

I had known this woman for a few years, and I know she never heard one prejudiced remark from me! I have many friends from different backgrounds. Some people are just hypocrites! Am I prejudiced just because I am white? I judge people by the way they act and the kind of person they are. We all make mistakes, so I am not talking about that but your heart. Two wrongs never make a right!

The northern states abolished slavery after the Revolution. However, the South kept it because they felt it was the basis of economic prosperity. Sounds like today with illegal immigrants. They did not have to pay higher wages. All they had to do was provide a place for them to stay, food, and clothing: not much of anything. However, some owners treated their slaves well, almost like family, but liberals do not bring that out either because they want discord. This gives them power.

Also, I will remind you the Northwest Ordinance prohibited slavery in the Northwest Territory. The Republicans and Democrats continued to debate the slave issue for some time. The Fugitive Slave Law of 1793 made provisions to return slaves that had run away. However, by 1807 a law passed stopping slaves from being imported.

The Republicans and those terrible religious groups that stand for what is right became very active against slavery. Some Democrats twisted the Bible and the Constitution to back their views, just like the liberals today twist the Constitution to promote separation of church and state, and change freedom of speech to freedom of expression, which caused violence and the desecration of our flag, trampling over the blood of those who died for freedom. What was that song they played while the FBI was killing those people at Waco? Oh yes: "These boots are made for walking … these boots are gonna walk all over you."

Just like the South tried to squash the literature of anti-slavery, the liberals try to squash the freedom of speech of anyone who disagrees with them. I see Democrats have not changed in this area either. The South in fact passed a gag rule so anything pertaining to slavery was put aside, no debates, no action. Now keep in mind that the South is mainly Democrats.

In 1850, there were 347,525 slave holders out of a total population of 6,000,000 in the slave states. Half of them owned four or fewer slaves. Fewer than 1,800 owned more than 100 slaves.[68]

In 1860, there were 250,000 free blacks in the South, and some of them owned slaves. Go ahead and get mad. I do not care, but it is true. Not all of them bought their families out of slavery. Remember I told you slavery was not unfamiliar with the people of Africa. Egypt had slaves, and you may find most countries have them today. That includes Kenya, where Obama spent his school years and where his father is from.

It was all in the name of fear just like the liberals are trying to get people afraid of Christians with lies and perversions. They even get some Christians to get onto other Christians because they are not tolerant of wrong.

These liberals know nothing about true Christianity, but they spout off like they are experts. That name, Christian, was given to the people who followed Christ's teachings. They were so much like Christ that they were given the name Christian, meaning "Christ like."[69] Plus they kept hearing the gospel about Jesus Christ. Christ is a title and not a last name. You are not a Christian because of the church you go to.

---

68   Robert Guisepi, American Civil War, http://history-world.org/american_civil_war.htm

69   Acts 11:23–27, 26:28; 1 Peter 4:16; South Asian Concern, http://www.southasianconcern.org/faith/detail/where_does_the_name_christian_come_from/

Just face it; they do not like the idea of there being any absolutes in the world. This would mean they would have to be responsible for their own actions. Therefore, they despise Christians because they are reminded that there are absolutes in our world. If there are no absolutes, then you have chaos, and you can see it today because of the falling away. Now I want to repeat, I am not saying this about all liberals but a lot of them. They do not know what they are giving up. They have been blinded to the truth.

President Millard Fillmore (Whig party) from New York favored a bill that made the Fugitive Law Act more effective. He declared California a free state, new territories of New Mexico and Utah were sovereignty states, slave trade was abolished in the District of Columbia, and the United States paid $10,000,000 to Mexico for New Mexico.

The Whig party faded out around 1852. The new Republican party was composed of anti-slavery, Whigs, Democrats, and the Free Soldiers in Michigan. John Fremont ran against Democrat James Buchanan. Buchanan won, even though he did not have a majority of popular votes.

The Dred Scott case was brought before the Supreme Court. Scott was a slave who declared he was a free man because he had been born on free soil. This was backed by anti-slavery men. However, the court declared that as a descendant of slaves, he was a slave and was returned to his owner. At this point, the North and South realized that slavery and freedom could no longer coexist in the United States. They should have realized this long ago. You cannot have a free nation and yet have the sin of slavery in it.

Stephen Douglas, a Democrat, wanted to open slavery in Kansas and Nebraska. This caused heated debates because that was part of the Northwest and that was supposed to be free.

Buchanan's platform in 1856 was against Catholics and foreigners while the newly formed Republican Party's platform was against extension of slavery. The Republicans nominated

John C. Fremont, an explorer from the free state of California. He was new to politics. He had gotten 359 votes while Lincoln only got 110.

This did not discourage the young Republican. He hammered at the slave issue constantly. He ran against Douglas, who believed in sovereignty. Douglas started his campaign for the Democrats by declaring slavery was all right. He said that Lincoln advocated war between the North and South, that all states would become free or slave. Democrats seem to be real good at scare tactics, but he was not far from the truth in this case. Also, this is probably where the idea came from that the war was between the North and South. Douglas won the Senate anyway.

At this time, John Brown seized the federal arsenal. He was hoping to start a rebellion to free the slaves. However, Robert E. Lee, a soldier in the US Army at the time, took the arsenal back from Brown and Brown was tried, convicted, and then hanged.

May I add that Robert E. Lee was against slavery but he went with the South because of his belief in the sovereignty of the states? The South tried to blame the North for what happened.

Lincoln again ran against Douglas but this time for the presidency. Senator Bell had decided to run Lincoln in 1860 because he had become nationally known for his debates with Douglas. The platform was about high tariffs, public works, and an end to the extension of slavery. Fillmore declared that if the Republicans won, it would dissolve the Union. Lincoln told him that they were the "disunionists" and not them. The attempt would have to be made by them because they did not want to dissolve it. The liberals are dissolving our country by their changing what our Constitution's meaning is and thinking Socialism or world federalism is the way.

Just like today, the Democrats were able to use fear to get

support, not that some Republicans do not also use that tactic, but liberals do it more and use the word "crisis."

The *New York Times* reported $150,000 from slave states went to Pennsylvania, $50,000 from Belmont, New York, Wall Street bankers and brokers sent $100,000 to the Democrats. The Democrats spent nearly $500,000. That was a lot of money in those days.[70]

Roger Brooke Taney (a white man) freed his own slaves. He supported those who were too old to work. However, he had one fault. He did not believe the Constitution meant blacks when it spoke of "citizens" or referred to them when the Declaration of Independence stated "all men are created equal." I am not sure what he thought the definition of "all" was, and why did the North give up their slaves after the Revolutionary War? Maybe they were smarter than he was or some Democrats.

Then there came the question that if those who wrote the documents believed slavery was not a good thing, why didn't they stop the slave trade in 1808? I myself say that the majority did not own slaves. Only about twelve of those who wrote the Constitution owned slaves, and there was a big debate ever since the Revolution over slavery. So it is not that they had not been trying to do so.

However, Lincoln responded that if it was only referring to the English, then the French, Germans, and all other white races gone to pot with the judge's inferior races. Now keep in mind that Karl Marx was living during this time and spreading his doctrine as well as Darwin. This is what Lincoln was fighting in the Democratic Party, and they are still hanging on to this doctrine even though it has proven to not work. They are still trying to spread the wealth and conquer us with those twenty-six lead soldiers and fear.

Bloodshed started. Pro-slavery people threatened anti-

---

70   A lot of the statistics came from the *Encylopedia Britannica* and *Black Freedom*, Carleton Mabee, 1970.

slavery people (just like the pro-choice threaten and have done violence against the pro-life). The pro-lifers have done the same to pro-choice people. At Pottawatomie Creek Massacre, five free-state men were killed.

John Brown decided to get even. The victims, however, were poor farmers and not pro-slavery. This is why you do not use violence to change things. It has never solved anything, and innocent people get hurt or killed. Violence should only be used when there is no other recourse, like when our forefathers faced the British.

The Democrats started to try and divide the Republican Party with suspicions and jealousies. This seems to be their modus operandi even in this election. They even tried a gag act to shut people up about slavery. Well, that tactic has not changed with the Democratic Party. They are trying that today to keep people from criticizing the government. It is unconstitutional now as it was then!

I want to tell the Republican Party today, "Stop listening to the Democrats and their exaggerated polls. Stick to the truth and what is right, like life being precious and not something to be discarded like an old shoe." The Republican Party held fast to what was right about slavery and did not waver. They *won*!

Henry Ward Beecher was a Presbyterian minister and a leader of the abolitionists. His lectures helped win people over to the Republican view on slavery.

On July 10, 1858, Lincoln said in a speech in Chicago, "The Republican party is made up of those who, as far as they can peaceably, will oppose the extension of slavery and who will hope for its ultimate extinction."

The first black American in Congress was Hiram Rhodes Revels, a Republican from Mississippi (1870–1871):

> Revels arrived in Washington at the end of January 1870, but could not present his credentials until Mississippi was readmitted to the United States on February 23. Senate Republicans sought

to swear in Revels immediately afterwards, but Senate Democrats were determined to block the effort. Led by Senator Garrett Davis of Kentucky and Senator Willard Saulsbury of Delaware, the Democrats claimed Revels's election was null and void, arguing that Mississippi was under military rule and lacked a civil government to confirm his election. Others claimed Revels were not a U.S. citizen until the passage of the 14th Amendment in 1868 and was therefore ineligible to become a U.S. Senator. Senate Republicans rallied to his defense.[13]

"During the 1992 elections alone the total black membership in Congress grew by one-third and Carol Moseley-Braun of Illinois (1993–1999) was elected as the first black woman and the first African-American Democrat to serve in the US Senate."[13] Look how long it took for Democrats to have a black person in Congress. Who are the real hypocrites? They probably thought Hillary Clinton would win over Obama.

Lincoln said in the same state on September 11, 1858, "The difference between the Republican and the Democratic parties on the leading issue of this contest, as I understand it, is that the former consider slavery a moral, social, and political wrong...I will not allege that the Democratic party consider slavery morally, socially, and politically right, though their tendency to that view has, in my opinion, been constant and unmistakable for the past five years."

When Lincoln was victorious, the Democrats took it as a sign for secession. Therefore, the Confederacy was formed, consisting of the southern states, and this again is because they were mostly Democrats in those states. Now I want you to know I am from Louisiana. So do not think I am some Yankee saying this. I am not from the North!

I do want you to think about how strange it is that a

black person would belong to the very party that wanted to keep them in slavery. Now they have them in slavery to the government for handouts instead of encouraging them to be self-sufficient. Of course, they are trying to make everyone dependent on them. They want to be everyone's master now.

I laugh when I hear Democrats say their favorite president was Lincoln. The reason I laugh is everything he stood for, they have condemned. He was a man who believed in the Bible and carried it wherever he went.[71]

Lincoln believed that the Bible should not only govern people's lives but the government, even though he believed that pastors should not use the pulpit for politics. He had forgotten that it was those preachers that brought about our independence. You often see pictures of Lincoln holding a book; it is the Bible. The liberals believe we should teach every religion on earth except Christianity (the truth).

He knew liberty came from God, but liberals believe the government can grant rights to whoever they please no matter if it steps on someone else's rights or liberty.

He condemned class hatred. The liberals adhere to Karl Marx's teachings not only in creating class envy but race hatred.[72] Yet these same liberals in office have more money than most of us will see in our lifetime. Lincoln said, "I don't believe in a law to prevent a man from getting rich; it would do more harm than good. So while we do not propose any war

---

71   The first site has many links about Abraham Lincoln: Abraham Lincoln Class Room, http://www.abrahamlincolnsclassroom. org/Library/newsletter.asp?ID=127&CRLI=175 , http:// www.greatamericanhistory.net/lincolnsfaith.htm , http:// www.abrahamlincolnsclassroom.org/Library/newsletter. asp?ID=111&CRLI=159

72   Karl Marx's American Triumph, http://arcofcc.freeservers. com/Documents/karlmarx.html , http://www.coeinc. org/allpages/materials/Articles/Articles/PDF%20Files/ AbrahamLincolnDeniesALoan.pdf , http://www.icl-fi.org/english/ wv/946/let-marx.html

upon capital, we do wish to allow the humblest man an equal chance to get rich with everybody else."[73]

Lincoln believed that you do not help men by doing for them what they should do for themselves. Did he not tell his brother to go find a job? He did not keep giving his brother money because his brother did not learn any lessons. His brother kept getting into the same mess. So he would keep asking for money. Is this not what the liberals are doing with all this stimulus money?

When Lincoln was postmaster at Salem, the office was closed but no agent came to close it. He ended up owing about $17. A friend offered to lend him the money, but he did not want to borrow it. He preferred to use his savings; he had the exact amount he owed. As the saying goes, "His honesty stayed intact."[74]

Isn't this what President Kennedy tried to say? In his speech he said, "Ask not what your country can do for you but what you can do for your country." As I understand it, his party did not like what he said, but he was right. If people are hungry, let them glean out in the fields like in the old days. They do that here in Colorado. I have seen it in Washington and California. I did it myself as a little girl and have done it as an adult.

Lincoln believed that you should not take away a man's incentive.

Even though a lot of quotes that people say are from Lincoln actually were said by Rev. Boetscher, a preacher, Lincoln believed these things.[75] He was not a friend of Karl Marx.

During the Reagan years, our country prospered, but you will find the Democrats and liberals lied about that because

73 Speech at New Haven, Connecticut, March 6, 1860, http://showcase.netins.net/web/creative/lincoln/speeches/quotes.htm

74 *America, The Birth of Freedom*, DVD, Millcreek.

75 Abraham Lincoln, A Legacy of Freedom, http://www.america.gov/media/pdf/books/lincoln.pdf

just like the Bolsheviks, they do not want you to know that capitalism works and Socialism does not work. Just keep in mind what Jamestown, Virginia, and the Pilgrims learned. In every country that went into Socialism, everyone became poor (except those in office or their families). No one teaches about this, but Calvin Coolidge believed in small government.

Okay, now that we have seen some of Lincoln's beliefs, let's talk about the Underground Railroad, which they have given the blacks all the credit for. It was actually whites and blacks working together. They risked their homes, freedom, and lives to help the slaves, and it makes me so mad when they are not given credit where credit is due.

The Underground Railroad was started up by northern abolitionists (whites) and philanthropists (free blacks and ex-slaves). Church leaders like Quaker Thomas Garrett helped. Harriet Beecher Stowe, who wrote *Uncle Tom's Cabin*, had contacts with the Underground Railroad in Cincinnati. With her book, she helped shape the opinions of the people.

Even though this system was a small operation, it helped gain sympathy in the North and convinced the South that the North would not allow slavery to go unchallenged.

Fourteen northern states were involved, as was Canada, which was beyond the reach of the slave hunters. Springdale-West Branch, east of Iowa City, was another stop for the Underground Railroad. John Brown often visited there.

Many whites gave up not only their lives but their possessions as well as spending time in jail just like our forefathers who wrote the Declaration of Independence and fought in the Revolution. These were real men and women in those days. If you are going to teach history, teach the whole truth. I think one of the best books I ever read is *Black Freedom* by Carleton Mabee, written in 1970. It is about nonviolent abolitionists from 1830 all the way through the Civil War.

This book talks about the boycotts against products made

by slaves as well as against segregated schools, and you thought that was something new in the 1960s.

The Garrisonians refused to compromise when it came to the blacks' education. Too bad people are willing to compromise on what is right today and let our society go down. The book talks about many other things including the Underground Railroad and John Brown's raid. If you can get your hands on it, read it. It will open your eyes to a lot of things that have been hidden by liberals when they took over the school systems.

When it came to the Underground Railroad, there were three major groups. There were the Garrisonians, which were led by William Lloyd Garrison in Boston. They were nonviolent in their abolitionist activities but not necessarily in other parts of their lives. The Garrisonians were identified with the American Antislavery Societies. Their strength came from not compromising. Republicans, take heed to this. However, they were not tactful in their methods or in what they said.

The Quakers, which many know, were a nonviolent Christian group not only in their abolitionist activities but also in their personal lives. They were careful in what they condemned. Their center was in Philadelphia. There were others in North Carolina and Indiana. They stressed forgiveness of one's enemies. This group did the most good in the Underground Railroad. They were also the ones that started it. They created private schools for the blacks.

Lastly, there were the Tappanites, named after Lewis Tappan. Tappan was a New York merchant. Their center was in New York. They were identified with the American Antislavery Society and the American Missionary Association.

This group varied in degrees of nonviolence. The nonviolence was strictly in their abolitionist activities. Lewis Tappan and S. S. Jocelyn would not even defend their property from the antiabolitionist mobs. However, Arthur Tappan and Alvin Stewart did use force.

The Tappanites worked through political parties and

churches. They were strong through the Liberty party, among Congregationalists and Presbyterians.

Again, the United States can thank God for godly men and women who stood up for liberty here in our country. So when the liberals say that Christians' principles are going to destroy America, it has been proven that these principles (God's word) have made this country and defended freedom. Humanism has only proven fatal to a country.

Going on, Frederick Douglass, an escaped slave, started as a nonviolent Garrisonian. The more violent were Nat Turner, a Virginia slave, who started a slave revolt; Cassius M. Clay, who used pistols and knives; and of course, John Brown, who ended up hanged.

Helping runaway slaves was dangerous for both whites and blacks. One free black who helped was sold into slavery herself, along with her two children. Charles T. Torrey, a young minister, was sentenced to six years of hard labor in prison. He died in the prison. Jonathon Walker, a sea captain, was branded by a red hot iron on the hand with the letters "SS" (meaning slave stealer).[76]

Many slaves carried weapons, but some did not, like James W. C. Pennington, a blacksmith. Later on, he became a Tappanite pastor. Henry Bibb, who became a leading abolitionist, wrote to his master and even invited him to visit after he escaped to freedom. Thomas Van Rensselaer went to his former master and dined with him. However, not all slaves were as forgiving.[77]

Although the Quakers pioneered the Underground Railroad, there were some who opposed it because it was illegal. Some Quaker Undergrounders were disowned because they were more zealous, like Isaac Hopper and Levi Coffin.

The fugitive slaves were hid in white and black homes.

---

76   African Americans, http://www.nps.gov/guis/historyculture/
        african-americans.htm

77   *Black Freedom*, Carleton Mabee, 1970.

Robert Purvis, a Garrisonian black, hid fugitives in his home. T. S. Writhe was a black Tappanite pastor, and Quaker Isaac T. Hopper was known as the "North Star." David Ruggles, a black Garrisonian, had to change his residence and wear disguises, for his life was endangered because he helped protect slaves from the slave catchers. These people even hid them in black communities. This is something that blacks and liberals are not going to like to hear, but it is the truth. Some blacks in these communities reported the fugitive slaves to the slave catchers for money.

I think you are beginning to get the idea. It was not just blacks that were in the Underground Railroad, there were whites; it was not just any whites but those nasty Christians that you hear about from the liberals, and they started it (Quakers). Both races lost their homes, lives, and freedom, and they both went to prison because of their work with the Underground Railroad.

Also, it was not just whites that turned slaves in but blacks turned them into the slave hunters. However, in the schools, they make it sound as though only blacks ran the Underground Railroad and all whites were callous and dragged slaves back to their masters. This is not true, as you can see.[78]

I want to tell you of one other person. His name was Seth Conklin; he went all the way to Alabama to help a slave family escape. He had been a soldier at one time. Pastor Turness of Philadelphia helped Conklin prepare for the mission.

Conklin got the family to the Tennessee River. He played the role of a slave master. The slave mother and daughter hid under blankets on a skiff while the slave boys rowed. Observers on the banks yelled and fired their guns at them but decided they could not hear them because of the wind. However, after they left the skiff and moved north into Indiana, they got captured. The family went back into slavery, and Conklin was put in chains for trial. Later Conklin was found in the river

---

78   *Black Freedom.*

with his skull broken. He still had his chains on. I want you to think about this very hard, and the next time you want to play the race card for your own gain, you remember those people that gave their lives for freedom from the Revolution and even up to today. Remember, when you point that finger you have three pointing right back at you.

Now you think about it, liberals, when you say only blacks worked the Underground Railroad. This white man was killed while being chained up for helping a slave family. He could not defend himself. He stood there while the very people who were supposed to keep him alive and bring him to justice smashed his head in. He is not the only one you trampled all over who has helped to give freedom to the blacks, but you have done it to the very ones that set up the United States, and for what? To get political power, that is for what, as I see it!

President Lincoln said, "In America up to now, all men are created equal except for Negroes."

By the way, since Abraham Lincoln used the word "Negroes" in his statement, I want to remind you that this word was used by the Spaniards because of the color of their skin, and it meant black, like it does even today, and not brain dead, like that militant Jamal X convinced the young people of color in his statement at Montebello High in Denver. Jamal X, a Muslim, was just trying to start trouble and start hatred; "he told students that, way back in the day, black people were building pyramids while whites ate their dead and slept with animals in caves," [79] but it was the Jews as well because they were slaves of Egypt at that time also. Remember, it was the Spaniards that brought the blacks over here and sold them to

---

79   Controversial Issues: They Belong in the Classroom, Dr. Arnold
      Burron, http://www.procon.org/sourcefiles/they_belong_in_the_
      classroom_4-06.pdf , Citizen X, http://www.westword.com/1999-
      12-23/music/citizen-x/ , All of the Newspapers in Colorado

us![80] I am not saying Lincoln was perfect, but that is how that name came about.

One thing I hate the most is a bunch of bigots; I do not care what race they are or what they look like. Someone should have pulled Jamal X off the podium the minute he started teaching race hatred. The thing is liberals go out of their way to create racial tension, and yet they do it in such a way to hide it from you. Then they go around and blame it on the Republicans, who had the first black Congressman, or Christians, who were willing to free the slaves. Sounds like a lot of finger pointing to me.

We all came from Adam and Eve. When the flood came, Noah and his family were the only ones left. So the human race comes from his descendents, and guess what? We are all related from the distant past. Therefore, all you people who think you are better than someone else, get off your high almighty attitude, because you are all human beings, and we all bleed red! Quit trying to create division here in America!

The Civil War was started to change equality to include people of color. During and after the Civil War, three amendments to the Constitution were ratified; now they just change it when it suits them, and we do not get a say.

In 1865, the Thirteenth Amendment officially abolished slavery. The Fourteenth Amendment, in 1868, guaranteed equality and civil rights to all citizens. You notice the word "citizens," and not foreigners, animals, trees, or plants.

In 1870, the Fifteenth Amendment guaranteed blacks the right to vote. This amendment came about because of what was known as the Black Codes, created by Democrats in the South. The freed blacks could not vote or serve on juries, and they were compelled to work even if the wages or conditions were bad. If they did not comply with these codes, it was off to the jail house. They could not have firearms or insult white

---

80   Slave Trade Kura Hulanda Resorts, http://www.kurahulanda.com/slavery/slave-trade

people. These codes were created because of fear of the blacks. When they got the right to vote, the Democrats said they had to register as Democrats. I got that from my grandparents when I grew up. By the way, they were Democrats.

Lincoln went to Congress in 1865 to create the Freedman's Bureau to protect the blacks from these abuses. However, when Andrew Johnson took office after President Lincoln's assassination, he opposed this bureau because of the claims made by the South that it was turning blacks against their former masters, but it stayed. By 1871, there were 250,000 blacks in colleges and universities. Johnson was also opposed to the Fourteenth Amendment. More than 620,000 people died in the Civil War.[81]

The Ku Klux Klan: Adolf Hitler must have learned some of their tactics. They claim to be Christians but do not show any Christian attributes. In Matthew 7, Christ says, "Beware of false prophets, which come to you in sheep's clothing, but inwardly they are ravening wolves. Ye shall know them by their fruits. Do men gather grapes of thorns, or figs of thistles? Even so every good tree bringeth forth good fruit; but a corrupt tree bringeth forth evil fruit … Wherefore by their fruits ye shall know them."

Galatians 5:22, 23 says, "But the fruit of the Spirit is love, joy, peace, longsuffering, gentleness, goodness, faith, meekness, temperance: against such there is no law." Are the KKK gentle, peacemakers, or meek (which doesn't mean weak but slow to anger)? Did they show love and goodness? Did they do anything that the Bible teaches? Not that I can see! Christ died for all.

The blacks were injured, whipped, and lynched by the KKK. Is this love? They did the same to whites who sympathized with the blacks. They called them "nigger lovers." Does this show temperance, meekness, or goodness? I know we all get

---

81   The Myth of the Civil War, History.com http://www.history.com/
      topics/ku-klux-klan/videos#civil-wars-greatest-myth

angry and our tempers are high sometimes, but their anger is just pure hate, like the Nation of Islam and the Million Man March.

Confederate officers started the KKK. Their first grand wizard was Nathan Bedford Forrest. Other leaders were General John B. Gordan and the governor of North Carolina, Zebulon B. Vance.

The Klansmen changed from a social club to a bunch of terrorists because of the Reconstruction, started by the North. They intimidated blacks and their allies from voting by riding at night in their white hooded robes. They erected crosses and lit them on fire, which now our great Supreme Court says is okay to do. Of course they did not call it terrorism but freedom of expression. They claim it is okay if done at a rally, but at some of these rallies, they beat and lynched blacks.

Also they have changed freedom of speech to freedom of expression. What is the difference? "Speech" is defined as "to make a speech; to harangue."[82] In other words, it is saying, using words to make your point. Now "expression" is defined as "the act of utterance, declaration; representation, a phrase, rhetoric, or mode of speech." This is the part that they use, the act of expressing, which means showing.

Now let's look at today's dictionary. "Speech" is defined as "the communication or expression of thoughts in spoken words; exchange or spoken words, conversation, something that is spoken." No actions. "Expression" is defined as "an act, process, or instance or representing in a medium" (includes words).

Our forefathers meant what they said; you have the right to make a speech, use words, lecture, address grievances, and criticize if you feel your government is going the wrong way. They deliberately did not use expression because this can lead to violence, and it has! Of course, that is liberals for you; for

---

82   *Webster's Dictionary* (1828 reprint).

they were the ones behind making it legal.[83] They are the ones changing our Constitution! So you think about that.

However, this did not stop the Reconstruction anyway. So the KKK started burning black people's homes and murdering them. In 1871, almost two hundred blacks were lynched in just Florida alone. More than three hundred were killed in New Orleans.

Hundreds of Klansmen were arrested but few went to trial and fewer were convicted. The downfall of the Reconstruction finally happened. So the South can thank the KKK for their lower education and other things during those times.[84]

By the way, the KKK lynched whites, also. Now I do not know where David Barton got his information but he said the blacks and whites that were lynched were Republicans; 1,300 white Republicans were lynched. That goes back to the Republicans against the Democrats. However, I did find some information that substantiates that whites and blacks were lynched by the KKK.[85]

Lucretia Coffin Mott, born of Quaker parents in 1793, was one of the important leaders in the campaign against slavery and for equal rights for women. She helped found the American Antislavery Society. It wasn't until June 4, 1919, that Congress finally passed the Nineteenth Amendment, giving women the right to vote.

When women's lib started in 1920, it was mainly about being treated fairly and having the right to hold jobs and get

---

83   The *Christian Science Monitor*, http://www.csmonitor. com/2003/0409/p10s03-comv.html

84   *The Encyclopedia Britannica*, The KKK in the 1920s, http://www1. assumption.edu/ahc/1920s/eugenics/klan.html ; the Ku Klux Klan (1866), http://www.pbs.org/wnet/jimcrow/stories_events_kkk.htm l; http://www.history.com/topics/ku-klux-klan/videos#the-kkk ; http://www.youtube.com/watch?v=n_YyLEjfQUg History Channel

85   David Barton, http://www.youtube.com/watch?v=VVzJ2RIlUwE , Bob Unruh, KKK's 1st targets were Republicans, 2011 WND, posted October 25, 2007, http://www.wnd.com/?pageId=44171

equal pay for equal work. You could have the choice to stay home or work. However, in 1960, when I was nine, militant females got into the National Organization for Women (NOW) and took over.

If I did further research, I would probably find that some of them were Communists. Communists believe in having both males and females work so they can indoctrinate the children. You see, if one has your children the majority of the time or all of the time, then they can get them to accept their philosophy and not yours.

Remember Franklin's quote: "Give me twenty-six lead soldiers and I will conquer the world." Karl Marx said something to that effect, also. They know that children are very impressionable. Remember the song that they were having children sing about Obama? This is brain washing, but no one said anything except Fox News. Now I am not saying that women should not work, but we need to guard our homes!

These women violently protested, claiming women wanted to be treated like men, which is not true. I do not like being talked to disrespectfully; have a door slammed in my face, or put up with foul language in the streets, in a public place, in movies, or on TV shows. You can have entertainment without foul language or sex. Because of these women, we have split families, disrespect for authorities (that includes parents), no morals, and the killing of unborn children as well as sick people that we've decided should not have any hope for a cure. It is better to just kill them off. Discard them as if they are nobodies.

Aileen Hernandez is a union organizer of the International Ladies' Garment Worker' Union and president of the National Organization for Women in 1970 and co-founder of Black Women Organized for Action in San Francisco who is committed to what she calls worldwide justice; she travels and meets with women throughout the world to gain a global perspective on humanitarian issues which includes women's lib issues.

Currently, she chairs the California Women's Agenda (CAWA), a network of 600 organizations dedicated to implementing the plan of action adopted at the Fourth World Conference on Women in Beijing, China in 1995. All this is part of women's lib and spreading it worldwide. However, I did not see any where she personally used violence in her approach.[86]

Look at what happened during Hurricane Katrina. They killed those people in the hospital. Why? Not because there was no hope but because we make these people kill babies and people all the time and for what, money? We have no respect for life anymore because the liberal Democrats are into dehumanizing anyone they want, including old folks. Yes, Hitler and Stalin, you have gotten your foothold here in the United States. If you were alive today, you would be laughing at us. But since you are in hell, you probably wish you could live your life over again and live it differently.

Nixon, the one people criticize, had conversations with King about many things. He worked hard on the Civil Rights Bill.[87] As Vice President he talked to the President on having a meeting with Dr. King. I dare you to look up http://images.nbra.info/docs/library/NationalBlackRepublicanAssociation2009/NBRA%20Civil%20Rights%20Newsletter%208Aug2011.pdf it will be an eye opener about Democrats and Republicans

---

86   Aileen Hernandez, *Union Organizer and Human Rights Activist*, http://www.nwhp.org/resourcecenter/biographycenter.php#hernandez : Women's History Month, http://nwhp.org/whm/hernandez_bio.php

87   Myth of the Racist Republicans, http://www.claremont.org/publications/crb/id.928/article_detail.asp , Letter to Nixon from King, http://mlk-kpp01.stanford.edu/primarydocuments/Vol4/30-Aug-1957_ToNixon.pdf , http://mlk-kpp01.stanford.edu/primarydocuments/Vol4/13-June-1957_StatementonMeetingwithRMN.pdf

when it comes to blacks and Civil Rights. This includes Obama and the Clintons. This site is done by the National Black Republican Association.

Richard Nixon with Martin Luther King sat down with KTCA to talk about the issues. King did most of the talking.[88]

When Nixon became president he issued Executive Order 11478 that adopted affirmative programs for equal employment and access to education for minorities that included blacks, Latinos, Asians, women, and disabled people.[89]

Yes he probably did make some mistakes but the thing is he did do things for civil rights and that should not be taken from him.

We know that Dr. King was a pastor at a local Baptist church. Get that, Baptist, Christian? Dr. King was born in 1929 and died in 1968 from an assassin's bullet in Memphis, Tennessee. He won the Nobel Peace Prize, which well deserved. He received a PhD in theology from Boston University.

He believed strongly in the nonviolent teachings of Henry David Thoreau and Mohandas K. Gandhi. King wrote, "I came to feel that nonviolent resistance was the only morally and practically sound method open to oppressed people in their struggle for freedom."[90]

During the Montgomery boycott, whites arrested King on trumped-up speeding charges and bombed his home; King responded with a Bible Scripture: "Love thy enemies."

88   http://www.mnvideovault.org/search_results.php?q=martin%20luther%20king&o=pg_obdate&d=DESC&limit=20

89   http://mlk-kpp01.stanford.edu/primarydocuments/Vol4/13-June-1957_StatementonMeetingwithRMN.pdf , HNN George Mason University, Why Richard Nixon Deserves to Be Remembered Along with "Brown", http://hnn.us/articles/5331.html

90   Martin Luther King Jr. http://www.designsbydaybreak.com/holidays/martinluther/index.html , History.com, http://www.history.com/topics/martin-luther-king-jr , http://www.history.com/topics/civil-rights-movement

Although Rosa Parks lost her case, in 1956, the Supreme Court ruled that segregation on buses was unconstitutional. On December 21, 1956, Dr. King and Reverend Ralph Abernathy rode together on the first desegregated bus through Montgomery's streets. They do not teach that in the schools.[91]

Dr. King helped make great strides for true freedom for blacks. The Civil Rights movement not only had blacks in it but whites also. I remember watching the news on TV, and Dr. King was surrounded by white people who truly believed "all men are created equal."

The one thing I admired most about Dr. King was that his demonstrations were peaceful, unlike protests by NOW and gay groups. He did not join Malcolm X in the violence. He did not have the prejudices that Malcolm had inside of him. I admire and have great respect even to this day for this man and what he did. This goes for Nixon also, for he really cared about all US citizens, not just pretending like some liberals. Some things he should be noted for is the SALT II treaty and affirmative action, but they took that away from him.

The march through Birmingham is well known. Dr. King planned a peaceful rally and march. However, the police, led by Chief Eugene Connor, had other plans. With dogs, fire hoses, and bully clubs, they broke up the march and made mass arrests, including Dr. King. King wrote to local white clergymen, "We still creep at a horse and buggy pace toward gaining a cup of coffee at a lunch counter."[92]

President Kennedy took up where Nixon left off. Kennedy told the nation:

---

91   Rosa Parks and E.D. Nixon, Dr. Ronald Walters, *The Black World Today,* June 15, 1999, http://www.hartford-hwp.com/archives/45a/448.html

92   Letter From Birmingham City Jail, Martin Luther King Jr., April 16, 1963, 7th paragraph, http://teachingamericanhistory.org/library/index.asp?document=100

One hundred years of delay have passed since President Lincoln freed the slaves, yet their heirs, their grandsons, are not fully free. They are not yet freed from the bonds of injustice; they are not yet freed from social and economic oppression.

Now the time has come for this nation to fulfill its promise. The events in Birmingham and elsewhere have so increased the cries for equality that no city or state or legislative body can prudently choose to ignore them.[93]

Unfortunately, in November of 1963, President John F. Kennedy was assassinated in Dallas; not only did he leave a mystery surrounding his death, but the civil rights program was not passed. President Lyndon B. Johnson pushed for its passage in honor of Kennedy.

The Civil Rights Act of 1964 promised the right to equality in public accommodations, to have federal funds, and the right to racial and sexual equality in employment. The Voting Rights Act of 1965 eliminated all discriminatory qualifying tests for registration to vote. Later in 1968, the year Dr. King was assassinated, a bill was passed outlawing discrimination in housing.

Dr. King accomplished a lot; his famous speech, "I have a dream," lives on, but some people of both colors do not take heed to what it said. I think Dr. King would be ashamed to know that some people of color are claiming prejudice to get off for rape, theft, and even murder. I think he would tell them that going around and telling other people of color to find them not guilty just because of their color is wrong, just as it is wrong for whites to say they are guilty just because they are black. I think he would tell them not to lower their standards.

---

93   John Fitzgerald Kennedy, Address, June 11, 1963, http://millercenter.org/president/speeches/detail/3375

These kinds of people (white or black) encourage violence and prejudices.

I think he might even be up there with God shaking his head because the liberals have done everything to keep race and class hatred alive, pitting one group against another. All he had accomplished has been taken a step backward. These people who have used their race to get away with murder while others cheer them on have trodden all over Dr. Martin L. King, Jr.'s grave.

Another way of changing history is doctoring photos. I heard that NOW was trying to change the photo of the Marines raising our flag on Iwo Jima, placing a woman in it. This is a deliberate changing of history. What an insult for those who were there. There are many things our women endured during the war, at home and abroad. I know that there are pictures of women that we can bring out without trying to change history and take away someone else's accomplishments.

Again photos are being changed to depict what they want; they changed the photo of three white firefighters who raised the American flag at Ground Zero after 9/11. Again they try to change history.[94] They just do not give up, and people are not on their toes or they would not support these people.

However, that is typical of militant liberals. They seem to like to take credit for what someone else did. They want things to be what they want it to be so they change history and teach it to our children. They do not care about the truth, just what they want. They talk about greedy corporate people, but they are just as bad if not worse because what they are doing is putting us into bondage not liberation!

So now I have shown you a few things that have been altered and changed due to the liberal's agenda. We need to remember the past, not to hold grudges but to keep it from

---

94   White Firefighters Who Raised Flag at WTC depicted "racially diverse" in New Statue, January 10, 2002, http://www.freerepublic.com/focus/fr/605601/posts

happening again. You cannot blame all for a few, and remember that blacks owned blacks. In addition, some Africans own slaves even today, so there is no need to have self-pity for what happened in the past. The past is the past, it cannot be changed, but we can keep it from happening again if we cling to the truth. You cannot be held accountable for the past doings of someone else. This is wrong.

I leave you with this quote from Deuteronomy 24:16–18:

> The fathers shall not be put to death for the children, neither the children be put to death for the fathers: every man shall be put to death for his own sin. Thou shalt not pervert the judgment of the stranger, nor of the fatherless; nor take a widow's raiment to pledge: But thou shalt remember that thou wast a bondman in Egypt, and the Lord thy God redeemed thee thence: therefore I command thee to do this thing.

Schools

*Those who provide much wealth for their Children, but
neglect to improve them in Virtue, do like those who feed
their horses High, but never train them to the manage.*
—Socrates

WHEN BENJAMIN FRANKLIN SAID HE could conquer the
world with twenty-six lead soldiers, he was talking about the
alphabet, the schools, and the news media. Like Karl Marx,
he knew that if you train the kids the first seven years of life
you would have them for life.

This is why seculars wanted to get hold of the schools. They
wanted God out of the country and have the children help turn
this government around from what it was meant to be: free.
We allowed people from the Nazi era and other Communists
into this country and let them teach in our schools. Now we
are seeing the results. Let's look into the background of our
schools.

In the beginning, our schools were handled by the church
and not the state. These were Christian schools, just like our
Constitution was based on Christian precepts, not Buddhist,
Hindu, Satanist, humanist, atheist, or any other beliefs because
Christianity does not enslave the people. The author of *Teaching
and Learning America's Christian History* stated "Christianity
alone is the citadel of America's freedom."

When our forefathers came over, the memories of the

civil atrocities done in the name of Christianity were fresh in their minds. They believed this happened because the common people did not know the Scriptures. So they passed a law called the "Old Deluder Satan Act"[95] in hopes that these atrocities would not happen in America, but these atrocities are happening through the liberals and the ACLU under the banner of civil liberties. They claim to be Christians but are not.

They have been able to delude the American people by taking them away from the Scriptures by that lie of separation of church and state. By the way, the schools are to be handled by individual states, not the federal government. Therefore, even that has been thrown out if you really think about it. The federal government has put their grubby hands in by saying they give grants and things; therefore they have the right to tell us what to do in the schools. Wrong! It is our money, not theirs!

> But there were false prophets also among the people, even as there shall be false teachers among you, who privily shall bring in damnable heresies, even denying the Lord that bought them, and bring upon themselves swift destruction. And many shall follow their pernicious ways; by reason of whom the way of truth shall be evil spoken of. And through covetousness shall they with feigned words make merchandise of you: whose judgment now of a long time lingereth not, and their damnation slumbereth not … But these, as natural brute beasts, made to be taken and destroyed, speak evil of the things that they understand not;

---

95   Matzat, Amy L., http://www.nd.edu/~rbarger/www7/
masslaws.html ; Old Deluder Satan Law (1647), http://www.
americareclaimed.org/elements/docs/documents/Old%20
Deluder%20Satan%20Law%281647%29p.pdf

> and shall utterly perish in their own corruption (2
> Peter 2:1–3, 12).

"There is a way which seemeth right unto a man, but the end thereof are the ways of death" (Proverbs 14:12).

Our forefathers would not have passed anything that violated what they put into the First Amendment. Nor would they do anything at all that went against the Constitution.

I was watching one of David Barton's shows. He said that he went to court about school prayer. He had showed them documents upon documents how our forefathers/framers had prayed at school functions and how they never meant to keep God out of the government. The judge said that they either were hypocrites or they did not know what the Constitution said.

What? The very people who drew up and voted on the Constitution do not know what they meant when they wrote it? Do you know how idiotic that sounds coming from a judge! What makes him think he knows more of what they meant than they who wrote it did? Such arrogance!

This judge is either very ignorant or he chooses to be ignorant!

The Northwest Ordinance was passed under the Constitution. So give that a thought for a while. We owe our free government to Christian principles, which were derived from the Bible. Our country prospered under these principles. Do you see any prosperity now under liberal laws?

There are two ways to control people. One is by self-government, which our forefathers believed in, and the other is by someone else, which includes government, which the liberals believe in.

Self-government is taught through the biblical principles, as I pointed out in the chapter on history. 2 Corinthians 3:17 states, "Now the Lord is that Spirit: and where the Spirit of the Lord is, there is liberty."

Why is the Spirit of the Lord where liberty is? It is because he teaches us self-government, and when we learn to control ourselves we do not need the government to control us. We do not have to have all these laws put upon us to oppress us. It lays burdens that should not be there. Therefore there is freedom and liberty under self-government.

Right now, because the liberals have taken God out of the schools, we have high crime and immorality, which breeds more crime.

They want the Ten Commandments out of the schools because children might obey them. So are they telling us that they want our children to kill, steal, covet, bear false witness, and not honor their parents? It would seem so the way they have taken the authority away from the parents like the Communists did overseas.

The courts go around and say it is okay to lie. Also, now it is okay to murder through abortion, and they are aiming for assistant suicides. They do not tell you that in the papers. However, *Reader's Digest* does. How communistic we have become where life has no meaning.

This new health bill indicates that old people are not worth keeping alive. That means your grandparents, parents, and eventually you! This is another way of getting rid of history, because we remember the truth. Oh, how far we have gotten away from the truth and what our country used to mean, cherishing life and not death.

However, I think it is more than desensitizing us to life and the other things mentioned, including the Ten Commandments. They do not want people to obey the first four ones and the seventh one. The first four commandments deal with man's relationship with God, and the seventh says, "Thou shalt not commit adultery."

Man must change within to curb crime. There must

be self-government. Benjamin Rush,[96] who was a surgeon, founder of Pennsylvania Hospital, and most of all a signer of the Declaration of Independence, said that we would spend more time punishing crime instead of preventing it (so don't take the Bible out of the schools). Bible and religion are the only things that deal with the heart.[97] Let's see what he might be talking about.

1 Samuel 16:7b says, "For the Lord seeth not as man seeth; for man looketh on the outward appearance, but the Lord looketh on the heart."

God deals with the heart. He does not care about how rich or poor you are or how pretty or ugly on the outside. He sees beauty in those whose hearts are toward him. Man does not care but judges by the outward appearance and not his character. This is why we end up with dishonest people in Washington. It is all about them, they think. They do not care about what the people want. They seem to put themselves before anyone else; they are very vain and arrogant. Otherwise, why would they say that we are not smart enough to understand the issues or that they do not care what the people want, they are going to vote the way they want?

Thomas Jefferson said, "I know of no safe depositor of the ultimate powers of society but the people themselves; and if we think them not enlightened enough to exercise their control with a wholesome discretion, the remedy is not to take it from

96   Rush, Benjamin (1746–1813), Alexander Leitch, *A Princeton Companion*, Princeton University Press, 1978, http://etcweb.princeton.edu/CampusWWW/Companion/rush_benjamin.html , Rush did the first mass production of the Bible in the United States; http://www.kjv400celebration.com/exhibit_print.php?id=3

97   The Value of Christian Education, Pastor Steve Proctor at Westwood Baptist Church, Poplar Bluff, Missouri, July 7, 2005, http://jcacardinals.org/THE%20VALUE%20OF%20CHRISTIAN%20EDUCATION.pdf , American History, Fun Facts, Founding Fathers Quotes, http://www.american-history-fun-facts.com/founding-fathers-quotes.html , http://www.vlrc.org/quotes.html

them, but to inform their discretion by education. This is the true corrective of abuses of constitutional power."[98]

Jeremiah cries out in chapter 17:9, 10, "The heart is deceitful above all things, and desperately wicked: Who can know it?" The Lord responds, "I the Lord search the heart, I try the reins, even to give every man according to his ways, and according to the fruit of his doings."

God had the men who wrote the books of the Bible put down what they had learned, like Solomon in Ecclesiastes. He lived the, eat, drink, and be merry life, only to find it is vanity (empty). He tried everything people said would make them happy. He had all the riches but it all was vanity. At the end of the book, he says, "Let us hear the conclusion of the whole matter: Fear God, and keep his commandments: for this is the whole duty of man:

"For God shall bring every work into judgment, with every secret thing, whether it is good, or whether it is evil." He had learned what man's sole purpose was; people keep asking why are we here on this earth. The Bible gives you that answer.

Proverbs mentions self-control a lot, like Proverbs 16: 32: "He that is slow to anger is better than the mighty; and he that ruleth his spirit than he that taketh a city," and Proverbs 25:28: "He that hath no rule over his own spirit is like a city that is broken down, and without walls."

James 3:2 says, "For in many things we offend all, If any man offend not in word, the same is a perfect man, and able also to bridle the whole body." What he was saying was that it is harder to hold one's tongue than anything else, and if a person can control what they say, they can control what they do.

One more example: Proverbs 20:1 says, "Wine is a mocker, strong drink is raging: and whosoever is deceived thereby is not

---

98   Section II-American Education, http://oregonstate.edu/instruct/
      ed416/ae2.html The Constitution of the United States, National
      Center for Constitutional Studies, © 2009, 2010

wise." Don't a lot of our crimes extend from alcohol and drugs (not guns)? Did not a lot of today's philosophy come from the hippies' generation; are they not in control of our schools and government today? Therefore, they are teaching our kids about "free sex" (nothing is free; there is always a price to pay.) and to do drugs by telling them they would do it again (inhaling, Bill Clinton?)? This is why we have more pregnancies, more sexually transmitted diseases, and more kids on drugs today.

Gouveneur Morris, who physically wrote the Constitution by writing down the ideas that were floating around on the floor, said, "Religion is the only solid basis of good morals. Therefore, education should teach the precepts of religion and the duties of man towards God."

John Witherspoon, who was head of Princeton University, said that anyone who was an enemy of God was an enemy of the United States. If they were a friend of America, they would bear down on immorality and profanity. Well, that takes care of the majority of Democrats up in Washington (and some of the Republicans).

Let's look at the one who proposed the wording of the First Amendment, Fisher Ames: "It has been the custom of this year, to put a number of little books into the hands of children containing fables and moral lessons. This is very well, because it is right to first raise curiosity and then to guide it. Many books for children, however, are injudicious compiled: Why then if these books for children must be retained, as they will be, should not the Bible regain the place it once held as a school book? Its morals are pure, its examples captivating and noble. The reverence for the sacred book that is thus impressed early, lasts long, and probably if not impressed to infancy, never takes firm hold of the mind."[99]

Here is what some of the early colleges said about education.

---

99   Fisher Ames, http://daniel.brogan.name/fisherames.html ; Do You Know, Founder's Original Intent, July 18, 2011, http://www. earstohear.net/Heritage/didyouknow.html

Harvard, where John Adams came from, said, "Let every student be plainly instructed and consider well the main end of his life and studies is to know God and Jesus Christ ... and therefore to lay Christ in the bottom as the only foundation of all sound knowledge and learning."

Yale stated, "Seeing God is the giver of all wisdom every scholar, besides private or secret prayer shall be present morning and evening at public prayer." Did you get that, public prayer? They believed students should have a life with prayer. Of course that has changed a lot today since secular people got their hands on the school board.

How about Princeton, where eighty-seven of our founding fathers attended? They said, "Cursed be all learning that is contrary to the cross of Christ."[100]

Out of the 250 founding fathers, only 6 to 12 were not that religious but believed in God.[101]

Jefferson wanted to attach a memorandum to set up a treaty to send missionaries to the Indians.[102] He used terms like *"in the year of our Lord Christ."*

When Washington took oath of office he kissed the Bible and said "so help me God."[103]

100   David Allbritton, Americans say ... Jesus, http://www. wincityonline.org/pages.asp?pageid=40507 ; Barton, David, Education & Founding Fathers; other quotes from Witherspoon, http://www.partyof1776.net/p1776/fathers/Witherspoon%20John/quotes/contents.html

101   http://www.freewill-predestination.com/files/constitution.pdf

102   John R. Guardiano, O'Donnell Bests Coons on First Amendment, http://spectator.org/blog/2010/10/19/odonnell-right-about-eparatio# ; Cherokee Removal—The Trail Where They Cried, nu na hi du na tlo hi lu i, http://www.powersource.com/cocinc/history/trail.htm ; http://www.emayzine.com/lectures/native%20 lecture1800-1828.htm

103   http://inaugural.senate.gov/history/video/video-sohelpmegod.cfm

When Woodrow Wilson set up law school, he said civil law needs to correlate with God's law.[104]

So now I hope you understand that they felt a need and urgency that the Bible should be taught in the schools. They did not believe in the separation of church and state, as the liberal Democrats put it. The word "separation" is nowhere in the Constitution.

The Democrats made up their own Constitution, and it is not the one our forefather wrote and ratified. Our forefathers wanted the Bible taught in the schools for two reasons. It deals with man's heart, and it shows them the right way to live. For if man's heart is right, then the chaos and destruction would not come to the nation but would make it strong.

Why do you think the Communists have tried so hard to get God out of our schools, bring in Communist beliefs, and label anyone who warns the American people? They just sucked you in like a big vacuum cleaner.

The other reason our forefathers wanted the Bible taught in the school, as I have stated before, is because they felt that the ignorance of the Bible brought about the atrocities in the Dark Ages. Don't you think it is strange that in all these years, no one had any problems understanding the Bible until now? So the Bible was changed because you are too stupid to read English or is it that they have brainwashed you into thinking it is too hard?

Even Thomas Jefferson, who helped start the Democratic Party, would scold them for taking up the Communist dogma of evolution and humanism. Then they put their religion in place of Christ and sanctified it with the government's blessings, which is what our forefathers were really guarding against.

Daniel Webster made an emotional appeal to the Supreme Court when the Philadelphia schools tried to teach morality without the Bible. During the appeal to the Supreme Court, he

---

104 The *Patriot Post*, The 50 US State Constitutions on God, http://patriotpost.us/reference/50-state-constitutions-on-god/

quoted the Bible where Christ said, "Suffer the little children to come unto me." He told the courts that Jesus did not say send them to the precepts of the Sadducees or the unbelieving Pharisees.

This addresses us today as we have sent our children to the unbelieving, Communists, atheists, and those who practice immorality and liberality.

The US Supreme Court afterward said, "Why may not the Bible and especially the New Testament be read and taught as a divine revelation in the schools? Its general precepts expounded, and its glorious principles of morality inculcated. Where can the purest principles of morality be learned so clearly or so perfectly as from the New Testament?" Wow! The Supreme Court already had ruled over this matter, and today our Supreme Court changed that ruling! The Supreme Court of that day knew more of what our forefathers intended than the one of today. They did not see anything wrong with teaching the Bible in the schools.[105]

When the liberal Supreme Court changed the Constitution in the twentieth century and declared separation of church and state, stating that teaching Scriptures and praying violated all laws and principles of our forefathers, they lied through their teeth like they always do to get what they want. The thing is most people were too ignorant to know it because most people never check things out. You sit there and just believe everything they tell you. The liberals are slowly taking your rights away, and you are too lazy to care. You will realize it one day, but then it will be too late.

When the liberal Supreme Court changed the Constitution and declared separation of church and state, they are the ones that violated all laws and principles of our founding fathers!

When elementary classes were being handed over to the state, even the teachers said that instead of taking the Bible

---

105   *Works of Daniel Webster.*

out of the schools, it would be better to hand them back to the churches.

The founding fathers never intended that God's word should not influence people's lives or not be infiltrated into the government and especially the schools!

The thing they wanted was that the government should not *establish* a religion or put their blessing on one religion, as the English did. They did not want the government to interfere with the church functions, telling them what they had to believe. However, the liberal Democrats have put in their religion (evolution, humanism, Marxism, atheism, and worship of nature) and teach it to our children while they have taken God out of our schools.

Noah Webster, who wrote the dictionary, read through the Bible by the age of four! When he reached six years old, he passed his minister in Greek, and by the time he was seven and a half, he passed the entrance exam to Yale. Were children smarter then than now? Emphatically no! The Bible was third grade level reading at that time.

Get this, they used to teach Latin in the schools here. They stopped doing that also. Now it has become a dead language. State mottos are actually in Latin. The motto of Colorado, where I live, is "Nil sin numine," which is Latin for "Nothing without God." On August 2, 2011, in an article by Patrick Crowder in the *Valley Courier,* he interviewed a friend of his and asked her how she knew Latin. I had to include this in my book. She said they use to teach it in the schools but quit teaching it. Latin is all over our country, yet no one knows what it means.

She said that they replaced Latin with English, but then she made a profound statement: "They are doing the same thing with God." Think about that statement for a while. She is a living history book. Liberals want to get rid of history books because they know the truth. She went on to say, "They pulled God out of science rooms, history rooms, math, and civics.

Parents aren't passing it on and churches have fifteen minutes of Sunday school per week if they are lucky and maybe eight hours of vacation Bible school a year."

Then Crowder asked what we would look like in fifty years if we continued to take Christianity out of our schools and government. He asked, "What do countries look like that have virtually no Christianity? If you are curious you may want to look at North Korea, Somalia, and Afghanistan for some examples." Think about that too. Look at all those Communists countries and dictatorships in the world. That is where we are headed if we continue the direction we are going.

Noah Webster made up the blue Back Speller because there was no wrong way or right way to spell. However, he knew the importance of unification so people could understand each other better. When you understand what people are saying, it cuts out arguments and misunderstandings.

The liberals are taking us back to what it used to be before a uniform education. This includes making up a language for the blacks here in America and keeping them under the slave forum. This gray area in math keeps our children ignorant and behind other countries. This is not progress! This is keeping them ignorant so they will follow liberals without question like a dog following its master with its tails wagging behind it. This is what they want.

Noah Webster used Scriptures for example sentences in his dictionary; he believed that God should be the center of education because he is the creator of all things including freedom.

He said, "The Christian religion is the most important and one of the first thing in which all children under a free government ought to be instructed. The Christian religion must be the basis of any government intended to secure the rights and privileges of a free people."[106]

---

106 *Webster's Dictionary* (1828 reprint).

The history of the United States declares the principles of the Bible are correct for a republic. However, the liberals do not want a republic. Haven't they kept saying this is a democracy? They even have Republicans saying the same thing. They know that if they keep saying the same thing over again, they can get the people to believe the lie. This is how we train our children, by repeating ourselves so they will learn. In a democracy, it is easy to step all over someone's rights.

Continuing with Webster's quote, "The moral principles and precepts contained in the Scriptures ought to form the basis of all our civil constitutions and laws, all the miseries and evils which men suffer from—vice, crime, ambition, injustice, oppression, slavery, and war—proceed from their despising and neglecting the precepts contained in the Bible."

Is this statement sounding like today? Are we not electing immoral people to the White House, people who dodge the draft and go to our enemies, protesting against the United States alongside of them, giving them aid and comfort, people who pretends to be a Christian, or they want to make history and not by what they believe?

Abraham Lincoln said, "The philosophy of the school room in one generation will be the philosophy of the government in the next."

Maybe this is why they replaced God with Karl Marx and Hitler's religion. After all, isn't that what Hitler was saying when he said that if he got control of the schools, he would have control of the country? Remember we had some of these people come here in the United States having influence upon our people and country. This was brought out in the news in 2010.

James Russell Lowell asked an American statesman, "How long will the American Republic endure?"

The statesman replied, "As long as the ideas of the men who founded it continue dominant," and as you can see, they have not. Karl Marx has replaced them.

Remember earlier I mentioned the atrocities that had been committed because of one's beliefs; let's look at what Jefferson said in 1786 on January 16th in a Virginia Assembly:

> Where as Almighty God has created the mind free, so that all attempts to influence it by temporal punishments or burdens, or by civil incapacitations, tend only to beget habits of hypocrisy and meanness [like the KKK] and are a departure from the plan of the Holy Author of our religion, who, being Lord both of body and mind, yet, chose not to propagate it by coercions on either, as was in His almighty power to do; that impious presumption of legislators and rulers. Civil as well as ecclesiastical, Who being themselves but fallible and uninspired men, have assumed dominion over the faith of others, setting up their own opinions and modes of thinking as the only true and infallible, and as such endeavoring to impose them on others has established and maintained false religions over the greatest part of the world, and through all time ...

> Be it ... enacted by the General Assembly that no man shall be compelled to frequent or support any religious worship, place or ministry whatsoever, nor shall be enforced, restrained, molested, or burdened in his body or goods, nor shall otherwise suffer on account of his religious opinions or belief;[107] but that all men shall be free to profess, and by argument to maintain, their opinion in matters of religion, and that the same shall in no wise diminish enlarge, or affect their civil capacities.[108]

---

107 Yet the ACLU does this and the government supports them.
108 Assembly of Virginia, Religious Freedom, http://www.loc.gov/exhibits/religion/f0510s.jpg

To put it into a nutshell, the government was not supposed to stop me from telling others about my beliefs. The government can't say keep Christianity out of the public or only non-Christian religions can be taught in the schools. If you Christians do not stop passing out tracts about your beliefs, you will be arrested, but it is okay for homosexuals to proselyte our children on the school grounds and teach them to experiment with different types of sex acts. They are approaching very young children.[109] It is only okay for non-Christians to pass out things about their religion and turn our youth.[110]

They come into our schools and have their church services on our school grounds under the banner of it being their culture. Well, if anything is part of our culture, it is Christianity because it is written all over our history, and it is what made the United States what it is. You can see Scriptures engraved all over our buildings in Washington. They even built a place to worship there on the grounds of Congress. Would they have done that if they want God out of our country?

All this is similar to Constantine[111], who went around and punished those who would not confess to be a Christian, missing out on who is a true Christian. The Roman Catholics and Catholics tortured people who refused to be Catholics and followed the true Christian faith. Yes there were Protestants that murdered Baptists and others.

---

109   Homosexuals brainwashing our children in elementary schools, http://www.massresistance.org/media/video/brainwashing.html ; "Gay" Groups: We have rights to your children! http://www.wnd.com/news/article.asp?ARTICLE_ID=52311 ; NEA Teachers Help Fund Pro-Homosexual Groups, Training, Linda Harvey, http://www.missionamerica.com/agenda.php?articlenum=70 ; Ground Spark, group to support Homosexuality in the class room, http://groundspark.org/trailers/itselementary.html

110   http://www.wnd.com/news/article.asp?ARTICLE_ID=55252

111   http://www.earlychurch.org.uk/constantine.php

There are two types of Catholics. There are the Roman Catholics and Catholics, which people refer to the Church of England or Anglican Church. Our forefathers did not trust either because both persecuted people that refused to be of their religion.

I came across a web site that talked about how the Catholics were not being treated right at the beginning of our history. Well look at what they had done to them. Would you trust people like that? Our forefathers did not trust them because they were afraid that the Roman Catholics and Catholics would take over the government and the persecutions would start all over! However this Catholic web site did not put that in! It's all half truths.

Anglican only means "relating to England". It was not a religion or faith at that time. It is like Anglican Saxon, Anglican singers, and so on. I know that some secular historians put Anglicanism to refer to the Church of England being white Anglo-Saxon Protestants. The word Anglicanism came around 1906. It was then considered a religious system separate from Royal Supremacy.

Roman Catholicism remands the main religion with the exception of loyalty to the pope under Henry. When he died King Edward VI was swayed to go a little more on the protestant side. However, when his half-sister took the throne she went back to Roman Catholicism. Then when Elizabeth took over she was excommunicated and the Roman Catholics were pushed out again but they still practice Catholicism.

When Charles I took over he married a Roman Catholic and let her practice her religion with the dislike of the Protestants. He dissolves Parliament. He supported the Huguenots[112] in France. Later he was beheaded.

During our forefathers the Church of England and Episcopal Church had their origins in the 16th –century

---

112   Huguenots-Suppression, http://www.infoplease.com/ce6/society/
      A0858696.html

England. They are as well as now the Protestant denomination closest to Roman Catholicism in theology and worship. However they call themselves Catholics because they are more Catholicism than Protestants in belief. I am from Louisiana where you have both forms of Catholics there. Our forefathers considered them Catholics that is the reason why a lot of our forefathers said that they did not trust any Catholics and I am sure that is why it took so long to have a Catholic President.

Even people today consider Lutherans Catholics even though they call themselves Lutherans. Have you ever been to a Lutheran church? I have. One of my uncles is Lutheran.

It is like you have American Baptist, Southern Baptist, Independent Baptist, Ana-Baptist, and so on. Each has their differences. I would have to write a whole book to explain this. I am not here to do a theological debate. I am no theologian but they do call themselves Catholics and so did our forefathers. So if I use the word Catholic by itself I am referring to the Church of England.[113]

Christ did not use torture to get people to follow him! It has to come from the heart! Come on, use your brain.

This statement did not say that the Bible was not to have influence in the government or in the schools. I just said that the government (or any other organization) was not to force people to believe what they believe. It does not mean one can't tell someone and let the person make a personal decision. He just can't threaten or do physical harm or throw them in prison because of his beliefs.

A movement started against truth. Harold Rugg could not

---

113   Church History, http://anglican.org/church/ChurchHistory. html ,Way of Life Literature, http://www.wayoflife.org/database/ protestantpersecutions.html ; David Cody, The Church of England (the Anglican Church), http://en.wikipedia.org/wiki/ Anglo-Catholicism ,Anglicanism, http://www.newadvent.org/ cathen/01498a.htm , http://en.wikipedia.org/wiki/Church_of_ England

understand why there was such a movement against his social science books.[114]

The reason was it had left out God's part in creation and morality. Look at what is happening to our children because we are teaching them they are nothing but an animal, so they can do what animals do. "Free sex" makes children wonder who their father is because he does not take responsibility for his action; after all, animals do not, so why should they, since they are an animal?

This produces anger and hatred in children, who may wonder if there is something wrong with them. They lash out in school, and the parent who is trying their best gets the blame. I know what I am talking about. I have to deal with it as a grandparent. I see it all around me. Children have a natural instinct that they are supposed to have a mother and father, so the schools now are trying to breed it out of them.

Social science deals with the science of origin (they had to get evolution in there), development, and the nature of problems confronting society. They take out our Christian heritage. If you hide the truth on these issues, then it is easy to lead people around by the ring in their noses.[115]

When they were able to get rid of these books, they replaced the vacuum with man-centered philosophies that took away the internal battles of conscience with the social, economic, and political struggles of society. The teachers were given a new history, which they passed along to our children, and this is why we lost our heritage. They are teaching us the heritage of other countries but not our own, and therefore we are losing America's true identity.

According to Veritas Foundation's *The Great Deceit, Social Pseudo-Sciences*, Socialists had to change the people's point of

---

114   Masonic Education, page 9, Communist Rules for Revolution, http://www.angelfire.com/music2/fullcircle/mas9.html ; New World Order, part 1, Education , http://www.asis.com/stag/starchiv/transcriptions/NWO/NWO2_Education.html

115   http://idioms.thefreedictionary.com/lead+by+the+nose

view about Washington, Jefferson, and all the other signers of the Declaration of Independence. They have to make the heroes look like villains. History was the forerunner of the social sciences. It showed that Socialism is inevitable. To do this, they had to destroy the forefathers' image and say that they were not patriotic. Once this is done, they can replace it with Marxism.

Charles Beard wrote *The Development of Modern Europe* with James Harvey Robinson. It popularized the socialistic teachings of Karl Marx and became widely accepted in American colleges. [116]

Beard, through the Intercollegiate Socialist Society (known today as the League for Industrial Democracy), brought Socialist branches into scores of universities and colleges in America.

Beard's book *An Economic Interpretation of the Constitution of the United States* tried to make it look like Madison's motivations were purely selfish and economic. He did this like a lot of people do, by taking things out of context. However, you have to leave things out to form people to your way of thinking. This is why they leave things out of our history books and only give one point of view. This is why I keep saying, "Do your own research."

The slant on history was continued by Carl Becker, Max Lerner, and Arthur Schlesinger (both Senior and Junior). This is why we have politicians who are socialistic in their views. They have been brainwashed in the schools and do not even know it. Socialism is taught in our schools' social science courses. Everything is put into social terms, including math! I went to a school and got a book that says everything is social:

---

116   Veritas, http://thegreatdeceit.com/?p=2047 ,Charles A. Beard's
       1913 Book, http://lexrex.com/enlightened/AmericanIdeal/
       add_beard.htm ,Langue Division, http://languedivision.blogspot.
       com/2008_10_01_archive.html

social math, social English, and so on (*Social Civics* by Munro, Kennelly, and McCarthy).

This is why you should not jump to conclusions when told something. This is why you should check things out because the lies have been out there for years, bringing us to a socialistic government. The Soviet Union did it for years. The Nazis did it for years. Yes they are still alive. This is being done out of your ignorance of not knowing what our Constitution really is about. I even confess that sometimes I do not check out what is said in the media and find out later that they left a lot out, making it look like something it is not.

Carl Becker, a progressive historian, wrote *The Declaration of Independence* (1922, 1942) and *The Heavenly City of the Eighteenth-Century Philosophers* (1932). He was born in Iowa and studied under Frederick Turner, famous for the Turner Thesis. Becker claimed that the Revolution was not a war for independence but a domestic war for equality. Yes, he is right to a point. They wanted equality but they were not getting it, so then they decided to break away from England and become a separate country. They were English citizens not given citizens rights. Like US citizens are being treated like foreigners and foreigners being treated like US citizens.

If it was not a war for independence why would they have made the Declaration of Independence? We would still be under England. If you really listen to these people, they do not make sense.

Max Lerner was born in Minsk, Russia, in 1902. He and his family came to New York in 1907. Later they moved to New Haven, Connecticut. He attended Yale Law School in 1923. He got a PhD from the Robert Booking Graduate School of Economics and Government in 1927. He wrote the best-selling *America as a Civilization*.

Lerner worked with the Democratic Party. He was a "neo-Marxian liberal." So you know what has been infiltrating the Democratic Party.

The Schlesingers were progressive politically. Arthur Sr. was a Prussian Jew who came to the United States in 1860. Arthur Jr. was born 1917 and was a special assistant and court historian to President Kennedy from 1961 to 1963. He was the one who came up with the term "the Imperial Presidency," saying that "the US presidency was out of control and had exceeded the constitutional limits" during the Nixon administration. I wonder what he would think about Obama.

Why don't they use that term about President Obama, since he is more out of control than Nixon ever was? President Obama has more czars and staff members than any other president in the history of the United States. In fact, I do not remember any czars except in the twentieth century. They also remind me of Hitler's little private army.

We do not know what these czars are up to; who's bidding are they doing, where did they come from, and how are they carrying out whatever these orders are? They report only to Obama.

How much are they getting of our tax dollars? Since they are getting paid by our tax money, why aren't they under Congressional supervision?

Schlesinger pioneered the new social history and women's history. He was coeditor and contributor of the *History of American Life*. As a historian of the rise of the city in American life, he argued that for a full understanding of the Jacksonian democratic movement, "It is necessary to consider the changed circumstances of life of the common man in the new industrial centers of the East since the opening years of the nineteenth century. This was a challenge to the frontier thesis of his Harvard colleague Frederick Jackson Turner. In Schlesinger's essay, the common man of the Mississippi Valley and the common man of eastern industrialism stood uneasily side by side."[117]

What has happened to our kids since the Communist

---

117   http://en.wikipedia.org/wiki/Arthur_M._Schlesinger,_Sr.

and the progressives' ideology has entered the schools? For one thing, our children can't read as well. The schools do not even guarantee they will be able to do the work like reading, writing, arithmetic, spelling, you know the general things, and this is after they have been in school for twelve years! Why?

There was a guarantee before the liberals took over our school system. It was there before they took the Bible out of the schools. There were no real problems then. Why has it all of a sudden changed? The children have not changed. I substituted at a kindergarten class, and they were reading. So there can be a guarantee but what is really going on?

Is it because they are more interested in brainwashing our children with these social subjects? That is right, social subjects. They do not really concentrate on the reading, writing, arithmetic, and spelling like they used to. Now that is not all the schools but quite a lot of them.

Why do we have more teen pregnancies than ever before since the liberals took God and morality out of the schools and replaced it with Karl Marx and other Socialist ideas?

On May 24, 1993, an article in *Time* magazine stated that about 30 percent of parents had taught their children thirteen to fifteen years old about sex; 22 percent of the children asked about sex were at the age of sixteen to seventeen years old. It seemed that most had learned from their friends.

It was founded that 61 percent of the sexually active girls had multiple partners, which was up from 38 percent in 1971.

They asked, "Have you ever had sexual intercourse?" 19 percent said yes between the ages of thirteen and fifteen and 55 percent said yes around the ages of sixteen to seventeen.

Then they were asked, "How old were you when you first had sex?" 23 percent were under fourteen years old; 24 percent were fourteen, 25 percent were fifteen years old, 20 percent were sixteen, and only 6 percent were seventeen.

This all comes from the pot-smoking, hippie, liberals' free

love in schools and in politics today. Sex is not love, and you are not making love! You are having sex, which is supposed to be the product of love; you need to know the difference, and so do our children.

They think that sex is love because of the mixed signals. It is a wonderful thing in the right context. We can thank the liberals for all the misery they have put upon our children and families.

One thing that makes me mad is when parents say, "Well, they are going to do it anyway so I just give them a condom to be safe." First of all, nothing is entirely safe except abstinence. The only reason my generation did not have so many sexually transmitted diseases is because sex was pretty much left to only one partner.

Second, these parents have been brainwashed into thinking that. Isn't this one of the liberals' rhetoric? Do they not say constantly they are going to do this anyway so let's give them condoms in the schools and give sex education? Funny that we did not have so many pregnancies outside marriage until liberal sex education came into play.

I had so-called sex education when I was young and close to that time of the month. However, it was nothing like what they are doing today.

One of the things our teens now say is it is different now with our generation and free love. First of all, nothing is free. The thing is it is the grandparents of these children that are paying for it. The fathers are not. They just take off and do not help with the finances but the grandparents on fixed incomes are the ones paying! Yes and the taxpayers are paying, also.

It all goes back to taking the Bible out of the schools and teaching morals, self-government, and parents not being an example. This drags other children into doing the same thing because of peer pressure. This is what the hard core liberals and Communists wanted to do.

Even during Prohibition, they said, "They are going to

drink anyway so let's go ahead and make it legal." It does not matter if they get drunk and beat up their wives and children, make them susceptible to homosexuality (we will just say they are born that way), and rob and kill people.

That is what they are saying underneath about drugs. They want it legal and it is coming about today. Again remember those in power are our drug-taking hippies of yesteryear. If you are all drugged up, you are ripe for the picking. I'll let you think about that one.

Another thing: our students are not really learning about the world around them. In *Reader's Digest* under "That's Outrageous," it talked about college students. It found out that half of the students do not even know who their home state's US senators are, and one third do not know the name of Britain's prime minister (by the way, the prime minister is David Cameron). I have taped the names of my senators and representatives near my computer. I write them constantly.

Most people do not know about the Ginsberg Address. This was a survey of 3,119 undergraduates at eight Ivy League campuses done by Frank Luntz. 44 percent of these students did not even know who the Speaker of the House was or the Supreme Court justices (I have to admit I did not know all of them myself).

Now I can see, if you have been out of school for a long time, like thirty years, that you might not know some of these things because you are busy making a living for your family, but everyone should know their US senators. We do know what time does to our memories. But then I keep remembering all those people that do not even know the Declaration of Independence when someone read it to them on the streets.

These people have done very well to keep the American people ignorant of history. Oh, that is right, social science is more important. We have to make sure that we change the values from one generation to another. We have to make sure they think, believe, and live their way and know what their right and wrong is instead of the truth.

Another thing that cropped up is disrespect for parents and anyone in authority. Today it is "work hard" and "helping others" above "obedience." By 1991, "to obey" ranked fourth in importance in child rearing. However, obedience is the root of child rearing. Working hard and helping others are just branches. Working hard comes from being able to obey instructions, either from your parents (the beginning of your learning) or your employer, which is what your parents are trying to gear you toward. Now what was it that Karl Marx said? Oh yes, something like he would destroy the hollow relationship between the parents and children and replace it with social relationship. Sounds like teaching them to be part of the collective, with no ambition, no individual thought, and so on.

Helping others comes from the philosophy "Charity starts at home." You learn to do things to help your family. When you learn to help your family and care for them, this passes over to helping other people. A child learns to care when they learn to obey and not give their parents such a hard time, especially when their parents are having hardships.

Obedience is the key for teaching children in order to get them prepared to be mature adults and not babies that have to have their way all the time (like some Democrats), gang banging, killing, stealing, road rage, and so on.

I am not saying they can't ask questions, because that is the process of learning, but they need to learn to do what they are told. When they get older, they will understand why their parents did what they did (if they matured enough). You have people like the Clintons and Obama, who never grew up and learned this. They want everything their way. Have oral sex in the Oval Office, pass a health bill that will put the American people more into poverty, and they do not seem to care. They seem to have the "me, myself, and I" syndrome.

We can look at some reasons by these examples: smaller families, higher divorce rates, more women working outside the home, and declines in church attendance (*San Jose Mercury News,* March 15, 1995).

Another is no respect for life and others' rights. We see a rise in our children getting caught up in gangs. How can we expect our children to respect life or others' rights if we do not respect life and other people's rights ourselves? The Constitution says that our rights end when they violate someone else's rights, but it is done every day by government and individuals because no one knows their Constitution.

When I first started this book, the United States had butchered about 35 million babies since *Roe vs. Wade* (by the way, I heard that woman who did the suit now wishes she never had done it). How can we expect our children to respect other people's rights when the law lets other people step over other people's rights? This includes the government doing it themselves. They are supposed to protect each individual's rights and not cater to special groups or individuals. Both parties are guilty of this!

All this has derived from humanism, the religion of liberals, which is also the Communists' religion and derived from evolution, which Hitler clung to.

What is humanism? It is the religion that puts man in place of God. It lifts man to the point of worship. This sure sounds like today, doesn't it?

My husband was talking to a man about God and this person told my husband he was his own god. My husband said ok if you are a god make this pebble out of nothing. The man got mad at him. Why? It is because man is not a god.

Humanism is the opposite of humanitarianism, which shows Christ-like love and caring for others, where humanists are concerned primarily for their own self than the needs of others. However, whatever we do, it does affect others around us. We do not live on an island where we are alone. Humanism is subtle and sneaks in unawares because the promoters make it sound so good, just like Satan makes sin sound good but it brings destruction.

This religion is what replaced the Bible in the schools, and the government has established it. Therefore, it is shown in other forms of communications to us and our children, in the news and entertainment media, friends, and family members.

If you do not belief their way and believe in God and the Bible, you are ridiculed. If you have any position like a radio show or a civil rights job, you are forced out of that job.[118]

This is what Thomas Jefferson was talking about, not what the liberals keep lying about what he said. They are the biggest offenders in placing another religion under a different banner, and that goes along with saving the frogs and so on. I'll get to that later.

First, let's go back to disrespect. Students in many schools are made to believe that they are not accountable to God, parents, teachers, or civil authorities. They are told, "Whatever you choose will be right for you because you chose it." I had a counselor tell my daughter that. So if my daughter chose to take drugs, that is right for her, even if it kills her. This is bull!

How about the phrase, "Anybody's values are as good as anybody else's"? So if a homosexual decides he likes your ten-year-old son and decides to make him into a homosexual, which is okay because it is his values to play around with young boys and sexually abuse them. I guess so, since they are now teaching homosexuality in some schools.

If people feel it is okay to steal, then they can go ahead and steal. What if their values are that if someone gets in their way, they can just kill them? But people just soaked it up and now we have more unruly people than ever before. Why? Because that is their values. This destroys a society, it does not build

---

118   http://caselaw.findlaw.com/us-9th-circuit/1384879.html

it up. Look at all those societies that died out because they started that kind of philosophy.

That is one of the things that destroyed Rome! They took on Greece's values, which were the very thing that helped bring them down.

Lastly, "No one can tell you what to do." Yet we are told every day what to do from the minute we get up by street signs, bosses, and the government. So do not say, "I cannot understand why kids are so disrespectful." You are teaching them to be disrespectful, and parents trying to teach their children what is right are being undermined by liberals. You cannot tell your kids anything or discipline them. We are seeing the results today of this line of thought.

Dr. Spock started this philosophy of not spanking your child. What experiments were done to prove this? I ran across a site that used *Leave It to Beaver* as an example. This was just a TV show where everything was controlled and they were told what to say and what to do. This is not real life! If you have kids, you know they do not listen to you and go ahead and do their own thing. They do what is known as selective hearing.[119]

Spock claimed that people took what he said in the wrong way. He did not mean for people to let their children rule them. He found out more mothers were afraid to give firm leadership. He believed that there should be firmness in raising children and not let them be unreasonable or rude; he did not mean parents should spoil them.[120] However, our government has taken it the wrong way, and the child, who has no idea of what life is really about, rules the roost.

I spent three days in my daughter's classroom because she had gotten two suspensions; I found out later that some girl

---

119   Parenting Techniques, http://www.leaveittobeaver.org/thesis/
          thesis_parenting.htm
120   Benjamin Spock, World's Pediatrician, Dies at 94, http://www.
          nytimes.com/learning/general/onthisday/bday/0502.html

right off the bat said she was going to beat her up. I have seen the chaos and disruptions by the students. I saw the disrespect because of the humanistic religion of the liberals of "do your own thing," "you cannot discipline the child." or "you cannot take something away from a child and return it to them later because it is their property."

One day when I was there, a student was playing with a balloon instead of watching a video. She started to bounce it to other students and disrupt the class. I asked the teacher why she did not take the balloon from her. This is what she said: "It is the student's property and I cannot take it from her." I said she could take it from her and tell her she can have it after class. She said she couldn't.

The liberals and some parents have tied the teachers' hands behind their backs. Now do not get me wrong, the schools have tied some parents' hands behind their backs and have gone overboard with some things too. This is why I said things are in total chaos.

That same day, I saw a boy right in class grab a girl in a certain area. This is unacceptable in public and at school! Wake up, people. The school should not be raising your children, and that goes for the government. We have the government so eager to take your kids from you. If anyone knows what real abuse is, it is me!

1 Corinthians 14:33 says, "For God is not *the author* of confusion, but of peace, as in all churches of the saints." If things had stayed God centered, there would not be this mass confusion and helplessness that people feel. It is all due to the movement that the Communist had put into play. Senator Joseph McCarthy (R-WI) was right about what was going on in America, but they ignored him.

Because of the lack of discipline in our society and the "do your own thing," we see the results. Their own thing is no education, fighting on the streets, killing, stealing, drugs, gangs, and control over others.

We as adults are supposed to teach them what is right and wrong, and that doing the wrong thing has bad consequences. It starts at the home and is to be backed up by the schools. It is not the school's place to raise the children; it is the parents' responsibility! The parents are to back up the teacher if they are right. Parents need to respect the rules of the school and, if they disagree, talk to the school board without the child being there, unless they want their child to be disobedient and end up on the streets. Maybe they even will be like one of those kids at Columbine.

This philosophy leads to a decline in academics, for when there is a decline in discipline, there is a decline in learning because they are not listening to the teacher. Why can't people see the forest for the trees?

Humanism brings about self-centeredness. They are taught to only look out for themselves. The Bible tells us to take care of ourselves and to help others. It teaches God first, then families, then others, and we are last. This is hard because our very nature starts out me, myself, and I. Any doctor will tell you that a baby is very selfish. You have to be taught to care about others and to share.

Total academic freedom is used to bring everything in for children to read or see (VCR, DVD) under this banner. It does not matter what is in it. Dr. Tim La Haye wrote, "Academic freedom in public education only means freedom to teach humanism." My daughter's school showed inappropriate films with naked people. Is this education? This is pornography under the banner of education. Sure, there was a substitute that day, but if I was a teacher and wanted to show that film, I would have found a way to play it with those parts taken out. The school just gave me a flimsy excuse. It should have been screened in advance.

Humanists say it is immoral to indoctrinate children about God and the Bible, but I say it is immoral to teach our children to be self-centered and not care about others; to have the "I" problem; to teach them about free sex so they can destroy their bodies either through sexually transmitted diseases or abortion as they torture babies; or to end up dead at fifteen because they ran away from home after being told "No one can tell you what to do." To teach them to be disrespectful and to ruin their lives by lack of education or become drug addicts, street walkers, or gang members. No one can tell me these are good things, but here we are trying to make marijuana legal, and the next thing will be heroin. Mark my words. They are using the same excuses that they used to make alcohol legal, and now you see the results: broken homes, abuse, more alcoholics, and so on.

You do not have to outright say go take this or do that. It is the liberals' ideology that teaches them; you have teachers smoking pot and selling it to students. If their kid was smoking, they would sit in the room to take in the second hand smoke from the joint!

We had a president who thinks there's nothing wrong with it. He fired Jocelyn Elders as surgeon general because it would have been political suicide if he did not. The liberals have not desensitized the people enough yet or gotten enough dope-head kids old enough to vote to go along with them, but it is getting there.

John Dewey, an atheist and father of progressive education, said, "There is no God and there is no soul." I bet he wishes he could take that back now. He was the first president of the American Humanist Association, who stated, "As non-theists, we begin with humans not God, nature not deity. No deity will save us; we must save ourselves."

Do you know how idiotic that sounds, being that man is naturally self-centered? How can someone who thinks of himself help save humanity?

Romans 1:20, 21 says, "For the invisible things of him from the creation of the work are clearly seen, being understood by the things that are made, even his eternal power and Godhead; so that they are without excuse: Because that, when they knew

God, they glorified him not as God, neither were thankful; but became vain in their imaginations, and their foolish heart was darkened."

When I was in my twenties, I watched a program on a scientific experiment. It was because they were trying to determine if man had a soul. They found out that when a person died, on the point of death they lost five pounds immediately. However, when an animal died, there was no weight loss. So you think about that one.

Dewey continued to state that teachers are social servants and they are to teach the right social order and social growth. Academics are on the bottom of the pole. He declared teachers as being the true prophets.

They use social science to pass on their ideology. If you do not believe me, get your hands on the book *General College Vision*. It provides the historical context for the influence of John Dewey. They have multicultural mathematics with social issues. All their courses seem to be around multiculturalism and social science.

The humanist religion put sex education in the schools, but has it cut down rape, crimes, VD, or teen pregnancies? No! Every single one of these has risen along with abortion. This was put in our schools to start desensitizing us to killing.

We are killing and torturing about 1.5 million babies a year. The next time you see a baby; just picture their limbs being torn apart.

Now abortion has gone down a little in one year. So now they want to put sex education in kindergarten and elementary schools. Why? Is it to brainwash more children that are more susceptible? They know they will have America captive to their philosophy and religion.

Dr. Sam Jones said in the *Los Angeles Times* that sexual freedom is the "death of innocence." We have taken the pure innocence of childhood and forced young people into adulthood with no intermission. [121]

No wonder our children are a mess today and families are faced with extinction. A strong family unit helps to make a strong country! Thank you, John Dewey, for helping to destroy our children and our country; thank you, Communists, for infiltrating our country's schools and government to destroy our children and families so you can destroy our country; thank you, Democrats and liberals, who helped them along. Yes, I am being sarcastic.

In January of 1996, Colorado voted to end the requirement that students learn about the documents our forefathers wrote. Now if that is not trying to hide history and the truth, I do not know what is. As far as I am concerned, it deliberately hides what freedoms we have lost and what our forefathers really had in mind. Read the Federalist Papers; that will be a real eye opener.

To take over a country, you have to strip it of its history and pride in one's country (patriotism, no respect for the national anthem or pledge of allegiance, disrespect the flag by wearing it as a diaper, and so on), and this is what is being done in our schools. If you really look into all the events that changed things, you will find that the movement was started by someone who believes in Communism or Socialism and has pulled naïve people into hiding it. This is what Communists do to change a nation.

They have said that if they destroy the home they would have the country. They only needed is to take over the school, news media, and entertainment. We are just handing it over to them.

They got you bucking the school and teachers instead of backing them up. This also teaches your child to be disrespectful

---

121   Dr. Paul A. Kienel, How Humanism Affects Children, http:// www.watke.org/resources/Humanism%20Affects%20Youth%20. pdf

and use you as a pawn to their benefit. Shame on you! I am not saying the teachers are always right, but if there are rules, you should teach your child to respect them. We now have students going to school in their PJs.

It is high time to start teaching our children the truth about history. Our nation was not perfect, but it did have the right beginning with God.

ACLU

A goodly apple rotten at the heart:
O, what a goodly outside falsehood hath!
—Shakespeare

THE AMERICAN CIVIL LIBERTIES UNION (ACLU) is not what you think it is. This chapter will explain where it came from, who started it, and who joined it. I think this is very important because they have been going around our nation, getting rid of Christian symbols in private or public, and taking Bibles and prayer out of schools.

Now according to the *Encyclopedia Britannica,* the ACLU was founded in 1920 by Jane Adams (a social reformer), Morris Hillquit, James Weldon Johnson, Helen Keller (in the midstream), Jeannette Ranken (the first woman elected to the House of Representatives), Norman Thomas (who ran for president five times on the Socialist party ticket), and Roger Baldwin, who was a Communist and also wrote *Liberty Under the Soviets.*

Roger Nash Baldwin, one of the ACLU's founders and its director, was a Communist. He even admitted that his goal was Communism in 1935:

> I have been to Europe several times, mostly in connection with international radical activities ... and have traveled in the United States to areas of conflict over workers rights to strike and organize.

My chief aversion is the system of greed, private profit, privilege and violence which makes up the control of the world today, and which has brought it to the tragic crisis of unprecedented hunger and unemployment ... Therefore, I am for Socialism, disarmament and ultimately, for the abolishing of the State itself ... I seek the social ownership of property, the abolition of the propertied class and sole control of those who produce wealth.

According to Wikipedia, Baldwin claimed that he purged the organization of Communists. After what he said, do you really believe that? Especially since they are still tearing down our Constitution?

Crystal Eastman, another founder, was a lawyer, antimilitarist, feminist, Socialist, and journalist. Then there was William Z. Foster, who was the author of *Toward Soviet America*. Others were Harold J. Laski, A. J. Muste, Scott Nearing, Eugene V. Debs, and John Dewey. You think Communists and Socialists do not have a hold on our schools?

In 1920, the ACLU held a party in New York City, and guess who attended? Norman Thomas, Elizabeth Gurley of the future Communist Party, and a Soviet agent named Agnes Smedley.

They make themselves look good while they change your way of thinking and our country into Communism. I found this information on this website: http://www.stoptheaclu. com/2005/07/12/american-communist-lawyers-union/. Either way, it was founded by Socialists and Communists in 1920.

In 1967, the ACLU joined up with the Lawyers Constitutional Defense Committee and went around the country to see who they could con into helping them question the Constitution. Of course, this is not what they are saying but it is exactly what they are doing.

The people that were not Socialists were easily influenced by them because they wanted to make things better for the people in the United States. Socialism sounds like a utopia, but it is not, as you have seen from our history and the history of other countries. This is why you need to learn history and do research because they are not giving the full story and have twisted the truth of our history. This twisted history is being taught to our children. Do not forget; teach it to your children.

They are still duping people into backing them up while they continue to destroy America little by little. Do they care if you find out the truth? No, they got what they wanted out of you. You were their little puppet to help get us closer to Socialism and eventually to Communism.

I remember talking to a lady about their history and she said, "But they have done a lot of good." Of course they do some good to make themselves look good, but eventually you will be under a dictatorship wondering what happened.

Shakespeare said, "The devil can cite Scripture for his purpose. An evil soul producing holy witness is like a villain with a smiling cheek, A goodly apple rotten at the heart."[122]

Christ said something similar: "Even so ye also outwardly appear righteous unto men, but within ye are full of hypocrisy and iniquity" (Matthew 23:28).

According to Fox News, the ACLU defends child molesters, attacks the use of the word "Christmas" (because it means Christ's high holyday; they want it out), and demands homosexual clubs in high schools, funded by your tax dollars! This is so they can indoctrinate your children into that kind of behavior. Remember it is not natural and therefore you have to teach that kind of behavior. They also go after people that do not follow them and use this money to tear down our social system.

So where do they get their funding? Well, they do get

---

122   *The Merchant of Venice*, I:3.

some from memberships but according to Fox News, they get some of their other funding from foundations like the Ford Foundation (which gave them $14 million), George Soros of the Open Society Institute gave $2 million (I looked up his site and it said, "to help countries make the transition from Communism. Our activities have grown to encompass the United States and more than 70 countries in Europe, Asia, Africa and Latin America. "[123] By the way, at the time Bill Moyers was a trustee), the Carnegie Corporation gave $800,000 (at the time Judy Woodruff of CNN was a trustee), and the Rockefeller Foundation gave $275,000 (one of the trustees was cellist Yo Yo Ma).

There is a more extensive list available from Morning Coffee (morningcoffee.wordpress.com).

The ACLU brings many suits against the government and wins attorney fees. That means the citizens pay with their tax dollars. We are paying the ACLU to destroy America!

Here are some other foundations that contribute to the ACLU:

Arca Foundation, established by Nancy Susan Reynolds in 1952. Her father founded the R. J. Reynolds tobacco company. In the 1980s, it funded pro-Cuban, pro-Sandinista, and anticorporate groups.

Reynolds Bagley's daughter, Nancy Bagley, worked on Clinton's campaign and then helped work on the health care that Hillary Clinton wanted. Arca also fund ACORN, Planned Parenthood, and Immigrant Workers Citizenship Project along with others.[124]

The Annie E. Casey Foundation, established in 1948 by Jim Casey along with his siblings in honor of their mother. He was also one of the founders of United Postal Service.

---

123 Who We Are, http://www.osiwa.org/index.php/en/about-us/who-we-are

124 http://www.discoverthenetworks.org/funderprofile.asp?fndid=5282&category=79

The foundation went from being devoted to child welfare and foster care to liberal agendas like multiculturalism, race-based programs for minorities, government control of health care, employment, and personal incomes of American citizens. They support the progressive movement. In a report called "Race Matters: Unequal Opportunity Within Criminal Justice," they claimed that the judicial system was prejudiced against people of color. Well, I guess they have not heard that there are different races in the judicial system!

Who else do they support? Well, they support the Rockefeller Family Fund, ACORN, National Immigration Law Center, Planned Parenthood, the American Bar Association, the Arab American Institute Foundation, and others.[125]

The Columbia Foundation, founded in 1940 by Madeleine Haas Russell (great-grandniece of Levi Strauss) and her brother to further welfare. The president of Levi Strauss and his business partner served for twenty years on the board. Supposedly it works to fight injustices of the American's capitalists economic system (I wonder if they did research on the injustices of Socialism and Communism) and solve environmental problems; it supports organizations that are anti-capitalist (yet they make millions off of this system; why don't they just give all that money away to people that are struggling if they are against capitalism?). Now hear this and you will understand the agenda of the liberals: Michael Berliner said, "Not clean air and clean water, [but] rather … the demolition of technology/industrial civilization."

> The Columbia Foundation also supports numerous anti-war groups that share a view of the United States as an aggressive, exploitative world power whose unjust policies lie at the root of many international disputes. Representative of such organizations is Global Exchange, led by

---

125   http://www.discoverthenetworks.org/funderProfile.asp?fndid=5202

the pro-Castro Communist revolutionary Medea Benjamin.

Other organizations they support are Open Society Institute, Foundation for Deep Ecology, and the National Abortion and Reproduction Rights Action League (NARAL).[126]

The William and Flora Hewlett Foundation, which was set up by William Hewlett's widow and son in 1966. When Hewlett (of Hewlett-Packard fame) died, he bequeathed the foundation $5 million. They support population control (now you know another reason why liberals want abortion; it is to make room for their god, nature), conflict resolution (I am not sure what conflicts they are talking about), US-Latin American relations, global affairs, and others.

Other organizations they support include Mexican American Legal Defense and Education Fund, ACORN, Amnesty International, National Urban League, Rockefeller Family Fund, Planned Parenthood, Harvard University, City University of New York, and Columbia University.[127]

Let's look at this Open Society Institute that a lot of them support; established in 1993; they claim to be "a nonpartisan, nonpolitical entity" but when you support the ACLU, you are a political group. So I do not know who they are fooling. They are affiliated with the Institute for Policy Studies and National Lawyers Guild.

Aryeh Neir, who is Open Society's president, worked for the ACLU from 1963 to 1978. Bill Moyers is a former trustee of Open Society Institute. Lani Guinier, who was Bill Clinton's nominee for assistant attorney general for civil rights, was a trustee until 2007. She favored proportional representation in elections based on race and ethnicity. Other groups they support are Catholics for Free Choice, Institute for Policy Studies,

---

126   http://www.discoverthenetworks.org/funderProfile.asp?fndid=5286
127   http://www.discoverthenetworks.org/funderProfile.asp?fndid=5337

Planned Parenthood, Center for American Progress, NARAL, Mexican American Legal Defense and Education Fund, and Immigrant Legal Resource Center; they gave $20,000 for the defense of Lynne Stewart, who was later convicted of helping Omar Abdel Rahman, who was connected with an Islamic group that did terrorist acts. They received about $30 million from US government agencies between 1998 and 2003.[128]

I am not going to put everyone but it is enough here to see the intertwinement of all these organizations; they are geared to destroy America. If you want to see the rest of the list, go to http://morningcoffee.wordpress.com/2006/10/06/who-funds-the-aclu/

---

128   http://www.discoverthenetworks.org/funderProfile.asp?fndid=5181

A Republic

*If angels were to govern men, neither external nor
internal controls on government would be necessary.*
—James Madison; Federalist Paper 51

MANY PEOPLE OF TODAY DO not know what a republic
government is because of the mixed signals they have been
given, especially from our politicians. The United States has
never been a democracy, it is a federal republic. Even our
pledge to the flag says, "and to the *republic* for which it stands."
Maybe that is the real reason they do not want the Pledge of
Allegiance said in the schools.

I have a reprint of *Webster's Dictionary* from 1828, and it
says that a republic is "a commonwealth; a state in which the
exercise of the sovereign power is lodged in representatives
elected by the people. In modern usage, it differs from a
democracy or democratic state; in which the people exercise
the powers of sovereignty in person. Yet the democracies of
Greece are often called republics."

In Latin, "republic" means "the public thing," but that was
corrupt in practice in that the concept that sovereignty is in the
people who delegated power to the representatives and officials.
George Carey made statements about Plato and Aristotle, so
I looked them up.

In the book *Political Thought of Plato and Aristotle*[129], it said the Latin word republic had two meanings: "the State," meaning government (Latin, *respublica*, hence the name by which it generally goes), or "concerning justice." Plato had a unique thought of a republic being a "philosophy" or man and laws in thought. Looking upon Greece's struggle between a few rulers and democracy, he found vivid evils and so came the attacks on property and abolishing their form of economics, which was based on gold.

Plato saw Athens as one pressing their will over the ignorant and the assembly as "demagogue," meaning someone who, in our day in time, would be called a smooth talker to influence people to adhere to him (*Webster's Dictionary*, 1828). Sounds like our president today, doesn't it? He is getting Congress to pass laws without knowing exactly what is in the bill. If a country can keep people ignorant, it is easier to get them behind you by what you say than what is actually the truth. That is why they have taken the Bible out of the schools and deny our Christian heritage. Plato thought the masses should not govern themselves; he also thought they shouldn't make the government.

Plato declared that the government is only as good as its members. If they are selfish, then the good of the people will not be looked after. This is the problem we have today with Congress. They do not care what the laws are doing to the people. All they care about is dictating our lives and leaving themselves exempt from the laws they make (which is illegal anyway but people do not know that).

At the conclusion, Plato declares that a republic isn't a utopia but a practical form of government. The thing is you have to get rid of immorality, ignorance, selfishness, corruption, and other things that bring down the government.

Aristotle talked about self-government, which goes hand

---

129 Sir Ernest Baker, *The Political Thought of Plato and Aristotle*, Dover Publications, New York 14, New York 1959

in hand with liberty. It was put this way: "Liberty, to a modern mind, often conveys the sense of freedom from interference of the State—a sense which implies that no man is free, in so far as he is a member of a State, and abides by its rules."

The forefathers of the United States believed in self-government. They believed that a person couldn't rule a country if he couldn't rule a smaller form of government, and he couldn't rule the smaller form of government if he couldn't rule his family, and he couldn't rule his family if he couldn't rule himself. If you couldn't control your anger, vanity, lust, self-centeredness, and so on, you are not fit to rule a country because you only care about yourself and not about the people and what they want to be done.

A prime example of selfishness is a representative who did what she wanted and not what the people wanted: Senator Dianne Feinstein from California. On TV, she out and out said she didn't care what the people thought about gun control; she was going to vote the way she wanted. This senator couldn't put aside her own feelings because of what had happened to her in the past. She voted the way she wanted, not considering what the people wanted or that there are millions of people who have guns and don't commit a crime. That's dangerous and we are seeing how dangerous it is today with the Obama administration.

Rome was called a republic at one time. When Marius and Caesar twisted the constitution for their own gain, it became a monarchy under the disguise of a commonwealth. (Gibbon, 1998).

Democrats have been twisting the Constitution to get the Bible out of every public place they can and restraining Christians from practicing their faith, trying to make them the enemy of the state, like Hitler did with the Jews, to be able to make people not care if they are immoral, selfish, and corrupt. Did you know that the Communists said that if they could destroy the family and the morals of our country that they could destroy this country and take it over? Oh, you were not taught that? Of course you were not taught that, because the liberals have taken that out along with what this country was built upon.

The United States of America is known as a federal republic and unique in its own rights. *Each state is a government in itself that has made a compact with each other, which is the Constitution.* This type of government was well planned and constructed. They put into consideration everything including the future. This is the reason for making amendments. Also they thought of a falling away. They insisted on self-government being taught in the schools but they do not do it today.

John Overton Choules wrote on August 12, 1843:

> We should never forget that the prison, the scaffold, and the stake were stages in the march of civil and religious liberty which our forefathers had to travel, in order that we might attain our present liberty… Before our children remove their religious connections … before they leave the old paths of God's Word … before they barter their birthright for a mess of pottage, let us place in their hands this chronicle of the glorious days of the suffering churches, and let them know that they are the sons of the men of whom the world was not worth; and whose sufferings for conscience sake are here monumentally recorded. (Hall, 1975, p. 8)

There was a great debate about what form of government we should have. Some didn't want a government (Anti-Federalists) and others did (Federalists). Essays came out from both groups. The most famous essays known were the Federalist Papers, which were written by most of our well-known forefathers, Adams and Hamilton being among them. They are no longer taught in the schools, because then the people would know exactly what our forefathers were thinking.

John Adams said that they needed to decide what the government's purpose was before deciding what form of government to have. He declared that happiness to the greatest number was the main purpose, not to a few. Today it is the opposite. The few are controlling the majority. Adams mentioned Socrates, Confucius, and other philosophers.

He declared that fear is the basis of most governments, and Americans wouldn't go for that type. Also, that all of society being able to assemble to administer laws was impossible.

The thirteen states only surrendered their power to make war and peace, and create foreign and domestic treaties, and such like items. They believed in what is called the "compact theory of the states." In other words, you have a dual citizenship of a sort.

In the Federalist Paper 10, James Madison claimed that a democracy wasn't a cure for parties trying to control the government. However, a republic could control the efforts of the parties. He stated:

> It may be concluded that a pure democracy, by which I mean a society consisting of a small number of citizens, who assemble and administer the government in person, can admit of no cure for the mischief of faction. A common passion or interest will, in almost every case, be felt by a majority of the whole... There is nothing to check the inducements to sacrifice the weaker party or an obnoxious individual... A republic, by which I mean a government in which the scheme of representation takes place, opens a different prospect, and promises the cure for which we are seeking, Let us examine the points in which it varies from pure democracy, and we shall comprehend both the nature of the cure and the efficacy which it must derive from the Union.

Daniel Webster noted that the US government was set on morality and religious sentiment and that without morality, there wasn't safety from government. Also you needed religious principles for morality. They wanted themselves and others to keep from being harassed because of their religion, like they had in England (Tefft, 1930, p. 111).

So they set up a republic on the compact theory. They came up with the Bill of Rights because a lot of people wanted to insure their rights. The First Amendment insured their religious freedom, which was very important to them; it states, "Congress shall make no law respecting an establishment of religion, or prohibiting the free exercise thereof." This means that they cannot set up a certain religion as a government religion, like England did, and punish people if they believed differently. People were tortured and put in prison because they believed otherwise, and that was the main reason most Christians came to the New World. They wanted to exercise their beliefs without fear of persecution. Now today they are starting to persecute the very religion that set this government up and made it a great nation. There is no separation of church and state in the Constitution in the manner that the Supreme Court has dictated. The liberals have their own Constitution, and they are forming our Constitution to theirs.

The three branches of government, legislative, executive, and judicial, are a check and balance system to make sure that one doesn't step over the line and contradict the Constitution. If they do and the other groups don't do anything, it is up to the citizens to say something. That is why it is important that you know about your government. We are not Nazis or any of the other things that the Democrats call us. It is our duty. By the way, when someone is doing a lot of name calling, you need to look even closer because it is their way of trying to hush you and trying to take the focus off of themselves. Usually they are doing something they are not supposed to be doing and trying to hide it. It is a military tactic called a diversion.

You get the enemy to look at something else while you attack from behind.

The president is elected and he selects the cabinet members, Supreme Court Justices, and other officials. They are to be confirmed. No czars without confirmation; they are accountable to the president and Congress! This helps from a takeover of the government. Both the House and Senate are elected.

Today the republic views are being muffled, and people are combining democracy with republic; this is a very dangerous thing, I believe this is because the schools have so many dropouts, so they are ignorant on what the difference is. Liberals are changing our history so people are ignorant and they can say anything. You also have politicians calling us a democracy. What gets me is that you even have Republicans calling us a democracy. What's with that? They should know better.

No government is perfect, as our forefathers stated. As long as man isn't perfect, there will be no perfect government because they are greedy and selfish. People want only what they want. They will increase when self-government is not taught. For if I am not taught that my rights end where others begin, then it is okay to steal, kill, and so on. Being taught self-government at home and in the schools is very important in a society and extremely so in a government. Our forefathers did not intend to keep God out of our schools and lives.

I want you to think about this: Karl Marx said that you can get people to do things if there is a crisis. If there is no crisis, then make one up and you can get them to do what you want them to do. Doesn't it seem that we are always in a crisis according to the liberals? Did you know that only about 10 percent of the animals and plants that they put on the endangered species list are actually endangered? That is right. They do not have to prove that they are endangered. So they take property away from people under falsehood. This is fraud and the government sanctions it. I learned that from a forest ranger.

Have you ever wondered why they do not teach the Constitution, the Declaration of Independence, or the Federalist Papers in depth any more in our schools? What I mean is they do not go into depth with our Constitution any more, they brush over the Declaration of Independence, and they do not even bring up the Federalist Papers. I keep remember people saying how terrible it was when the Declaration of Independence was read to them. Remember what I said about keeping people ignorant?

I got this chart from a teacher years ago. This gives a great understanding of what our forefathers had in mind. We are a federal republic, not a democracy! The longer they can fool people, the sooner they can put us under a dictatorship!

Ye shall know the truth and the truth shall set you free
John 8:32

Democracy	Federal Republic
Sovereignty rest collectively in the majority.	Recognizes the individual importance and property as a God-given, not government granted.
Each individual exercise power collectively.	Individuals represented no matter their point of view.
The group controls, not the individual.	Control is by the individual by electing representatives who make laws but must live by them also.
One can force the will of the majority.	Individual self-government, love for neighbor, and respect for others' rights and property. (Your rights end when they violate someone else's.)
Everyone is assembled and voting is direct by individuals.	Political power is in the individual delegating authority to elected representatives to act for the individual.
The majority (50+1) may rule; the majority administers authority or power directly in assembly.	Power is exercised by representatives in assembly.
Role of law: It is a government of man who make the laws, thus laws are subject to the whims and passions of the majority, maybe a mob.	Role of law: It is a government of law, written law and subject to amendments. It is administered by elected officials for a limited time during good behavior.
Individual rights, liberty, and property are subject to the majority's will	Liberty and property are expressly declared to be secured by written laws, which representatives must follow and be governed by.
Public views are expressed by a majority.	Public views and wishes refined by passing through a chosen body of citizens elected for their qualifications and character.
Individual rights not secured.	Individual rights most secured.

The Environment

Professing themselves to be wise, they became fools, and Changed the glory of the incorruptible God into an image made like To corruptible man, and to birds, and four footed beasts, and Creeping things ... Who changed the truth of God into a lie, and Worshipped and served the creature more than the Creator, who is Blessed for ever. A-men.
—Romans 1:22, 23, 25

I WANT TO SAY RIGHT off the bat that I believe in keeping our environment and protecting endangered species, for God has made us stewards of this earth. However, I do not believe in using them to make our country into a totalitarianism state.

As I said, about 10 percent of the species on the endangered species list are really endangered. We are teaching our kids about the environment and endangered species, but what is not being taught is that any animal or plant can be put on the list, even if it is not really endangered. It is just a way for liberals to take people's land from them and herd them into cities so they can keep track of them.

I was camping in California one summer and we went on a nature walk with a forest ranger. On the walk she talked about how someone brought in a bullfrog, which chased the red legged frog from the area.

They weren't becoming extinct! These red-legged frogs just did not like living with the bullfrogs. Because the liberals did not like the idea of these frogs moving, they decided to put them on the endangered list just because the red-legged frog was not where they wanted them to be.

Someone asked if they would be able to put the red-legged frog on the endangered list. She said, "Sure, because if the government questioned it they could be sued." In other words, she was saying that any species they decided to put on the list, the government had to do it or they could sue them. There are no guidelines to prove whether or not the species is really endangered. They can put any animal or plant on this list no matter what. This is a great opening for liberals to use the government for power over the citizens, and they have. This is a small group telling the American people what to do! Illegal, illegal, illegal!

Example: In *Reader's Digest,* they told about a struggling family in Winchester, California, that wanted to build a larger home. They had two sons, fifteen and thirteen, and a ten-year-old daughter. They lived in a one-bedroom home. This means the girl was not able to have any privacy from her brothers and vice versa.

The parents' applied for a building permit but it was denied because their twenty acres was in a kangaroo-rat study area; this disease-infested rat is on the endangered species list and there is a $100,000 fine if you injure one. Remember that rodents—rats and mice—brought about the plagues and famines in the old days before people learned how to put them under control. The liberals want to put us back to that time because they really think we ought to be exterminated. In other words, they are trying to genocide the human race for their god, nature. As far as they are concerned, there is no room for us! Of course they exempt themselves like the Democrats exempt themselves from the Obama health care, which is illegal.

The parents had to put out $5,000 for someone to survey the property to show there were no kangaroo-rats. If one was found, they could not build but had to give the government $40,000 to buy land for a rat's preservation.

What? They had to give the government money just because that diseased rat was living on their property! I would start killing every one of them and go to jail because it is wrong to penalize someone for having an animal on their property. This is against what our forefathers set up: liberty and the pursuit of happiness! Animals come before humans, and this is what they are teaching our children.

This is a typical liberal Democrat, and the Republicans are no better because they have not corrected this problem. No one is making it mandatory to prove that these animals are extinct.

The hard-earned money that this family scraped together for years so they could build and live comfortably had to be given to the government! This is outrageous! This is outright robbery!

I do not know how it finally came out because nothing more was said. That is typical also. Hush, hush, anything that might get people mad or people realize they are wronging people.

A family in the San Joaquin Valley of California who raised dairy cows had a run-in with the Fish and Wildlife Service (FWS). They wanted to plant barley for feed.

The FWS insisted that the blunt-nose leopard lizard was on their 160 acre section of the farm. They ended up having to hand over sixty acres to the FWS to avoid expensive legal fees to fight them, even though no lizards were found. All this is extortion, and nobody does anything about it. The government seems to say, "We will leave you alone if you give us this or that. Otherwise we will make life miserable and cost you a lot of money even if what we say is not true." The government is greedy and so are the people of these organizations. They are bullies. This is how a dictatorship starts, when the people of a country do not stand up together for what is right. This is like protection money that the mob gets. If we did any of this, we would be thrown in prison. It is against the law!

Beth Morian, an environmentalist and a member of the Zoological Society of Houston's board of directors, was nabbed by the EPA. Their family donated sixty-two acres, worth $1.9 million, to the city of Austin for a nature preserve. Then they started to sell home sites only to have everything put to a halt because the FWS put a bird on the endangered species list. I agree with Morian that preserving species is good but people have a place here on earth, too. I'll bet they lost her support after that.

Right here in Colorado, they have been talking about having to do construction work around a rodent's habitat because these animal activists have decided to put it on the list. Everyone is still forgetting what happens when you have too many of them around.

I think it was a couple of years ago they complained about there being too many cranes, and they said they needed to get it off the list. It was in the *Valley Courier* in Alamosa, Colorado.

To show the ignorance of these people, they decided to put an animal where it had never been before. They put a lynx cat in the valley here. Do you know that that cat was brought over on ships around the late 1700s? They are messing with nature and making a mess of things on top of it. They do not know what they are doing and they do not seem to care.

They sit there and make you think they know everything, and every once in a while, something will be published in the news that shows they are just doing whatever to make money off our taxes and give them power.

It is our property, and we have the right to do with it what we please, as long as it does not create a health hazard. Did you know that our forefathers did not believe in property tax or require permits to build on your property? This is just another way of taking money from you because they do not know how to quit spending or budget right.

Some environmental laws are geared toward dictating people's lives. They talk about depleting the ozone, destroying the watershed in some areas, global warming, and so on and so forth. They are all geared to political power and cutting on people's freedom.

Let's take the ozone. By now you have heard that a volcano's chlorine is not like CFC; it comes down like rain, and natural chlorine dissolves in water. It never reaches the ozone, which is hard to believe on the grounds that it spurts out a lot higher than a spray can. Logic tells me that if one reaches the stratosphere, so does the other. Chlorine is chlorine. This would be one thing someone would have to prove to me. I do not really mind the ban on CFC because it really has not changed anything that I can see in the way of our lifestyle. Some people are probably allergic to it anyway.

This is a known fact: there is a hole in the ozone every time a volcano erupts. Then after a while, it goes away. So who is fooling who?

So what about global warming? Some of the warming is from the tilt of the earth. Now I am no scientist but we have countries towing icebergs down to their countries for drinking water and farming. That is weight, and if you take weight from one end to put it at another end, things will shift. That is a fact. Just look at an old-fashioned scale and how they measured things out with weights. Just think about it. It cannot help but shift the earth. I do not believe it is from all this stuff that the liberals claim.

So should we be alarmed about global warning? According to NASA, we are not warming at the great rate that our liberals want us to think we are. It has been shown that more energy is lost after warming than our liberal alarmists' models show. The carbon dioxide being trapped is far less than they say.[130]

Let's talk about logging. There was an article in the *San Jose Mercury News* on July 1, 1993, about logging on federal lands. Clinton permitted logging but limited it, and I agree with these limits. After all, these are federal trees.

However, when you start getting into private land, this is a different matter. I am going to give a prime example in the San Luis Valley area in Colorado, where I live.

A man acquired 1,700 acres of land by paying back taxes. He does logging on the property. He is a farmer of timber. I put it that way because that is his crop. Just like a farmer plants corn, or tomatoes, or any other crop, he logs trees and plants new ones in their place. He has to, or he will be out of business. The land is divided so one section is logged and then trees are planted. Then the next year another section is logged and trees are planted. Now I grant that people new in the business do not realize they need to keep the stumps in the ground until the young trees get big enough in order to cut out the erosion. That is when someone has the right to say something.

People came in from outside and started protesting. Now these people make a living from protesting. It has become a business. This is wrong. This man had the right to harvest his crop. A lot of things are made out of wood that we use.

Plastic bags? Yes, we had a discussion about plastic bags in my college class. I have to hit on this subject because of "save the trees." This girl said that we ought to buy these canvas bags; by the way, it is advertising for the company and you pay, because the plastic does not dissolve very well into the ground. Well duh! My husband and I told people that when they were

130 NASA Data Blows Gaping Holes in Global Warming Hysteria, http://reddogreport.com/2011/07/nasa-data-blows-gaping-holes-in-global-warming-hysteria/ ; Global Warming a Hoax? NASA Reveals Warmth Releasing Heat into Space, http://sanfrancisco.ibtimes.com/articles/189649/20110730/global-warming-hoax-nasa-earth-releasing-heat-space.htm

talking about getting rid of paper bags and replacing them with plastic bags. They wanted to save the trees.

Paper bags are natural things. What I mean by that is they can be used afterward for people who want compost or as trash bags, and they decompose fast. You can burn them without putting any toxic chemicals into the air. But no, we are too dumb and we did not know what we are talking about. Plastic bags are made from petroleum, bad for the environment.

I told the class that I would not go out and buy canvas bags. The girl asked me why. Well, the first thing I thought was, "You arrogant people deserve what you get for not listening to people who know what they are talking about." We should go back to the paper bags but I knew that would not go over big. I did tell them that I used them for trash bags, which is true, and therefore I do not have to buy plastic trash bags. Now they are talking about plastic bottles and how they are bad for you. Not only are they bad, but they do not keep your drinks cold either.

Common sense tells you that if plastic, when heated, gives off a smell, it is probably melting into whatever you have in the container. This is petroleum and it is not good for your health. If the government is so concerned about our health, why don't they cut out the plastic and all those chemicals in our food? How about those hormones they give cows, which make us fat!

Have you read things on the label of some foods? It has agents that cause cancer. I know people are beginning to wake up but common sense should have told them so. The government agency says it is not enough to harm anyone. Come on, this stuff builds up in one's system, but you do not see the schools teaching you that in science class. This is another reason cancer is on the rise. You do not need a PhD, just use your common sense!

Another thing with trees is letting them rot and not clearing out the dead trees. You want to know why we have more fires that are harder to control nowadays? Well, just think about it. What do you need for a fire? Heat, oxygen, and fuel. The more fuel, the greater the fire. All those dead trees that used to be cleared out are just fuel to make the fire bigger and stronger. Did you know that before these great environmentalists decided to have all that wood lying around, there were fewer fires and they were easier to manage. Now I know that some people have started fires, but they would not have gained momentum if the woods had been cleared. What has happened to common sense?

In my next book I will get into Agenda 21 which Bush on up to Obama is trying to push on the American people and they are not aware of it.

Presidents of the United States

He that answereth a matter before he heareth
it, it is folly and shame unto him.
—Proverbs 18:13

"I DO SOLEMNLY SWEAR (OR affirm) that I will faithfully execute the Office of President of the United States, and will to the best of my ability, preserve, protect and defend the Constitution of the United States" (United States Constitution, Article II, Section 1, Clause 8).

Have you wondered why some presidents are talked about and others are not? Have you ever wondered why for some presidents, we only hear about their good points, not what they did wrong and what happened by making the decision they had made? Have you wondered which president and Congress that brought about certain policies really helped the economy? I am only going to hit on some presidents in this book; I will talk about the others in Part II.

George Washington was the first president we had. But what were his policies or faith? Not much is talked about that.

First we need to know that he was a tobacco farmer and owned a plantation. He was a great strategist and did negotiating between Congress, the colonial states, and the French allies. He was also the only president that did not want to be president and did not want to be elected.

Washington, people claim, was a deist. A deist believes in God based on reason rather than revelation and involving the view that God has set the universe in motion and does not interfere.

Well, he definitely believed in God and read the Bible. If he did not believe in the Bible, he would not have asked to be baptized or read it. He was baptized by a Baptist minister, Chaplin Gano.[131]

Also, if he did not believe in the Bible, why would he insist on putting his hand on the Bible and adding the phrase "I swear, so help me God"? Then he kissed the Bible. None of this was required of him. He did this on his own. It then became a tradition. This shows reverence for God and his word!

He talked about God's intervention in his writings. You see pictures of him praying as well as making it clear that God is needed. They even have a picture of him praying in the "prayer room" at the White House. If one believes that God abandoned everything and left it on its own, there would be no reason to pray for wisdom or pray to God at all, but Washington did pray to God for guidance.[132]

Washington presided over the Philadelphia Convention, which drafted the Constitution. As president, he established many of the customs and usages of the Executive branch of the government. He provided a basis for avoiding any involvement in foreign conflicts. This was due to the conflict between France and Great Britain. Today, we get involved all the time.

---

131 George Washington's Baptism, Act of Congress 7-16-1894 Accepts, http://www.ministers-best-friend.com/George-Washingtons-Baptism-Three-AFFADAVITS-and-Eyewitnesses-Act-of-Congress-7-16-1894-Accepts-Evidence.html , http://www.sluiceboxadventures.com/history26_washington_john_gano_circumstantial_evidence1.htm

132 Patricia Zapor, Catholic News Service, http://www.catholicnews.com/data/stories/cns/0500250.htm ; Was George Washington a Christian? http://www.christiananswers.net/q-wall/wal-g011.html

He supported the Federalist party, even though he did not join. This was the opposite of the Jeffersonians.[133]

He made sure that he did not cross the line between what his duties were and what Congress was supposed to do. He would recommend things to Congress even though Congress disagreed with a lot of those things.

Washington considered the Treasury Department the center of the new government, and all debts incurred during the Revolution were valid. Hamilton's report was in three divisions; foreign debt, $11.7 million; domestic debt, $40.4 million; and states' debt, $25 million.

Hamilton wanted them to discharge foreign debt with interest, pay domestic debt at face value, and postpone states' debt for a while.

Madison had a different thought, but people argued that it was discrimination because he wanted those who bought securities to be paid a higher return. Madison's plan was turned down.

Washington signed the bill to charter the Bank of the United States but only after he sent letters to Attorney General Edmund Randolph, who said it was unconstitutional; Jefferson thought it would strangle the government, and Hamilton said it was constitutional.

Washington did not go along with Hamilton all the time, like trying to industrialize the nation. The main thing he had to deal with was the war between Hamilton and Jefferson. Hamilton began slandering Jefferson in the papers. So you see this kind of thing has been going on in our nation since the beginning.

Washington sounded like he was unsure about a lot of things, but then this was new to them all. However, he got the Congressional Gold Medal and the Thanks of Congress.

In his farewell address, Washington said that the people

---

133   The Democrat/Republican Party; which is the Democrat Party of today?

should beware of the branches encroaching on each other and consolidating powers; he reminded them that man has the love of power and is prone to abuse it.

He also concluded:

> Of all the dispositions and habits which lead to political prosperity, religion and morality are indispensable supports. In vain would that man claim the tribute of patriotism, who should labor to subvert these great pillars of human happiness, these firmest props of the duties of men and citizens. The mere politician, equally with the pious man, ought to respect and to cherish them.

He warned of foreign powers and said to let them have as little political connection as possible. I wish I could go on but this can give you a little more insight into our first president.[134]

John Adams was George Washington's vice president. He ran against Jefferson and won by only three electoral votes. As president, he was attacked by the Jeffersonian Republicans and the Federalist Party, led by Alexander Hamilton. He built up the army and navy because he was faced with an undeclared naval war with France. He did find a peaceful resolution.

The Alien and Sedition Acts were passed because of this war. Congress was controlled by the Federalists. One act increased citizenship residency requirements from five to fourteen years.[135] This act was repealed by the Democratic-Republican Party when they won in the 1800 elections.

Other acts passed were the Act concerning Aliens, Respecting Alien Enemies and Punishment of Certain Crimes against the United States, which the new Congress let elapse. These dealt with being able to confine alien enemies and it

---

134   Yale Law School, Lillian Goldman Law Library, http://avalon.law. yale.edu/18th_century/washing.asp

135   Fifth Congress Sess. II Ch. 54 1798, p. 566.

was not necessary to call in the aid of judicial authority;[136] one could not sustain a suit or take property of an alien enemy in court;[137] the last act dealt with a list of crimes and the imprisonment for committing these crimes was not less than six months nor exceeding five years.[138]

It has been said that Adams was suspicious of Catholics,[139] but it was because of the atrocities that the Church of England committed and probably the Roman Catholics. Any church that looks like it is taking over the government and being showed favoritism will be looked upon with suspicions, like Muslims being exempt from Obamacare.[140] The thing is everyone including Congress must adhere to the law.

Adams was against debt of any kind and dishonest paper money. However, Congress did issue checks on anticipated borrowing, not money granted. Some businessmen would try to redeem these checks to find out the loans did not exist. This was not his fault, but people took it as being his fault. Later on down the road, money became backed with gold. Today we have gone back to the past, and our money is not backed with anything. No one has learned. Why? Because it is not taught that you have to have something of value to back up your paper money to make it strong.

Thomas Jefferson's words have been taken out of context; I read what he said and what he was trying to say. The state should not interfere with the church, and there should be a wall between the two so the state does not tell the church what to do.

Second, he was not even in the States when he wrote that letter. You read it and decided for yourself. You have to take what is written beforehand and after to understand what he is saying. Those that wrote the Bill of Rights understood.

---

136   Fifth Congress Sess. II Ch. 58 1798, p. 570.

137   Fifth Congress Sess. II Ch. 66 1798, p. 577.

138   Fifth Congress Sess. II Ch. 74 1798, p. 596.

139   http://americandaily.com/s-farrell-6-21-05.htm

140   http://www.snopes.com/politics/medical/exemptions.asp

They wrote it the way they did so there would not be any misunderstanding. The Bill of Rights is what the state government cannot do. It is our rights that the government is not to infringe upon:

Mr. President

To messers Nehemiah Dodge, Ephraim Robbins, & Stephen S. Nelson, a committee of the Danbury Baptist association in the state of Connecticut.

Gentlemen

The affectionate sentiments of esteem and approbation which you are so good as to express towards me, on behalf of the Danbury Baptist association, give me the highest satisfaction. My duties dictate a faithful and zealous pursuit of the interests of my constituents, & in proportion as they are persuaded of my fidelity to those duties, the discharge of them becomes more and more pleasing.

Believing with you that religion is a matter which lies solely between man & his God, that he owes account to none other for his faith or his worship, that the legitimate powers of government reach actions only, & not opinions, I contemplate with sovereign reverence that act of the whole American people which declared that <u>their</u> legislature should "make no law respecting an establishment of religion, or prohibiting the free exercise thereof," thus building a wall of separation between Church & State. [*Congress thus inhibited from acts respecting religion, and the Executive authorised only to execute their acts, I have refrained from prescribing even those occasional performances of devotion, practiced indeed by the Executive of another nation as the legal head of its church, but subject here, as religious exercises only to the voluntary regulations and discipline of each respective sect.*] Adhering to this expression of the supreme will of the nation in behalf of the rights of conscience, I shall see with sincere satisfaction the progress of those sentiments which tend to restore to man all his natural rights, convinced he has no natural right in opposition to his social duties.

I reciprocate your kind prayers for the protection & blessing of the common father and creator of man, and tender you for yourselves & your religious association assurances of my high respect & esteem.

(signed) Thomas Jefferson

Jan. 1, 1802.[141]

Do you see anything where it is the other way around or that God was supposed to be out of the government? No, you do not. He talked the whole time about the state not establishing a religion or prohibiting the church from worshiping. He explains this wall, and he stated it was so that the state does not infringe on their religious rights, not that God was to be taken out of government. It was the state that changed what he was saying! They lied to the American people. Oh, that is right, it is okay to lie now according to the courts. What is right is wrong now, and what is wrong is right. Oh, what chaos.

Yet Congress and the president today are doing the very thing Jefferson said he did not want to happen. They are showing preference to Muslims. Did they not exempt them from this health care program? Everyone should be under it.

---

141   U.S. Constitution Online. Jefferson's Wall of Separation Letter, http://www.usconstitution.net/jeffwall.html

Pelosi told the churches what to say in their pulpits. The ACLU tried to get rid of the very faith that set up this country.

Jefferson said, "A Bill of Rights is what the people are entitled to against every government, and what no just government should refuse, or rest on inference." He also said, "All tyranny needs to gain a foothold is for people of good conscience to remain silent." (Brainy Quote) And people have been silent too long.

Jefferson believed that the God that gave us life had given us liberty, also. He said, "Enlighten the people generally, and tyranny and oppressions of body and mind will vanish like evil spirits at the dawn of day." This is what I am trying to do.

He also believed every citizen should be a soldier because this was needed for every free state. How do you think he would feel with the court ruling that it is okay? He said that honesty is the first chapter of the book of wisdom; so much for that court ruling. He believed that ignorant people (lacking in knowledge) will not be able to stay free. Are you getting the point?

I will leave Thomas Jefferson with this quote: "When a man assumes a public trust he should consider himself a public property. "

James Madison, principle author of the Constitution, wrote over a third of the Federalist Papers. He was responsible for the first ten amendments, which were based on the Virginia Declaration of Rights.[142] He believed strongly in checks and balances (which our government today has crossed the line), to protect people from the tyranny of the majority. This chart shows how our government is supposed to work under the checks and balances:

---

142 The Virginia Declaration of Rights, http://www.usconstitution. net/vdeclar.html

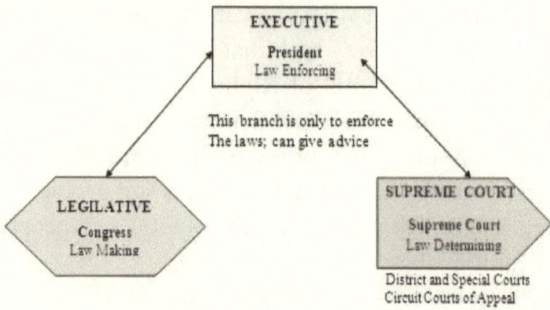

Each branch is supposed to make sure the other branch does not step over the line. The executive is not to tell the legislative or judicial branch what to do! Congress is supposed to do the will of the people! The judicial branch only makes sure laws are constitutional by what is exactly written in the Constitution, not letters of what people thought.

As you can see, the branches have crossed the lines. The thing is the legislative is supposed to keep the executive and judicial in check when they cross the line.

The executive is to keep the legislative and judicial in check when they cross the line, and the judicial is to keep the legislative and executive in check when they cross the line.

The thing is no one is doing their duty. This is why the judicial is changing the Constitution and making up their own laws. They were never to make policies at all! They are to uphold the Constitution, not change it!

We have had two presidents in my time that have broken their oath, and no one has done anything!

Madison ordered an embargo against France and Britain because of the seizing of American ships. All it did was put the American people into a depression. Napoleon acted like he was complying and Britain kept American seamen in prison and kept seizing cargoes. Madison declared war.

Washington DC was invaded by the British, and the

Madisons had to flee. The White House and Capitol were set on fire. Dolly Madison was able to save some things.

During this battle, Francis Scott Key went to the British to negotiate peace but they kept him prisoner on one of their ships. The British started bombarding Fort McHenry in Baltimore. When daylight came, the American flag was still flying. Because of this, Key wrote *The Star-Spangled Banner*. Do you know where the "In God We Trust" came from? That's right, from this song. That is why we have liberals trying to change our national anthem. They do not want people to know the truth about our country and God. It says in the second verse; "And this be our motto: 'In God is our trust!'"

The Federalist Party disappeared after the war. They had been against the war at the beginning.

James Monroe opposed ratification of the Constitution, saying the government was given too much power. He tried to cut partisan tensions. You need to look at what is really good for the American people. There should be no parties in Congress, the White House, or the Supreme Court. They are to work for the people that elect them not their party!

Monroe developed the Monroe Doctrine, which stated that European countries were not to colonize land in the Western Hemisphere. It would be conceived as an act of aggression if they did. Yet we have illegal immigrants doing it today, and our government puts Arizona on the chopping block. We have foreigners buying land here.[143]

He recommended that the Constitution be amended so the federal government could authorize construction of roads and canals. Madison had vetoed a bill for this, calling it unconstitutional because it would use federal funds. However, he had signed a bill like it to construct the Cumberland Road.

---

143   Monroe Doctrine and the Roosevelt Corollary. http://www.theodoreroosevelt.org/life/rooseveltcorollary.htm , Monroe Doctrine, http://www.u-s-history.com/pages/h255.html

When Monroe asked about it, Madison said he had signed the bill in haste and did not examine it in depth.

Sounds like the health care bill today. No one read it, so it should be unconstitutional on the grounds that they did not know what they were really voting on!

Monroe was criticized for meddling in legislative matters. He vetoed a bill to collect tolls on the Cumberland Road.

Monroe wanted to strengthen the defenses but Congress disagreed and reduced the army instead. However, Monroe pleaded to help defend Florida so Congress raised the annual appropriation in 1822 after they had cut it in response to the Panic of 1819.

Then there was an attack to reduce governmental expenditures, and it was directed toward the military because they took up most of the budget. No one seems to understand that military personnel get less pay than their counterparts in the civilian world. People forget that the men also have to support their families. They did reduce the military and it was made permanent even when the revenues improved.

I will remind people that the government had no income tax at this time; revenues came from sales and tariffs. The first sales tax was in 1817. The first income tax was not until 1862 to support the Civil War. The IRS was set up at this time. The Sixteenth Amendment in 1713 made it a permanent system in the United States.

President Reagan eliminated tax preferences to help keep revenue levels when he reduced taxes. Other presidents tried to cut taxes after Reagan.[144]

John Quincy Adams, a member of the Federalist, Democratic-Republican, National Republican, and later the Whig party, was the son of John Adams. He helped formulate the Monroe Doctrine. He tried to get programs of modernization and educational advancement. He was against

---

144   History of the Income Tax in the U.S., http://history1900s.about. com/od/1910s/a/incometax

slavery. He had problems because Congress was controlled by the opposite party.

He brought messages to the people of religious revival, social reform, party politics, and being able to move goods, money, and people more rapidly.

His economic beliefs were a central government to promote economic growth. He wanted a high tariff to support his programs of science, economic development like a national university, roads, canals, observatories, and exploration. Of course this made the Jeffersonians mad because they believed in limited government. A lot of this was fear of getting into states' affairs of slavery.

He tried to acquire Texas from Mexico but failed when trying to get more trade with the British West Indies. On top of that, he tried to use the government to stimulate the economy, which included a high tariff to promote industry and a national bank to regulate the economy. The protective tariff raised the cost of goods, which upset the southerners.

That is what happens when taxes are imposed. The companies raise the prices up to keep their profits at a certain level. Let's say their profit floor is $18 per item and their cost is $23 per item. Then they have to sell things to where everything will come up to at least $41 per item.

Now here comes the government with their great taxes to pay for, let's say, a government health care program. So now instead of it costing the American people $41, it costs about $45. Now the state decides to up their sales taxes, and instead of being 6.9 percent, it goes up to 8 percent. So there is another $3.60. So now it costs the American people $48.60. I put it simply but in general, that is how it works.

You say tax the rich but it always comes back to us. We lose when the government raises tariffs, taxes on companies, restrictions, and so on. The cost is always handed down to us. I am not saying they should not be taxed, but if you keep raising the cost, we the people get penalized. I think this flat tax thing going around should be analyzed very closely.

Friends of Andrew Jackson in Congress decided to exploit the sentiments of the southerners over the tariff. They came up with the Tariff of Abominations. This raised duties on iron, hemp, and flax. However, it lowered tariffs on woolen goods. All this was done to embarrass Adams.

So look closely before blaming the president for everything. People in Washington even today do things like this to discredit someone. Anyhow, the people in the South got all upset with this tariff. They declared that the tariff was unconstitutional and discriminatory. South Carolina declared that they could nullify the law in its own territory. However, they waited for the next president to see what his attitude would be toward the tariff.

Andrew Jackson was for individual liberty but supported slavery and Indian removal. He did have a nickname, "Old Hickory," for his toughness. He survived an attempt on his life.

Also, during his campaign against Adams, they tried to make him look like he was unfit to be president. They dredged up the same old things that the liberals have done to tear down those who formed this country.

Lets look at Jackson and his wife. Rachel Jackson's first husband was abusive and constantly accused her of adultery (even though he was unfaithful). She tried to get back with him several times but because of his violent behavior, she decided to leave him permanently. Believing that she had been divorced, she married Jackson. They found out that her husband had not gotten the divorce, so she was divorced on the grounds of adultery.

Rachel and Jefferson got married again. Adams's friends spread the rumor that Jackson had lived with her before she was divorced. They called him all kinds of names.

There was a picture of twelve coffins of people Jackson had

supposedly killed in duels, one being a man that had attacked Rachel's reputation. So you see that is why you check things out.

The ridicule did not stop with Rachel; they also called Jackson's mother a prostitute. The doctors had ordered Rachel to smoke a corncob pipe for her shortness of breath, which was part of the ridicule.

Rachel finally died of a heart attack. She got her wish. She really did not want to go to the White House and who could blame her with all those self-righteous people. She was buried on Christmas Eve in the gown that she was going to wear to the inaugural.

If Obama meant what he said that families should be off limits, that is one thing I do agree with, especially if you are not telling the total truth about them. Rachel probably died because of these people!

Jackson vetoed on twelve bills during his time in office. One was the Maysville Road Bill, which would have funded a sixty-mile road in Kentucky from Maysville to Lexington. However, he did approve the extension of the Cumberland Road.

Another bill he vetoed was the new charter for the bank. He felt control of the nation's money was bad for private businesses and to the country's ideals. Bank notes contributed to credit abuses and paper money's value was hard to control.

Jackson said that when they sold public lands, the payment had to be in gold or silver. Inflation soared because the demand for gold and silver was higher than supplies, so many banks failed.

Jackson did not want to get rid of the tariff that was passed because it was paying the bills, but in hopes of appeasing South Carolina, he tried to reform the tariff law so it would not be so burdensome.

In spite of that, Jackson signed another tariff; South Carolina passed a nullification bill on the federal tariff laws and declared them unconstitutional. However, Jackson threatened to send in federal troops.

These laws were making northern manufacturers rich, while South Carolina grew poorer. They even said they would secede from the Union if force was used against them. Jackson sent troops and pleaded with the people to reconsider. He told them that they were on the brink of treason.

When Senator Henry Clay came up with a compromise, South Carolina rescinded. The compromise was any duties in excess of 20 percent would decrease in time. Clay also came up with the Force Bill that said that the president could use the military to enforce bills.

Vice President John Calhoun resigned from office because he was displeased; he became South Carolina's senator. Martin Van Buren became vice president.

Van Buren was the key figure in organizing the Democratic party along with Andrew Jackson. He also organized political organizations, one being Jacksonian Democracy.[145]

During Van Buren's time, there was economic hardship. The Caroline Affair took place under him; look it up to get the whole thing, but it had to do with a group of Canadian rebels seeking a Canadian republic. He lost popularity.[146]

The American economy was bad during this time, but it started in 1836. This became his primary concern. What started this downfall was that the English banks stop pumping money into the American economy. This was because of the troubles they were having at home. So the US banks started calling in loans because the banks overextended credit; get that? They overextended credit to their clients. The other was Jackson's policies that land purchases must be made with precious metal and not paper money.[147]

---

145   Martin Van Buren, http://virtualology.com/uspresidents/
       presidentvanburen.com/

146   http://www.u-s-history.com/pages/h156.html

147   http://www.digitalhistory.uh.edu/database/article_display.
       cfm?HHID=6

When Van Buren took office, the New York banks refused to convert paper money into gold or silver because they were running out of hard currency. After that, other banks followed them and did the same thing. This became known as the Panic of 1837. So Van Buren called for a special session of Congress. He wanted to reverse Jackson's decision to have federal funds in state banks. He asked for an independent treasury system to put federal funds in. However, it was not warmly welcomed, even by his own party. The Whigs had traced the downfall to Jackson's decision not to recharter the national bank. They said that there needed to be a strong institution like a national bank to manage the economy and have a stable economy.

Finally, after much debt and resistance, Congress passed an independent treasury bill. However, four years had passed, and the country's economy had gotten worse. This became a great debate during the 1840 presidential election.

William Henry Harrison was a Whig. Democrats ridiculed him, calling him "Granny Harrison, the petticoat general" because he resigned from the army before the War of 1812 ended. However, he tried to present himself as a humble frontiersman when he was from a wealthy, slave holding family. He served the shortest term as president.

One interesting thing I read is that when the Whigs went to Harrison to get rid of all Democrats, he refused. He said that he would resign before he committed such an injustice. Also, he called a special session because he was told by the secretary of treasury that the federal funds were in trouble and something needed to be done. He definitely did not believe in the spoils to the winner philosophy.

Harrison believed that the president should not exceed his power but that he was to veto any laws he felt were unconstitutional. He was someone else that understood what the presidency's position was supposed to be, and that is not a dictator telling Congress what to do.

His death tested Article II of the Constitution, which

covers who will take over in case the president dies in office; Harrison died one month after taking the oath of office.

John Tyler was Harrison's vice president and became president after him. Even though he was a Democratic-Republican, he had been Harrison's vice president on the Whig ticket. However, when he became president, he went against his party's platform. Most of the cabinet resigned, and the Whigs expelled him from their party. After he was not reelected, he retired from politics but then was elected to the House of Representatives of the Confederacy during the Civil War.

As president, Tyler set a constitutional standard that the vice president had all the powers of the president if something happened to the president. This was done because when Harrison died, they would not recognize him as a full president. He was the first president to have his veto on a bill overridden. It was a bill on funding on building ships for the federal government. They overrode his veto on his last day in office.

Tyler did not get rid of any of Harrison's cabinet people. However, Clay told Tyler that the cabinet made major policy decisions but Tyler did not go for that. He said that he wanted them there but he would accept any resignations. All did except Daniel Webster, who was secretary of state.

There was no great love between Tyler and Congress. Congress sent a bill resurrecting the same national bank that Jackson had dismantled. Tyler claimed it was unconstitutional not because he believed in Jackson's policies but he believed in the doctrine of states' rights. Congress changed the wording but Tyler vetoed that bill also. The Whigs wanted him to resign.

Because he vetoed a tariff bill, Congress initiated impeachment proceedings, because it was based on policy grounds and not constitutional grounds. A veto was only supposed to be used if Congress passed an unconstitutional law or a bill that put too much burden on the people or cut into one's liberty. The Whigs lost control of the House, so it did not go any further.

The governor of Rhode Island wanted him to bring in troops because of Thomas Dorr, who wanted to install a new state constitution. He did not send in any federal troops. Dorr and his followers left when faced with the state militia.

Tyler was in office when they were trying to get Texas to join the Union. Texas accepted the terms on December 29, 1845, and became the twenty-eight state.

I will skip Polk and Taylor and go to Millard Fillmore, who took office upon Taylor's death. He was the last Whig president. He also believed in a strong legislative branch, as did Taylor and previous presidents. I do want to note that when he took the oath of vice president, Fillmore waited until Monday to observe the Christian Sabbath.

He opposed having Texas as a slave territory. Taylor's cabinet rarely spoke to Fillmore and resigned when he became president. He appointed his own cabinet members that were pro-Union and pro-compromise. He had to deal with divisions in the Whig party. He tried to deal with the slavery debate. He abolished slave trade but not slavery itself. He signed the Fugitive Slave Law, which stated that slaves were to be returned to their masters.

He was totally for the Compromise of 1850 and had told Taylor so.

Stephen Douglas came on the scene and headed the Committee on Territories. Douglas was smart and instead of fighting big battles, he worked on small ones. They started to pass bills on border lines; California became a state; and they passed the Fugitive Slave Law, deciding who would be a Free State or a Slave State and other such issues.

However, many Americans disliked it for one reason or another. Abolitionists did not like the Fugitive Slave Law and therefore some states passed laws prohibiting its enforcement.

Southerners did not like the idea that new territories were Free States.

It became a mess, and one incident brought Fillmore to the point of having to charge forty people, black and white, with treason. A man was going after runaway slaves after one killed his master. Fillmore brought the charges against those involved in this killing. However, the Supreme Court said that resistance to the law was not a treasonous act. So what is treason? Today no one talks about treason.

According to *Webster's Dictionary* 1828 reprint, "treason" is "to draw in, to betray, to commit treason." In general, it is the offense of attempting to overthrow the government of the state the offender owes allegiance to, or of betraying the state into the hands of a foreign power. In the United States, it includes actual levying of war against the United States or giving aid and comfort to their enemies.

So what do you think about handing our country over to the UN? Saying the countries that are our enemies have precedence over our Constitution? What about going to the UN to get them to make a treaty so our guns can be taken away and leaving us defenseless against invading forces, including the enemy within?

In foreign affairs, Fillmore decided to stay neutral despite Lojos Kossuth, who wanted him to abandon its nonintervention policies into overseas affairs.

He sent Commodore Matthew C. Perry to negotiate trade between the United States and Japan. Perry never made it over there in Fillmore's time. He also started the White House library.

Franklin Pierce was a Democrat. He affirmed his oath instead of being sworn in. His cabinet included personal colleagues he knew and Democratic politicians. His vice president, William King, died of tuberculosis before taking office. It seemed that his beginning was full of tragedies.

He believed like Jefferson and our founding fathers in

self-determination, individual political and economic rights, and limiting centralized government, emphasizing state sovereignty.

Pierce developed the Ostend Manifesto, under which he wanted to purchase Cuba from Spain; if they would not sell, he wanted to go to war with them. It never came to pass but was a black mark against him.

However, the issue of slavery continued. Senator Stephen Douglas would not let things go. With new territories coming under the government with the Louisiana Purchase and land taken from Mexico, the issue became hotter. The Slave States wanted half the new territories to be slave and half free. I suspect to hopefully secure themselves from being turned on and made Free States, losing their slaves.

Pierce tried to get Douglas to let the Supreme Court decide, but I think that he had some ambitions of his own. He wanted to make a name for himself so he continued the debate.

The Kansas-Nebraska Act, allowing the settlers to determine if they would allow slavery and the Missouri Compromise were repealed.

Kansas became the battleground over slavery. The Whig party disbanded and the Republican Party was born, led by Abraham Lincoln. The Kansas governor was sympathetic toward those who were antislavery. Kansas became known as "Bleeding Kansas" because of all the violence.

He opened the trade with Japan, he gained advantage over Britain in Central America, but he was unable to attend too much of anything because of what was going on in Kansas.

James Buchanan was a Democrat that people saw as a compromise on the slavery issue. In his inaugural address in 1857, he said, "In entering upon this great office I must humbly invoke the God of our fathers for wisdom and firmness to execute its high and responsible duties in such a manner as to restore harmony and ancient friendship among the people of the several States and to preserve our free institutions throughout many generations."[148]

Of course this did not happen. His efforts to maintain peace between both sides ended up with him being alienated. He believed in self-government. A bill that he vetoed allegedly showed his disinterest on education, but like today, there was an attachment that federal land donation would benefit Rep. John Covode's railroad company. Yes, there were crooks in those days too. It was all a ruse.

There was a division between the northern and southern Democrats. Republicans got hold of the House. Buchanan vetoed six pieces of Republican legislation. He wanted the ideologies of the United States to bring peace and prosperity to other countries, but major European powers intervened.

Buchanan thought if he got the Supreme Court to rule that Congress had no right to outlaw slavery in the Dred Scott case, Americans would accept it, and the dispute over slavery would end. Wrong! However, I read that in his memoirs he put the blame on the abolitionists for the Civil War and not his lack of understanding.

The government kept coming short of revenue. Treasury Secretary Howell Cobb started issuing deficit financing. Democrats supported hard-money policies. The Republicans used this to attack Buchanan for mismanagement.

The Democratic Party split and one part elected their own candidate, whom Buchanan refused to support. The other part nominated Douglas. Buchanan did nothing when South Carolina and six other states seceded from the union and formed the Confederate States of America. Buchanan was in denial of the rights for states to secede but said that the federal government legally could do nothing about it.

I really debated with myself on whether I should go down this path of everyone asking if he was a homosexual or not,

---

148   James Buchanan inaugural speech, http://www.bartleby.com/124/pres30.html

because he lived with a very good friend because he never got married. Come on, give it a break.

You know how many people that do not get married or live with friends that are not homosexuals. This is just another way of trying to tear down people of the past and justify themselves. There is no evidence of such a thing but people keep hashing it over and over. Put it to rest.

He loved someone but her father thought he was only interested in her money. It is the old, "You are on one side of the tracks and I am on the other side of the tracks" thing. He never got over her so he never got married. It has happened to people before, so get over it!

Buchanan said, "There is nothing stable but heaven and the Constitution." Well, the latter is more correct than the other because man can corrupt the Constitution but man cannot touch heaven.

John Covode's group leaked damaging information about Buchanan but there was not enough evidence to start impeaching procedures. Covode's nickname was "Honest John." Well, I say he was not so honest if the information was not founded.

Covode attended public schools and even though he engaged in agricultural, manufacturing, and transportation pursuits, his main interest was coal trade. He was elected as an Opposition party to the 34th Congress and as a Republican to the 35th, 36th, and 37th Congress. He remained in Congress until his death.

During the next election, Abraham Lincoln's name only appeared in the Free States. Did anyone tell you that? No one ever told me this, and I got a lot of Civil War history in school. Commanding General Winfield Scott told Buchanan that if Lincoln won, it would likely lead to the secession of about seven states.

In late December, Buchanan ousted Confederate sympathizers and replaced them with Nationalists. The secretary of the treasury said, "If any man pulls down the American flag, shoot him on the spot." (wikipedia.org)

Today there is no respect for the flag. You can do anything with it, including wearing it like a diaper! Again the courts are making policy and not enforcing what the Constitution really says. It says freedom of speech, not freedom of expression! There is a big difference, and there is a reason for what they wrote and how they wrote it. They were highly educated! They deliberately put it the way they did. This is just another way of creating chaos in our country and tearing it down.

You have to have chaos so you can say, "Oh this form of government does not work. Let's go to Communism or Socialism. The government has to have full control over the people to have peace." Please use your common sense. I can see it; why can't people who are following liberalism see it? I feel it is because they have not been taught everything that went on in the past, so they do not see how people can bring a downfall to a country.

I will not go into great depth about Abraham Lincoln because you learn a lot about him in school and I have gone into depth about him already. He refused to compromise on the slave issue. The Democrats hated him for that. He was a Republican president and the first and only one elected with only having his name on part of the country's ballots.

He defused the *Trent* Affair and the possibility of war between the United Kingdom of Great Britain and Ireland. The *Trent* Affair involved two Confederate envoys who were going to Britain to get diplomatic recognition. The ship was the *Trent*. People wanted to go to war with Britain because of this. The Confederates were hoping to get the United States to go to war with Britain, and the British were outraged because one of their ships was boarded. They considered it a violation of rights and an insult to their honor. To cut the tension Lincoln released the prisoners, and they went to Britain but failed in their mission.

Lincoln depended on God to give him direction. He not only prayed before his meal but after he ate. He claimed the Bible was the best gift God gave man because all the good of Christ is given in that book.[149]

How about his proclamation, "Whereas, the Senate of the United States, devoutly recognizing the Supreme Authority and just Government of Almighty God, in all the affairs of men and of nations"? He mentioned that they had forgotten God and His grace (unmerited favor; favorable influence of God). They hide all this nowadays also.[150]

During Reconstruction, most of the time was tranquil and not this big upheaval that people imagine. Everyone was ready to go back home and get on with their lives. Each state that had seceded had to take an oath of future loyalty to the Union and the Constitution of the United States, and promise to emancipate their slaves in order to be readmitted. The main reason of the Civil War was for the preservation of the Union. Under Lincoln's plan, Tennessee and Arkansas sought readmission into the Union.[21, p. 971]

I will leave with this quote from Lincoln, which we need to heed because a division is being created through political correctness and other things: "A house divided against itself cannot stand. I believe this government cannot endure permanently half slave and half free. I do not expect the Union to be dissolved—I do not expect the house to fall—but I do expect it will cease to be divided. It will become all one thing, or all the other."

Today we will all be free or we will all fall under a

149   Lincoln at Prayer, http://www.ccel.us/trueblood1.ch4.html
150   Never Give Up, http://www.dianedew.com/lincoln.htm ; Lincoln's Proclamation, http://www.crossroadsinitiative.com/library_article/807/Proclamation_of_National_Day_of_Prayer_and_Fasting_Abraham_Lincoln.html

dictatorship. It is up to you. Will we have liberty or will we be slaves under a dictatorship?

Lincoln said, "Those who deny freedom to others deserve it not for themselves" (Quotes). Remember the old saying, "What goes around comes around."

I want to note that not all southerners believed in slavery and that some northerners believed in slavery. We had brothers against brothers, sons against fathers, and so on.

When I was in an English class, they got to talking about prejudices against blacks. The teacher found out I was born in Louisiana and asked me when I got over my prejudices against blacks. He had made a judgment about me just because of where I was from. I just told him and the class that I had never been prejudiced against blacks. When I was young, I played with blacks. I had even pushed a white boy into the bayou because he told me I should not invite my black friend over to my house.

Andrew Johnson took over after Lincoln was assassinated. He hurried to reincorporate the former Confederate states back into the Union. He vetoed civil rights bills, causing a friction between him and Radical Republicans. They impeached him on charges of violating the Tenure of Office Act. However, he was acquitted by one vote in the Senate.

President Andrew Johnson vetoed the Tenure of Office Act in 1867, but it was overridden. The bill said you could not remove from office anyone appointed by past presidents without the advice and consent of the Senate unless they approved the removal during next session.

President Johnson believed it was unconstitutional. He and Edwin Stanton, secretary of war, were consistently at odds with each other. Stanton refused to resign, so Johnson suspended him from office and put Ulysses Grant in charge. When the new Congress met, they refused to remove Stanton. Johnson was unwilling to accept it and appointed General Lorenzo Thomas secretary of war. This is what started the impeachment. The law stayed until 1926 and was declared unconstitutional to have the consent of the Senate to remove non-cabinet officials (*Myers vs. United States*).

He did not identify with the Republican or the Democratic parties, but his past party was Democrat so the Radicals put their trust in him. He had pardoned and gave amnesty to most Confederates. Also, he authorized North Carolina's governor to proceed with the reorganization of the state. When asked why he did not join the Democratic party, he said, "It is true I am asked why don't I join the Democratic party. Why don't they join me ... if I have administered the office of president so well?"

It is counted that he was among the worst presidents, but since he refused to be identified among the two parties, I at least count that to him as being honorable because he was doing what he thought was best and not what the parties wanted him to do, like a puppet, which we have today.

Now do not jump to conclusions that I agree with his prejudices toward blacks, because I do not, but when you go into office, you are supposed to be for the people who elected you and not your party.

During his time, southern states adopted what were called the Black Codes. These codes limited blacks' freedoms because they considered them inferior. Some of these codes restricted land ownership, and blacks could not bear arms. This led to riots in Memphis and New Orleans.

Because of these codes, northern Republicans decided to pass a bill to protect the rights of ex-slaves by extending the Freedmen's Bureau. This bureau was set up to help the freed slaves and could be considered the first federal welfare agency in America. Johnson vetoed the bill, but it was overridden by Congress. This made the northern Democrats, white southerners, and the president very unhappy. The Republicans were called "traitors" by Johnson.[21, p. 972]

The Republicans then tried to pass the Fourteenth

Amendment, which states that no citizen could be denied their rights regardless of color. The president urged the southern states to reject it.

The Republicans did not trust the president to carry out the Act of 1867. He had vetoed everything they were trying to pass. They tried to limit his power as well as his control over the Army. Later on, they started impeachment proceedings but the Senate acquitted him by one vote. So if you think your vote does not count, think again because a lot of things have come about by one vote.

Ulysses Grant was a Republican. When he first voted for a president, he voted for James Buchanan because he said he did not know Buchanan but did know his opponent. He wanted to be a mathematics teacher but did not want the military to be a career; surprise, surprise.

Did you know that on the same day that Lincoln was assassinated, John Wilkes Booth also stalked Grant's wife Julia? However, they did not attend the presidential party and went to Burlington, New Jersey, to see their children.

As for his drinking, I learned that when he was young, he drank no more than any other man, and logic dictates (as well as the letters written about his drinking) that to be precise in his orders, so that the men did not have to ask twice, he needed to have a clear head, which drunks do not have. Look up *Ulysses S. Grant: The Myth of His Drinking.*[151]

He was president over the last half of the Reconstruction. Andrew Johnson wanted a more moderate approach to the Reconstruction in the South. He signed the Amnesty Act of 1872. He limited troops in the South and suppressed the Ku Klux Klan's violence. He enforced civil rights for people of color. Unfortunately, he suffered from scandals mostly because of corrupt appointees and personal associates, and they blamed him for the ruined economy caused by the Panic of 1873.

Panic of 1873 was a worldwide depression like today.

---

151   http://faculty.css.edu/mkelsey/usgrant/alcohol.htm l

It started in Vienna and then spread to Berlin and then throughout Europe. Later it reached the United States. Banks stopped making payments, and then the New York Stock Exchange shut down for ten days. Unemployment went up 14 percent, and many railroads went bankrupt.

There were also fires in Chicago and Boston, which created great losses. Grant had to rely on bankers for advice because he was not knowledgeable about finances. Outstanding bonds were liquidated; $50,000 was released without undermining the value of the dollar. A lot of this sounds like today, but the money they are printing today, I do not think they are calculating the value. Also, they did not learn history because they would know that the same tactics they are using did not work. All this only curbed the panic on Wall Streets. It did not end the depression.

You cannot go printing money without monetary value backing. This just devalues the money and makes things worse! You cannot keep spending and borrowing money, because this makes the economy worse, not better. The route that our Democratic Congress is going with all this spending and borrowing, they are either trying to bankrupt this country so they can say that our system does not work or they are ignorant.

All this is superficial, and even though it makes them look good, it is only brief. Either way, they do not deserve to be in the position they are in. You cannot keep spending more than you take in! So guess what? Taxes have to go up to pay for all those loans because our people in Congress do not know how to cut costs and stop spending! Where are our economists and accountants? They know you cannot keep doing this!

No one would want me for president, because the first thing I would do is try and get rid of the health bill, then make a law that all these animals and plants have to be proven endangered, cut grants to the Endowment of the Arts, and other things I feel are unwarranted.

They can get people to donate, like everyone else. Did you know that we pay people not to grow things? Do you know how many people take advantage of that and get rich off of your tax dollars? Can you imagine how much money we could save and pay our debt so later we can have better programs for the American people? I bet I could find a lot of fat instead of cutting our military benefits and paychecks.

I am tired of hearing people in Congress talk about this surplus. There is no surplus when you have a debt! That is why our Social Security is in trouble.

Let's talk about the Washington treaty. Great Britain aided the Confederates, so the United States claimed that Great Britain was responsible for half of the debt. Great Britain was lax in coming up with any resolution, so they handed it over to an international arbitrator. The United States said that they would consider taking Canada for payment. Britain decided to make an agreement fast. Finally, the arbitration committee declared that Britain owed the United States $15,500,000 for all of their disputes.

When it came to civil service reform, Congress passed the buck to Grant. They said for him to appoint someone to set up the rules, so he appointed Curtis.

There was resistance when it came to something they wanted to keep. Grant eventually abandoned civil service procedures because Congress failed to act. So remember, not all things are the president's fault.

Grant got reelected because the economy was looking up: the debt was reduced, tariffs were temporarily lowered, and the income tax was repealed. All this had hurt the opposition. Under his second term, the nation was going from farming to great industrial growth. People were beginning to feel the effects of this rapid growth. The railroads were overbuilding and pushing the farmers to the side.

Grant had been seen with two speculators, Jay Gould and James Fisk. These men had a scheme to corner the gold market.

When he found out, he had the secretary of the treasury sell a lot of gold to stop their plans. However, it was too late and havoc was brought to the business place.

Rutherford Hayes was the first to win by electoral votes but not popular vote. He was a Republican like Grant was. He also had been a military man.

In 1864, he was nominated to Congress but he refused, saying, "I have other business just now. Any man who would leave the army at this time to electioneer for Congress ought to be scalped." So he did not campaign but won anyway.

He believed that blacks should have the right to vote. He took the oath of office in secrecy because of fear that the Democrats would attempt to hijack the public inauguration ceremony. Later he took the oath publicly. In his inaugural address, he said, "He serves his party best who serves his country best." I wish our politicians believed that because then we would get representatives and presidents that would do right.

Hayes supported the Radical Reconstruction while in Congress. The South continued to fall to a Democratic party. He also had a Democratic House of Representatives, who did not want to fund the Reconstruction. The northern voters were more concerned about the economy than Reconstruction.

The Confederate officers came back into power in the form of the Democratic Party. The Reconstruction was pretty much on the downhill when he took office. The blame, as far as I see it, was because of the Democratic and Republican parties and not because of Hayes's policies.[152]

You may want to know where the executive order came from. Well, Hayes is your man. Because of the scandals that went on during Grant's presidency, his hope was to "depoliticize the civil service" and not destroy the Republican Party. It

---

152   http://isaacmmcphee.suite101.com/the-rutherford-b-hayes-
        presidency-a52957 , http://americanhistory.about.com/od/
        reconstruction/a/Reconstruction.htm

was the Pendleton Civil Service Reform Act of 1883. Chester Arthur ended up signing the act after it had been sacked during Hayes's time.

Under him, he made things a little more stable for the greenbacks by using more gold to back up the paper money. So in 1879, the value of gold was attached to the paper money. The economy's growth contributed to the return of the gold standard. They did not say anything about the correlation between gold and our paper money in my college class on economics. I did get it in junior high though. But again we have veered away from having gold as backing, and our present administration is printing paper money right and left, not giving consideration that they are making our money useless and therefore wrecking our economic system.

Have you wondered how we got to the point that they put attachments onto bills? Well, it started when the Democrats had control of both House and Senate. It became known as the "Battle of the Riders." They would put these attachments on federal election enforcement laws that prevented fraud and voter intimidation. Now remember, at this time, if you were black you had to register Democrat and vote for their candidate or things would happen. This I got from my grandmother. Hayes would veto these bills, mainly because of the attachments.

Hayes said, "Every citizen has the right to cast one uninitiated ballot and to have his ballot honestly counted and the riders were an unconstitutional attempt to force legislation on the president." The Democrats finally gave up because they could not overcome his vetoes, and it united Republicans. I think we should tell Congress today, no riders! They all do it.

We think we have immigration problems today. Hayes allowed unrestricted flow of Chinese immigrants, which caused a lot of problems. The railroad cut costs by employing Chinese workers.

People were not able to find work; those lucky enough to have a job had their pay cut. There were riots in California.

The people called to end immigration, but Hayes vetoed the bill, which would be a violation of the Burlingame Treaty. This did not make him popular. They revised the treaty so that the government could regulate, limit, and suspend but to prohibit the coming of Chinese laborers.

Look at today. The companies want illegal immigrants because they can cut costs. The whole thing is back again but instead of legal immigrants, it's illegal immigrants; with legal ones, companies have to pay at least minimum wage.

I found it interesting that he won by one electoral vote, Hayes's wife refused to serve alcohol in the White House, she was the first First Lady to have a college education, he signed an act to let women plead before the Supreme Court, and he was the first law school graduate as president.

His biggest economic problem he faced, other than the Panic of 1873, was the railroad strike. Wages had increased in the beginning, but they were working long hours. Even with the wage increases, the workers were not making enough even for the basics needed for living.

Later, because of the economy, the railroad shortened hours and cut wages, then came the unemployment. Of course, this was not the first time they had cut wages. It started to get hard for the organizations to help people because they were poorly equipped; they did not have the resources to help themselves.

This left an opening for the Socialists to step in and indoctrinate people with class hatred. There were strikes on the Baltimore and Ohio (B&O) Railroad because of a 10 percent cut in wages. From there, the strikes spread to West Virginia, Pennsylvania, Ohio, Illinois, and then all the way to Omaha, St. Louis, and the West.

The governor of Maryland and the president of the B&O asked Hayes to bring in the military. Some of the worst violence happened in Pittsburgh. The crowd had trapped the military and burned the roundhouse. There were mass arrests of protesters and Socialist leaders. There were about eighteen deaths. Six companies of the US Army had been sent in. The incident did damage to Hayes, and unions became more popular.

Hayes was smart; he exploited the issues and appealed to the public. He would travel often giving speeches because he knew that he would get the publicity. He was much like Theodore Roosevelt in his tactics. He had refused to appoint Conklings and Blaines to his cabinet. Before he died, he said that he was a radical by thought but a conservative in method.[36]

James A. Garfield was a Republican and was only in office for four months. He was shot by Charles J. Guiteau, reportedly a deranged political office seeker. Guiteau believed he was responsible for Garfield's victory and felt he should have been rewarded with an ambassadorship but did not get it.

Chester Arthur was the Republican president who finally got the Pendleton Civil Service Reform Act passed. He entered the presidency being distrusted but when he got out, he became well respected. Why was that? First he was the vice president and took office when Garfield died. When he got into office, he went his own way and became independent of both parties.

He asked Garfield's cabinet to delay their resignations until December when Congress convened. Slowly they resigned before December, and he had to appoint new cabinet members as they resigned.

Arthur tried to lower tariff rates. He signed the Tariff Act of 1883. This became the political issue between both parties. This was a tax on all imported vegetables (however, fruit was exempt). On February 4, 1887, during *Nix vs. Hedden* (149 U.S. 304), he argued that the tomato was a fruit. I had that argument with some girl in my college. She said it was a vegetable, but Nix was right; by genre, it is a fruit, and it says so in the dictionary. It is a fruit often used as a vegetable. Well, that is what the Supreme Court said, also. However, they said that since it was treated as a vegetable, it can be taxed as a vegetable.

Arthur was not really for the civil service reform but later found out how vital it was after the Republicans lost a lot of seats in the midterm election. The Pendleton Act was written by a Democrat, Senator George Pendleton. It banned salary kickbacks, apportioned federal appointments among the states, and new employees started their service at the bottom of the ladder to advance by merit exams. Now Congress has signed in a bill to make their pay 50 percent retroactive every ten years.[153]

Arthur signed the Edmunds Act to ban bigamists and polygamists from voting or holding office. The first immigration law was passed under him. Congress had passed the Chinese Exclusion Act, which denied citizenship to Chinese people residing in the United States who were not already citizens and not born here. He was reluctant to enforce the Fifteenth Amendment, which says you cannot keep a citizen from voting because of race or color. He also never attempted to overthrow Jim Crow laws.[154]

Grover Cleveland, a Democrat, was the twenty-second and twenty-fourth president; he had no formal education and was pro-business. He believed that the president was in the position of stopping bad things. He had more vetoes than any president (584) and believed that the government does not support the people. He opposed high tariffs, free silver, inflation, imperialism,[155] and subsidies to business, farmers, or veterans.

He has been praised for his honesty, independence, integrity, and commitment to classical liberalism. He worked against political corruption, patronage, and bossism.[156] Wait!

---

153 UsLegal.com, Retroactive, a delayed pay for work already done at a lower pay. A kind of back pay. Some laws and constitutions prohibit retroactive pay, even when a mistake had been made on calculations.
154 Segregation in all public facilities.
155 Pertaining to an emperor, a dictatorship.
156 A boss figure.

Wait! This does not sound like liberals of today, who want people dependent on them.

In his 1885 inaugural speech, he said:

> In the presence of this vast assemblage of my countrymen I am about to supplement and seal by the oath which I shall take the manifestation of the will of a great and free people. In the exercise of their power and right of self-government they have committed to one of their fellow-citizens a supreme and sacred trust, and he here consecrates himself to their service.

You notice that he said the will of the people, not the will of the politicians! He also knew we have the right of self-government. When you read further, he stated that the people had put a trust in just another citizen like themselves, no better or worse than them. Politicians today think they are better than the people that voted for them, that they know more than them, but Cleveland knew better.

Cleveland was not able to reverse the depression. The Third Party System ended and brought about the Fourth Party System and the beginning of the Progressive Era. He did not fire any Republican that did his job. He reduced the number of federal employees. Politicians can take lessons here. You cut spending, you cut taxes; the more you cut taxes, the more people can spend, and then it will help the economy.

Soon, he started to replace Republicans with Democrats because they felt they were not getting enough of the spoils. Oh, if only we could have politicians like that today. Too bad he gave into the Democrats and their greed.

There were no appointed blacks but Cleveland allowed Frederick Douglass to continue as recorder of deeds.

They debated whether the US currency should be backed with gold or silver or both. Of course, we know that gold won out. He even had the government purchase 3,500,000 ounces of gold to take care of the declining gold supply.

He struggled with tariff reform. Tariffs were too high. During his first term, he passed the Pendleton Civil Service Act, which detached about 12,000 federal jobs from political influence. He used his veto power to stop high protective tariffs and private pension bills. Congress could not even pass low tariffs because of attachments that were put on them by the Republican-led Senate

Lands were returned because the railroads failed to extend their lines according to the agreement. He vetoed hundreds of private pension bills for veterans of the Civil War.

He even vetoed a bill to help farmers to buy seed because of the crops that were ruined by a drought. He felt there should be limited government. He said:

> I can find no warrant for such an appropriation in the Constitution, and I do not believe that the power and duty of the general government ought to be extended to the relief of individual suffering which is in no manner properly related to the public service or benefit ... though the people support the government, the government should not support the people... The friendliness and charity of our countrymen can always be relied upon to relieve their fellow-citizens in misfortune. This has been repeatedly and quite lately demonstrated. Federal aid in such cases encourages the expectation of paternal care on the part of the government and weakens the sturdiness of our national character.

There is a great website called "Is Welfare Unconstitutional?"[56] Read it.

Thomas Jefferson said that Congress did not have unlimited powers to grant general welfare, except those specifically mentioned. Cleveland had come to the same conclusion, yet he became unpopular for his views, even though they coincided with our forefathers.[(40)]

Cleveland was right; many people came to the farmers' aid. Many people had been helped by the communities and people from other communities when help was needed. We did not need all these programs. As I mentioned before, some programs I can see because people do lose their jobs, but a lot of these programs should be under state and not federal control. Each state should take care of its own people, not the federal government.

Every president has the right to pardon someone if they feel injustice has been done. However, some presidents pardoned relatives and abused this power. President Grover Cleveland looked over a case that involved an Indian. The incident happened on Indian Territory. One Indian had killed another one in a drunken brawl. The case seemed straightforward but President Cleveland stayed the execution until he could look over the case. Neither one of the Indians were of great character. He claimed he would not be able to sleep if this person was hanged because of a failure to look into the case. The Indian was poor and had no one to see that his rights were not violated.

However, in another incident he refused to pardon a man who had robbed a bank; he considered the man had robbed the poor. This is true because it is our money that is put in the bank and yet for some odd reason people who rob banks think that they are robbing the stockholders, which is not true. Yet today a lot of our politicians think that downing the big companies is good. They fail to realize that it is our money that they are looking at. When they penalize them, they penalize us. By the way, they are rich. How much are they paying? We have a president that has a million dollar mansion! Do you? They are the pot calling the kettle black!

On page 212 of *Recollections of Grover Cleveland*, he states that there is a God and patriotism is not dead. You can find this book in the archives.[40] During his last interview, Cleveland said that the country seemed ready to return to the Democrat party if the party was true to themselves. He talked about the old-fashioned Democrats not supporting the candidate that the party had.

The Democrat party turned on him because he did not follow their progressive agenda. He had battled against corruption in Washington. He tried to lower the tariff but Democrats in the Senate raised the tariff and even added a 2 percent tax on incomes over $4,000. So Cleveland was not able to keep his promise. This is why politicians should not promise anything except that they will try to do this or that.

He saved money by answering the phone himself, drafted routine letters, and kept away from the wheeling and dealing and compromising that politicians do so much of. Defiantly not like our Politian of today.

He vetoed so many bills that had those tag-on extras that cost millions of dollars. In doing so, he saved the taxpayers money. It also cut down on corruption. You know those back-door deals our politicians do.

Also, America began to be recognized by the world during his presidency. He served as arbitrator between British Guiana and Venezuela.

He did a lot that people could have learned from. Yet they do not even speak about him in your history class. Why?

He knew that our history was founded upon the Christian faith. That when we depart from it the nation surfers. He said, "While slavery remained we could not hope fully to work out Christian ideals, and whenever we overlook the fact that "righteousness exalteth a nation," we must pay the penalty."[40, pg383]

Benjamin Harrison was a Republican. He had made no political bargains but supporters did on his behalf. Cleveland attended his inauguration ceremony. He also held an umbrella over Harrison's head. Harrison supported the merit system and opposed the spoils system. He got to see the enactment of the Dependent and Disability Pension Act.

Under him, the first Pan American Congress[157] met and established an information center. The United States was represented at the Berlin Conference, which kept the Samoa Islands independent. He also wanted to annex Hawaii but Cleveland stopped that when he got into office. Two American seamen had been killed in Valparaiso, which created conflict between Chile and the United States.

The high tariffs had created a surplus of money in the treasury. This made many Democrats and Populists want to lower the tariffs. However, Harrison urged Congress to add reciprocity (treaties) provisions. This backfired on him.

This Congress ended up being the highest spending in American history at the time. The spending was so high that the administration became known as the Billion-Dollar Congress. So I guess the Obama administration will be known as the multitrillion-dollar Congress?

Before Cleveland took office the second time, a group of Americans, with the aid of Marines from the USS *Boston,* managed to oust the queen of Hawaii. There seemed to be enthusiasm from the American people to have Hawaii as a state; a treaty was to be offered.[(21)]

However, Cleveland wanted the Senate to wait. James Blount was sent to the islands to study the situation. When he reported what had happened and said Americans helped the rebels but the population did not want the new government, the treaty was withdrawn.

The majority of Americans accepted the president's reason for doing so. Get this, politicians: he claimed it was wrong to overthrow a government for the idea of expansion. We need

---

157 Pan-American Union: organized to form cooperation between
     Latin America and the United States. The first conference was
     to reach an agreement on commercial and juridical problems. In
     1948, it became known as the Organization of American States.

to stay out of other people's affairs. We have helped people to overthrow governments in hopes for a puppet government to do our bidding. Yet every time, they have turned on us. Obama is doing it today. When are you going to get the message? Do not do it! You seem to never learn! It is wrong and it never works.

William McKinley was a Republican as well as a Methodist and an abolitionist. However, McKinley did not enforce the Fifteenth Amendment. So there was a lot of violence against people of color under his presidency. He stated:

> It must not be equality and justice in the written law only. It must be equality and justice in the law's administration everywhere, and alike administered in every part of the Republic to every citizen thereof. It must not be the cold formality of constitutional enactment. It must be a living birthright.

William McKinley did not use the Antitrust Act like Theodore Roosevelt, and therefore trusts grew. 1897 was the year of business, agriculture, and general prosperity; the Panic of 1893 ended, mainly due to underconsumption. The deflation ended due to the Gold Standard Act of 1900, setting the value of the dollar. I guess they need to go back to that. You see, people continue to make the same mistakes and yet we still do not teach these lessons in our schools.

The annexing of Hawaii was accomplished under his administration but not until after a long turmoil. American businessmen overthrew the queen. When the United States said something, they said it was none of their business. Well, if it is American citizens, it is their business. A petition was signed by the natives against the annexing. Later violence spread out over the islands.

Queen Lili'uokalani was already in Washington trying to get them to not annex Hawaii. Even the secretary of state was against the annexation. The treaty was defeated in February of 1898.

The treaty was eventually ratified in July of 1898 because of another event: the Spanish-American War. Part of that war was fought in the Philippines, which made the Hawaiian Islands a great spot to resupply US military ships. Then the battleship *Maine* was destroyed in Cuba. The islands became a state in 1959.[158]

During the Spanish-American War, journalists told stories of brutal concentration camps in Cuba, which developed conflict between the two countries. Democrats along with the newspapers of William Randolph Hearst pushed American public opinion to want war. The United States gained ownership of Guam, the Philippines, and Puerto Rico and temporary control over Cuba.

McKinley died after being shot. There were two bullets; doctors removed one but left the other in. They believed he would recover but he went into shock and then died from gangrene around his wounds.

Theodore Roosevelt was mentioned a lot in history class; his slogan was "Speak softly and carry a big stick." He was a Republican but in the later years he became part of the Progressive party. Now did you ever hear of the Progressive party? I never did. It was not told to me in class.

In 1912, the Progressive party grew out of the Republican party. Roosevelt was disappointed by Taft's conservative policies. Hostility developed between the two. Roosevelt decided to seek the presidency again after retiring in 1909. Taft, however, controlled the party organization. Roosevelt ordered his delegates to not vote. The next day, the new party was formed. There was great reluctance to join this party.

---

158 http://www.archives.gov/education/lessons/hawaii-petition/

Even his son-in-law Nicholas Longworth supported Taft. The Pinchots[159] joined.

The Democrats picked Woodrow Wilson, a prominent progressive, as their nominee. Many of the Progressive Republicans favored Wilson over Roosevelt.

Now "progressive" in *Webster's Dictionary* is defined as, "moving forward; proceeding onward; advancing; as progressive motion or course." The progressive era brought about the growth of government, and the government continues to grow. Now it is in every aspect of our lives. Read *The Progressive Era* by Gregory M. Browne. He states at the beginning that the Revolution of our founders was probably canceled by the progressive era and that the progressive era was the true revolution on American soil. It is a small thing consisting of about five paragraphs but he has references you can go to and read.

Most of all, read about Horace Mann, who is considered the "father of progressive education." My reprint of Noah *Webster's Dictionary* (1828) says that he was responsible for the new American philosophy of government. He did not believe in the fundamental conceptions of our Constitution, property, self-government, and voluntary union.

According to them, this man took the Bible out of the schools long before liberals talked about "Separation of Church and State". However, I say it is his philosophy that brought about "Separation of Church and State". He planted that seed here in the United States.

You want to know why people of today call us a democracy instead of what it is? That's right, we can blame it on Mann. They stopped teaching in the schools why a federal republic is a better form of government. This is why we have congressmen, presidents, and the Supreme Court trying to turn us into not only a democracy but a dictatorship. They continue to repeat

---

159   Someone who came from a rich family and became a progressive reformer from Pennsylvania.

that we are a democracy, but very few people know what kind of government we are supposed to be.

Roosevelt was the one that started putting regulations on businesses. He was responsible for child labor laws, better working conditions, inspections of meat, the Pure Food and Drug Act, not to mention the breakup of monopolies. However, companies found a way to get around the monopoly thing by putting them in different names and separate accounts.

The oil industry does that. I wish that they had never split Ma Bell because now we get lousy phone service. I am glad for the child labor laws because children need to be children first.

However, the liberals want to take that innocence away by giving them sex education. Some places want school twelve months out of the year. So now instead of the businesses destroying them, we have the liberals that want to destroy them. In my psychology class, they said that a child needs to go through certain stages to develop into a healthy human. So why are the liberals trying to take some of these stages away?

Theodore Roosevelt also wanted Social Security, regulation of stock trading, and the minimum wage (which I showed does not work). Of course, these did not get adopted until Franklin Roosevelt took office. Theodore became the first president to make environmentalism a political issue. However, and it is my guess only, he never meant to take land from people under the falsehood of endangered species.

William H. Taft was a Republican. He passed the Seventeenth Amendment, which US Senators passed by popular vote. This is the guy who started using our tax dollars to develop other countries. It was considered economic development. But economic development does not necessarily give economic growth. Economic development is social and technological progress. Economic growth is the increase of output. It may not involve development at all. Growth is measured by the change rate of GDP.[160]

Roosevelt thought that Taft was a progressive. He alienated the Republican party with the Payne-Aldrich Tariff Act. This act was started by Sereno E. Payne (R-NY) in the House of Representatives. It was supposed to lower tariffs on incoming goods. However, Senator Nelson Aldrich (R-RI) called for less reduction and to increase the tariffs. The bill finally lowered 650 tariffs, it raised 220 tariffs, and 1,150 tariffs were unchanged. Taft believed that the president should not dictate lawmaking (which they are not supposed to, but he can give an opinion like every citizen); he said that Congress was supposed to act as they deemed best. They blamed him for the bill.

This bill created the corporation tax or income tax on people doing business as a corporation.

Under Taft's presidency, the Mann-Elkins Act was passed in 1910. This gave the Interstate Commerce Commission power to set rates and suspend hikes in railroad rates. They had jurisdiction over telephones, telegraphs, radio, and postmasters. Skilled workers in the Navy were put under civil service protection.

There was more antitrust prosecution for violations under Taft than under Roosevelt; one of the companies prosecuted was the American Sugar Refining Company, which had rigged prices. He did start backing off because, according to what I read, conservative businessmen supported him and he did not know what the long-range effect would be on the economy.

Taft saw the role of judges to defend people's private property from undue governmental interference, and maintain law and order. Now all the judicial branch seems to do is to hand over property to these liberal groups.

His liberal Republicans turned on him, including Roosevelt, because he was not going through the progressive program that they wanted. Roosevelt wanted what he called

---

160   GDP is the gross domestic product of a country.

"the new nationalism." Roosevelt started the Progressive party. He decided to run himself. The Democrats decided on Woodrow Wilson. He lost but later when Harding became president; Taft was appointed to the Supreme Court.

Woodrow Wilson was a Democrat and the leader of the Progressive Era in the United States. Yes, he is the one that gave us the progressive income tax. Income tax was unheard of except in the time of war (except for the income tax of corporations that came under Taft). Most revenue was generated through tariffs and consumption. Wilson got Congress to pass what is known as the Federal Reserve Act, the Federal Trade Commission, the Clayton Antitrust Act, the Federal Farm Loan Act, as well as the Revenue Act.

"The Federal Reserve Act (ch. 6, 38 Stat. 251, enacted December 23, 1913, 12 U.S.C. ch.3) is the Act of Congress that created the Federal Reserve System, the central banking system of the United States of America, and granted it the legal authority to issue legal tender. The Act was signed into law by President Woodrow Wilson."[75] This was done in hopes to curb the financial panics. Now we have Congress bailing out these banks with billions of our tax dollars. This should be used to pay off our federal debt!

The Federal Trade Commission was supposed to be independent of the government and protect consumers and regulate harmful business practices. It seems to me that today the government pretty well controls them too. After all, aren't the commissioners nominated by the president and confirmed by the Senate? So you cannot tell me that they are independent of the government. Use your common sense.

That goes for these so-called advocates that are supposed to help you if you are having problems with the IRS. They are not for you. They pretend they are while they are not helping you at all. They get paid by the government or the IRS themselves, so they do what these people tell them to do. I had to deal with them, and the lady was not doing anything to really help. After I sold my land to my mom for $10, they finally dealt with me. So that tells me that they are not there to help us! They lie when they say they are, and you want them in control of your health care?

The Clayton Antitrust Act was to strengthen the antitrust law already in place.[7] Some of it dealt with price discrimination among customers and price fixing. It was to cut out monopolies. This just expanded government's role in regulating businesses' competition. I have read some things on whether these antitrust bills were squashing true capitalism and so on. So you think about whether these laws are good or not. However, I can see the point of the big companies squeezing out the small businesses, but they still seem to manage it.

The Federal Farm Loan Act allowed farmers to borrow money depending on the value of land and improvements. This was to help small farmers compete with big businesses. This brought back the income tax with the ratification of the Sixteenth Amendment and lowered tariff rates, because now all the citizens were paying, even though they were not making money like companies.

Wilson thought the Constitution was open to corruption. He favored the parliamentary system and thought the United States should be under that system.

Talk about corruption. That system is more open to corruption. Wilson said:

> I ask you to put this question to yourselves, should we not draw the executive and legislature closer together? Should we not, on the one hand, give the individual leaders of opinion in Congress a better chance to have an intimate part in determining who should be president, and the president, on the other hand, a better chance to approve himself a statesman, and his advisers' capable men of affairs, in the guidance of Congress?[76]

That was a shocker to me. I did not even know that. Now I know where the president telling Congress what to do came from.

Wilson believed that checks and balances were the reason for the problems in American governance. Now we have courts, the executive branch, and the legislative branch doing what he thought should be done, and we are losing our freedom. This is the very reason our forefathers put in the checks and balances, but people have forgotten. I bet if I ask my daughter about checks and balances, she will know nothing about it. She probably will think it is a checkbook or something of that nature.

However, later Wilson changed his mind. He realized the importance of the system of checks and balances; it depends on the person in office as to how much influence he would have in Congress.

Wilson accommodated the South and did not reappoint a person of color to the position of register of the treasury and other positions.

Wilson was also the one who went for internationalism, which is having economic and political cooperation among the nations to benefit all. Everyone should be equal. Is this the reason for NAFTA, which cut our companies and pushed up the economy of Mexico? It was hoped that it would bring world peace, but all it has done is make people here in the United States poorer and lose jobs.

Even though the term "middle class" is ambiguous, the following is from a chart that I found. In 2002, the upper class was 1 percent, upper middle was 15 percent, lower middle was 30 percent, working class 30 percent, working poor 13 percent, and underclass 12 percent. In 2004, you had the super rich .9 percent, rich 5 percent, middle class 46 percent, working class 40-45 percent, and poor 12 percent. In 2005, the upper class was 1 percent (so we went to growth to lower upper class), upper middle 15 percent (2004 there was no upper or lower class), lower middle 32 percent, working class 32 percent (but no division here anymore either), lower class 14 percent to 20 percent (you can constitute for the poor).[161]

You might look this up. Some Libertarian answered a question about whether the middle class is shrinking.[162] I am not saying I agree with everything he said, but he did say some interesting things. Go through a lot of those questions and answers. You might find out a lot of things. One thing he is definitely right about: if you tax the rich, they will only raise the price of the product and this makes your dollar smaller.

I talked to my professor in economics class about raising the minimum wage. I told him that it did not make sense for them to raise the minimum wage because the companies would raise the cost of their products. Also, I could not understand why people did not get it. They do not accomplish anything. You have to cut costs for prices to go down, not make more cost for the companies. He agreed with me.

The more the government gets into our business and taxes us to death, the more the middle class will cease to exist. So Wilson did not help with his progressive tax, but you will not get this in the history books.

One thing I did believe in was what he said about liberty: "Liberty has never come from the government. Liberty has always come from the subjects of it. The history of liberty is a history of resistance."

Warren Harding was a Republican. His cabinet included Charles Evans Hughes, Andrew Mellon, and Herbert Hoover. However, because he and his associates rewarded his close friends with high positions, scandals finally found their way. I

---

161   http://en.wikipedia.org/wiki/American_middle_class . I will remind you that even though I have used Wikipedia, sometimes their information is not complete.

162   http://askville.amazon.com/middle-class-United-States-disappearing-part-question-details%E2%80%A6/AnswerViewer.do?requestId=4927619

remember the old saying when I was growing up: "Do not go into business with your friends."

The secretary of the interior was jailed because of his involvement in the Teapot Dome scandal. This dealt with an oil field on public land. It was transferred from the US Navy to be under the secretary of the interior. It had been reserved for the Navy by Taft. The secretary of the interior leased the land without competitive bidding. There was bribery also in the making.

Harding rejected the League of Nations. I feel he got that right because look at what is happening now with the United Nations. Obama has put this country under them and no one realizes it. Did Obama not say that they take precedence over our Constitution? Obama took an oath but it meant nothing to him!

Protocol states that our flag should not be displayed lower than any other flag. This includes the United Nations flag. The reason for this is because if you do, it is showing servitude[163] to that country or organization.

That is putting us under all the nations that are members of the United Nations. That is handing us over to our enemies.

> No other flag or pennant should be placed above or, if on the same level, to the right of the flag of the United States of America, except during church services conducted by naval chaplains at sea, when the church pennant may be flown above the flag during church services for the personnel of the Navy. No person shall display the flag of the United Nations or any other national or international flag equal, above, or in a position of superior prominence or honor to, or in place of, the flag of the United States at any place within

---

163 "The condition of a conquered nation. A slave, the state of involuntary subjection to a master." *Webster's Dictionary* (1828 reprint).

the United States or any Territory or possession thereof: Provided, That nothing in this section shall make unlawful the continuance of the practice heretofore followed of displaying the flag of the United Nations in a position of superior prominence or honor, and other national flags in positions of equal prominence or honor, with that of the flag of the United States at the headquarters of the United Nations.[164]

Hillary Clinton is trying to pass what is known as the Small Arms Treaty so the UN can come invade our homes to see if we have any weapons. Wake up, America!

President Harding ended World War I by signing a single peace treaty with Germany and Austria. He also signed the first child welfare program.

When he took office, there was a postwar economic depression. Harding cut taxes and a series of actions by the Federal Reserve lowered rates. The recovery went on its way. But the recession remained all the way to the next presidency.

He wanted people of color in federal positions and favored the anti-lynching bill. Also, he supported an international commission to improve relationships between whites and blacks, but the southern Democrats blocked these initiatives! The anti-lynching bill passed the House but not the Senate.

Harding died a sudden death, and Calvin Coolidge took his place. Coolidge was a Republican lawyer. He believed in small government. Under him, public confidence was restored, and he was popular when he left office. Later they tried to assassinate his character, saying he had a laissez-faire government. This means that the government should not interfere with economics unless it goes to the courts. This included regulations, taxes, tariffs, and enforced monopolies. It literally means "Let do."

---

164   http://www.steve4u.com/flagcode.htm

However, the truth is the truth. It was a time of prosperity and thrift. People were happy. Yes, it was the time of the Roaring Twenties. Why? Because they did not try and punish the businesses, technology was developing, and there was production and distribution on a mass scale. Many people felt their standard of living rise, no matter what their income level was. President Coolidge knew big government was the death of a nation. You could not penalize industry and expect the economy to be good. You cannot raise taxes and expect the economy to be good. You cannot penalize people with fines and expect the economy to be good. Why cannot our politicians get that through their thick skulls?

He was for immigration restrictions. The Immigration Act excluded Japanese, which he was not happy about. The Bonus Bill World War Adjusted Compensation Act (43 Stat. 121) was passed by a Republican Congress over his veto. This was to create a benefit plan for WWI veterans.

The Revenue Act of 1924 lowered the income tax rates, increased the estate tax, and created the gift tax. Coolidge proposed reductions on spending as well as reducing taxes. Income tax was paid by 2 percent of the richest people.

Coolidge vetoed a bill that would allow the government to buy surplus crops and sell it later or to people overseas. Coolidge was a farmer's son and believed it would not help the farmers. Plus it could give government control.

Our government already controls what is grown. They pay people to not grow certain crops and to grow certain crops. People are getting rich off of this. They find out what the government does not want grown and say they are going to grow it. Then the government pays them not to grow it. Then farmers get paid to grow what the government wants them to grow. This is a program that needs to stop![165]

---

165 http://www.pbs.org/newshour/businessdesk/2009/08/why-does-
the-govt-pay-farmers.htm l; http://www.washingtonpost.com/wp-
dyn/content/article/2006/07/01/AR2006070100962.html

Coolidge was in favor of civil rights for blacks and Catholics. He tried to make sure no Klan people were in office. He tried to pass the anti-lynching law that Harding wanted passed, but again the Democrats filibustered it. He kept trying but it was no use.[166]

He did not want to get into foreign alliances. He did not push for joining the League of Nations. Whether he was a good president or a bad president depends on whether you want Big Brother watching or you want small government. The fact is he brought the economy through with cutting taxes and little interference in the economy by the government. It is unlike the government today with big spending, taxes, fines, large regulations, and taking over companies. You decide for your own, but before you decide, look at today and look at then.

I know that some people say his policies were the reason for the stock market crash in 1929, but was he really to blame? We shall see as we go on.

He made a speech to the Boy Scouts in which he said that while being on a farm, one learned three fundamentals of scouting: reverence for nature, reverence for law, and courage; he talked about the courage of our forefathers who set up our country.

In this speech, Coolidge said that material things did not create our independence and that we should be like our forefathers that brought us into a nation. He said that we as a nation should not put material things before the spiritual and moral leadership that our forefathers had.[167]

Last but not least, there is reverence for God. He stated, "Doubters do not achieve; skeptics do not contribute; cynics do not create." He continued to say that faith motivates, it shows man his full potential, and life is important. He said that one

---

166   Alvin S. Felzenberg, Calvin Coolidge Essay, 1988, http://www.calvin-coolidge.org/html/calvin_coolidge_and_race.html

167   The Inspiration of the Declaration of Independence, July 5, 1926, http://www.calvin-coolidge.org/html/the_inspiration_of_the_declara.html

should keep them close because it would make for a better understanding of our country. Coolidge told the scouts that they should strive for the truth and live by it.[168]

Herbert Hoover is very well known, by name at least. He was the son of a Quaker blacksmith and was secretary of commerce under Harding and Coolidge. I read that he believed in the efficiency movement. Now I had never heard of this movement, so I looked it up.

The efficiency movement was "a major dimension of the Progressive Era in the United States."[169] [21] It claims that the economy, society, and government all have waste and inefficiency. Experts ought to identify problems and fix them.

Well, the problem is there are people who think they are better than others and that they know everything. In other words, they are arrogant and selfish. They like to spend other people's money and raise taxes for their indulgencies. This seems to be the way politicians are: "I know more than the other guy."

Hoover was blamed for the Great Depression and discredited the movement. Now either Coolidge was to blame or Hoover. Come on, give me a break.

John D. Rockefeller was also a supporter of this movement. The Great Depression happened eight months after Hoover took office. Wall Street crashed. It had a major impact on the US and world economy.

Many blamed the banks because they had invested in the stock market. Even economists and historians are not really sure what caused the crash. But many do believe that the Depression started long before the crash.

We look at the market today, and this administration is blaming Bush, but if we go back to the Clinton administration,

168 Address to a group of Boy Scouts, July 25, 1924, http://www.
     calvin-coolidge.org/html/address_to_a_group_of_boy_scou.html
169 http://en.citizendium.org/wiki/Efficiency_Movement

the market was already going down. The Clinton administration had put 500,000 people out of work in his first year of office with those cuts. The market went down several times during his term.

How about the reason being bad business practices and taking too many risks as well as the government meddling. Now government encourages this by bailing them out.

Let's see what kind of man Hoover was. He helped organize the return of 120,000 Americans when World War I began. He helped with the relief effort when Belgium was faced with food shortages after the invasion by Germany. He had to negotiate with the German authorities to get the food there. Wilson appointed Hoover head of the US Food Administration. After the war, he used a Quaker organization to manage the supply chain in Europe.

As secretary of commerce, he promoted ownership of single-family dwellings. He promoted long-term home mortgages, which stimulated constructions of homes.

He broadcast news conferences over radio, which played a role in developing the radio industry.[21] He also addressed the amount of traffic accidents. During a flood of the Mississippi River, he was sent to mobilize state and local authorities, military, army engineers, Coast Guard, and the American Red Cross. Because of his appeals to the public, a lot of people responded to help.

However, there was mistreatment of blacks. Hoover struck a deal with Robert Moton, president of the Tuskegee Institute. Moton was to suppress the fact that blacks were mistreated. He said he would help the blacks when he got into office. But he broke his promise when he became president, and it backfired on him. They shifted to the Democrats. He ousted many black leaders in the Republican Party and put whites in their place. Now I know why a lot of blacks voluntarily became Democrats later.

He believed in a limited role for the government in

economics. But he saw government as a way to improve the condition of Americans by regulation and volunteerism.

Well, that was wrong. Too much regulation stifles growth, and that has been proven. Families, however, used to take care of each other with the help of the church and other people, not the government.

Hoover pulled US troops from Nicaragua and Haiti and wanted an embargo against Latin America. He said that the United States would not recognize territories gained by force.

Hoover said that people of color needed education to improve them and assimilate them into the white culture. The Senate rejected John J. Parker as a Supreme Court judge because they felt he discriminated against people of color.

Hoover's wife invited Oscar DePriest, a black Republican, to dinner at the White House, which was unheard of in those days.

Charles Curtis was the first Native American to be elected vice president. Hoover believed that the Native Americans needed to achieve self-sufficiency.

Let's get deeper into the Great Depression. Hoover believed that public-private cooperation would achieve long-term growth, because if the government got into it, this would destroy individuality and self-reliance. In his memoirs, he said he had rejected Andrew Mellon's suggestion to leave it alone. He tried to get business leaders to come and talk to him. He urged them not to lay off workers or cut wages.

"But something entirely outside the workshops of the nation has affected this hired employment very seriously. The word 'unemployment' has become one of the most dreadful words in the language. The condition itself has become the concern of every person in this country."[170] This was from a great speech by Henry Ford on June 11, 1932.

---

170   Gale Encyclopedia of US History; http://www.answers.com/topic/
       a-pub-caret1-dvice-to-the-unemployed-in-the-great-depression-11-
       june-1932-by-henry-ford

There came a great cry for government assistance as the economy kept declining. Hoover did not want to do bailouts. He felt that this would reduce the initiative to self-sufficiency. To try and pull the country out, he authorized the Mexican repatriation program.

This forced migration of approximately 500,000 Mexicans and American Mexicans to Mexico; 60 percent of those forced without due process were Americans.

So even though I feel that illegal immigrants should be sent back, we do need to make sure they are illegal because we are now at the point of repeating history. I do think that Arizona has the right to protect themselves and that the law is not an infringement on our rights since you have to have broken the law for them to ask where you were born. It is easy to verify. Again Obama wants to pass a law so states cannot protect themselves and that law would be unconstitutional.

However, I thought it was important to put this part of history in hopes not to make the same mistake again. Also, amnesty and citizenship is not the answer either.

Most do not want to be citizens. These people come here to send money back to Mexico so they can live like kings when they return there. Many are drug traffickers. However, we also need to realize that Mexicans are not the only illegal immigrants in this country.

I think that if a person is an immigrant, legal or otherwise, they have to pay taxes. They are benefiting from coming here, so they need to pay. They need to pay for the health care they get instead of us paying for it.

They get Social Security after working two years, not thirty like us. This is one of the reasons Social Security is failing along with our politicians taking from it for their pet projects. It should be the same for them as for us. Why do they get precedence over us? The government is supposed to be for us, not every noncitizen!

During the Great Depression, Hoover said that he would

try and keep a balanced budget while cutting taxes. He felt that caring for the people must be a local and voluntary thing. Hoover thought that his opponents were sabotaging his programs for political gain and calling him a callous and cruel president. He was definitely used as a scapegoat for the Depression, and he lost the election the next time around. This is why I think politicians care for only power and money.

Unemployment reached 24.9 percent, and there was a drought, which hurt the crops (I'd like to know how Hoover had anything to do with the drought).

Congress wanted to raise taxes, so it passed the Revenue Act of 1932. The top earners were taxed at 63 percent and increased 12 percent to 13.75 on corporations' income. This was the largest income tax that Congress had passed.

I believe that Obama will surpass that with all this health care and arms treaty changes, not to mention a few other things. People who cheer for these programs that the Obama administration comes up with, I do not want to hear any complaints from you when you find out that most of your pay is gone.[171]

Hoover commissioned the Hoover Damn to be built but it was a Republican Congress later on had it named that. When it was authorized, many unemployed tried to get in on it. There was a camp established for men and their families hoping to get work. Later on they cut wages for tunnel workers. It was proposed to be built at Boulder, Colorado, but the pass was on a fault. This is why it was built where it is today. This was a project to help put people to work.

Everyone has heard the old quote, "The only thing we have to fear is fear itself." This came from Franklin D. Roosevelt, and he was very right. We need to be cautious, but if we let fear take over, we end up making mistakes. I think that people let these fear tactics get to them, and instead of checking things out, they go on what they say: global warming, endangered

---

171   http://en.wikipedia.org/wiki/Herbert_Hoover

species, liberalism, Christians, Jews, and so on. These are just tactics to lead people in the direction they want them to go.

Franklin was the fifth cousin to Theodore Roosevelt. He had married his cousin, Eleanor Roosevelt. Her father was Theodore Roosevelt's brother. They were both Democrats. As James Cox's running mate, they had lost to Warren Harding. But it was an opening for him to later become president.

A fifth of all banks had closed and many people had lost their savings since the Depression, so he decided to try and help out. Sounds like today, does it not? Although unlike then, when people were withdrawing their money, people today are not going through the same panic. Roosevelt made all banks close and asked Congress to make a law so where savers would not lose their money if another crisis came up. Unemployment went from 4 to 25 percent by 1933. Roosevelt dealt with unemployment by having the government recruit, and he came up with the New Deal.

As I explain the New Deal, think about what Obama is doing today. Stimulus programs to supposedly create jobs. Roosevelt had Harry Hopkins run a program called the NY State Emergency Relief Commission, and Frances Perkins was the state industrial commissioner.

Within about 100 days, he had enacted the Emergency Banking Act so he could reopen and regulate banks. The Economy Act cut costs in salaries and veterans' pensions. Now they never say this in history class: veterans got lower pensions than their civilian counterparts, and this is why they get these benefits. They were promised to them. Yet I find that politicians are always willing to cut veterans' salaries and benefits all the time when they can cut other things like support to the arts, animal activists, and such organizations that can get their money from donations.

We have so many dead-wood programs that can be cut out, but they keep holding on to them. We have programs we do not need and should be controlled by individual states if they want it. We do not need an individual health care program no more than we need Social Security, because the government just thinks it is another form of income to use. By the way you pay Medicare for years not using it and then when you become eligible you have to pay out of your social security paycheck which is hardly anything! If you opt out when you become eligible at sixty five so you can have money to pay rent or bills you still lose all that money you put in so why are we paying into it?!

Social Security was not asked for by the people, just like a whole national health care system was not asked for. The elderly were taken care of by family, friends, and people of the church or other organizations.

The majority of pension plans were working well during that time. The majority of the people today are happy with what they have. It is evident that Congress is happy with their plan or they would not have exempted themselves. Social Security just became another supply for welfare. Now they are going to have health care money for them to spend on other things too. Don't you get it?

Just like Roosevelt embraced the Germans' social insurance, which is not really insurance because they would not be able to borrow from it but is really a social tax, the Democrats of today have embraced the social health care overseas. They will be borrowing from it just like they have with Social Security!

We have been told over and over again by Britain and Canada that we should not want socialized medicine. The care is not as good and it takes forever to even see anyone. This is why our congressmen do not want to be on this health care program. They know but are ignoring it.

The Beer-Wine Revenue Act passed, which legalized and taxed alcohol. The Civilian Conservation Corps (CCC) Act made work for construction, mainly roads, forestry, and flood control. Sounds like today with Obama stimulus for construction.

The Federal Emergency Relief Act spread $500 million to the states. The agency ended up paying out $3 billion. That is a lot smaller than the trillions that Obama has spent. Stop blaming Bush. The Obama administration has spent more than any administration in the history of this country! Do you really want him for a second term?

The Agricultural Adjustment Act subsidized farmers who would cut back on production. This gave government control of economics, supply and demand. If there is less of a product but high demand, then the cost goes up. This gives less in people's pockets so they can buy other things they need. If there is more than what is demanded, the price goes down.

Yes, it is not just the oil companies, it is the good old government. We have enough oil in this country, it has been estimated, to supply us for a hundred years!

However, the Thomas Amendment let the president inflate currency. So now we know where we get the president playing around with the economy. This is why we get into more trouble than what we started off with.

The Tennessee Valley Authority Act gave the government permission to build dams and power plants along with agricultural and industrial planning in Tennessee. This was to help improve the economy.

The Securities Act of 1933 required that offers or sales of securities had to be registered. This was to make sure investors received information about the securities, which cut down on fraud or misrepresentations. There were many other acts passed to try and help the economy.

The CCC did not last very long. Then you had the Social Security Act. Yes, Franklin Roosevelt was the one who set up the Social Security. We all know that later on it became another welfare program.[34]

However, none of these programs really worked, so why is Obama doing the same thing? They even raised taxes on the wealthy, just like Obama and our Democrats in Congress want to do. History clearly states that unemployment continued to rise until World War II.

So let's see, Bill Clinton apologizes for us bombing Japan when they bombed the United States first. I call it self-defense; we have the right to defend ourselves. Where does he get off apologizing? Now do not get me wrong. I lived in Japan for four years, and the people are beautiful people, even when some protested against the USS *Midway* aircraft carrier being there. They were thinking it was a nuclear run aircraft carrier, but it wasn't. I got to know them very well.

World War II cost more lives and money, inflicted more damage, and affected more lives than any war. That includes the Vietnam War. People of today remind me of a child that cries when he falls and does not even have a scrape on his knee. People must be willing to give their property, lives, and whatever to have freedom.

Our forefathers gave up their wealth, homes, property, families, and even their lives. Nothing is free! Everything has a price. What was it Patton said about having to pay for the same property twice? We have to go back to war with the same countries because we pull back without finishing what we started.

I remember when the Berlin Wall came down and the cold war was supposedly over. A coworker asked me if I thought the cold war was over. I said, "No, they still hate our guts and are trying new tactics." What did we find not too long ago in our country? Spies! So do you really think the cold war is over? Yet we are giving military secrets to them!

Many people feel that the conflict in World War I just escalated and so we went into World War II. Go to http://www.u-s-history.com/pages/h1104.html to get the time table for World War I.

World War II began with Germany taking over six countries in three months. Japan wanted to conquer the United States, so they bombed Pearl Harbor. Now they do not tell this in the history books: about seven Japanese submarines made it into Pearl Harbor. In fact, not too long ago they published photos that showed a splash in the water that could only have been from a mini submarine and not from a plane torpedo.

Also, a Japanese plane made it to the California coastline, so that dispels what those people have been saying that Japan did not want to take over the United States and that they were only interested in Asia. They would not have had submarines and a plane off our coast if that were true. Come on, use your common sense. In fact, I remember something about our troops having found special printed money for when they took over the United States.

Yet President Clinton closed a base there on the coast of California to save money, and shortly after that, a Chinese ship dumped HIV prisoners in a California port. The authorities managed to capture some but a lot escaped, and as far as I know, they are still running around our country.

I never heard of anyone reopening our bases. So our coastline is still exposed. We did not bomb Japan first! They bombed us first, and yet Clinton had the gall to apologize to them! He stepped all over our military and the ones that died, not only during the war but those that were slaughtered that day in December when the Japanese declared war on us!

My dad was one of the first people sent to Pearl Harbor right after they were bombed. What about my life because of his PTSD (which they did not recognize during that time)? He became a drunk and beat on us kids.

That is what they did to a lot of families, and I do not see them apologizing for what they caused! No liberal wants to hear what they did to families here or that they were the ones who started it in the first place. They are out of touch with reality! Again, I do not hate the Japanese, but I feel we should not be the ones apologizing. I know that they are not getting the full history, like we are not.

Many historians believe that the war was due to the

Treaty of Versailles. In that treaty, which ended World War I, Germany's army, navy, and air force were limited.[172]

Wilson knew that the treaty was taking colonies from Germany and totally cutting their military. This, of course, made Germany mad. The people blamed the government, and they drifted to Communism. This made Adolf Hitler and his party stronger. By the way, I did tell you not to say your one vote does not count. Hitler won by one vote.

They took advantage of the Great Depression. Germany, Italy, and Japan decided to conquer other lands to get their share of the wealth. By the way, there is no share. Wealth is not like a pie, fruit, or something that can be divided. Wealth comes when people do right in government and do not hinder it. Japan invaded China first to get raw materials and markets for her factories, because the Depression destroyed the silk market. Germany ignored the treaty and built up their military, and the war was on.

The United States placed an embargo on Japan for what they did. They froze assets in the United States. Japan finally decided to bomb Pearl Harbor. They were supposedly negotiating with us. About 3,000 people died at Pearl Harbor. This is almost half of our casualties in all the years in Afghanistan and Iraq. From 2003 to 2010, the total has been 5,701.[173] Now I do not like having lives lost any more than anyone else, and that includes children dying in the womb from abortions. These lives are just important.

On February 23, 1942, a Japanese submarine hit the Ellwood oil production site near Santa Barbara, California. It did not do much damage but still it was on our coastal line. Then on June 3, 1942, Japanese forces attacked the Aleutian Islands, near Alaska, as a diversion. Because the United States knew the real target, they did not respond with strength. However, some civilians were captured and taken to Japan

---

172 http://www.u-s-history.com/pages/h1334.html
173 http://icasualties.org/

as prisoners of war. Then you had Fort Stevens and so on, yet Clinton did not think it was necessary to have our bases there in that area.

There are others, but did you ever hear about that? Look up "Attacks on North America during World War II." You may be surprised by this website and agree with me that our borders need to be protected![174]

Roosevelt came up with a second New Deal. He ended up being attacked by conservative Democrats. Roosevelt told the people that they were self-serving and wealthy people who opposed the New Deal. Roosevelt won the election with that lie. Remember, Socialists turn people against the wealthy. They are into distributing the wealth (as long as it is not their wealth) and everyone gets to be poor—except them.

Clarence Darrow is the lawyer that tore into William Jennings Bryan in the Scopes trial. He is the one whose name is in the Soviet Comintern Archives[175] on the Communist Party USA (CPUSA for short). He was the person who defended the Communists, especially Ben Gitlow.[176] Even he was critical of the New Deal. However, was he doing it because he was trying to hide who he really was and what he believed?

Just like Obama, Franklin Roosevelt got Congress to spend more money on programs at that time than any administration before him: new taxes, payroll taxes, Social Security, and a lot more.

He sought ways to help Britain and France. He started thinking we ought to be the "Arsenal of Democracy" and try and make every country a democracy no matter what. This was a phrase French economist Jean Monnet used and was asked

---

174   California Military History, http://www.militarymuseum.org/
      HistoryWWII.html
175   Founded March 1919, it is a Soviet-sponsored agency formed to
      overthrow capitalism worldwide.
176   The one that wanted to turn America into a Socialist America,
      http://darrow.law.umn.edu/documents/NY_versus_Gitlow_
      Larkin_1919_McAdoo_order_Optimized_cropped.pdf

not to use it again so Roosevelt could use it in his speeches. This is wrong!

When we went to war, Roosevelt signed Executive Order 9066, and this is one of the reasons why I do not believe in executive orders; it stated that first generation Japanese immigrants (not US citizens) or those who had dual citizenship must be relocated. Now I can understand noncitizens, but people with dual citizenship?

Roosevelt's health started to decline in 1944. He finally died in 1945. However, he had a legacy that some consider defines today's liberalism; he served three terms and three months of his fourth term as president.

Franklin D. Roosevelt said, "In the truest sense, freedom cannot be bestowed; it must be achieved" (Quotes). Well, I believe that. The people have to be like watchdogs to make sure their freedoms are not taken away, but they must know what to watch for. They must know the truth.

Harry Truman, a Democrat, ended up facing a lot of domestic problems because of the war, shortages, strikes, and the passage of the Taft-Hartley Act.

Truman was only able to pass one of his proposals in his Fair Deal. In this deal came, guess what? Universal health care! That is right, universal health care! So Obama care and Hillary care are not new concepts by the Democrats. Truman wanted one too![177]

You need to be reading this stuff. The Democrats have been slowly nudging us in this direction, and no one is the wiser. Kids keep saying, "Why do I need to learn history?" Well, this is why people need to learn history. It is still out there. Learn it while it is still out there. It may not be long before our politicians get rid of it.

After the atomic bomb was used, Truman said, "We have discovered the most terrible bomb in the history of the world.

---

177   Fair Deal, http://www.americaslibrary.gov/jb/modern/jb_modern_fairdeal_1.html

It may be the fired destruction prophesied in the Euphrates Valley Era, after Noah and his fabulous Ark."

Now I want you to get this. Truman told Stalin that the United States was going to use the atomic bomb on Japan. However, Stalin already knew through espionage. The United States warned Japan in the Potsdam Declaration. They said there would be prompt and utter destruction. They are the ones who decided not to sign. They knew!

The Republicans fought with Truman on tax cuts and the removal of price controls. The Republicans won. The Taft-Hartley Act regulated the labor unions. It amended the National Labor Relations Act, and this upset labor unions. Truman sided with the labor unions but his veto was overridden, and the act was made law. There were "unfair labor practices" added to it. It would be good to read about this act.

You know while we are here on labor unions, let's talk about them. Did you know Russia had labor unions? Yes, they had thought to get better conditions through labor unions. However, the government formed the unions to control wages and companies. This is where Hitler was able to gain power and get elected. So it would not take long for our government to do the same thing. Labor unions get a lot of your money that you could be using for your family. Are you really getting the best out of labor unions? They dictate your life indirectly. If they want you to strike, you have to strike; where does that leave you and your family for food, a home, and other necessities? What about who you vote for? They want an open vote so they can penalize you if you did not vote for who they want you to vote for.

After World War II, they cut back defense spending to fund domestic spending. The Republican majority approved the "hold the line" defense spending.

Truman integrated the US Armed Services. This upset the main Democrats because they believed it would destroy the

Democratic party. Strom Thurmond ran for the presidency and declared Southern "states rights."

During his second term, Truman was in full support of NATO. Now I get to tell you what NATO was really about. It was an alliance with Canada and many of democratic European nations not under Soviet control after World War II. The purpose is to watch the Soviets in Europe to make sure they did not expand and to send a message to Communist leaders to beware. However, we have now let Communists into NATO. So who is watching the fox now? It cannot be NATO any longer, because Communists are in it. We have forgotten what it is for. It is to watch the Communists, and you cannot do that if you have Communists in the organization. We have let the fox into the hen house. So what are they saying their purpose is today?

I read a book about the life of Senator Joseph McCarthy. No one took him seriously. They claimed his warnings were "red herrings." Well, they should not have dismissed them as ridiculous. Now we have Communist doctors, organizations, and yes probably in our government. There are known Socialists in Congress, according to Fox News, and no one denied it when Fox News brought it up. By the way, Socialism is not that far from Communism.

With Truman having to worry about the Soviets having their own nuclear bomb, things started to go a little crazy. Some people tried to make McCarthy look like a fear monger, trying to put hysteria among the people. It was not hysteria he was trying to convey but awareness. That tactic was used by liberals on some of our Republican presidents if my memory serves me right. Now we have them in organizations and in our policies. Their philosophies are in our schools and hospitals.

The next thing that came about was the Korean War. Truman did not consult Congress (just like Clinton did not consult Congress when he fired those missiles into Afghanistan). I am doing this so you can see that the same mistakes are being repeated. He ordered a naval blockade of Korea, but because he had done cutbacks, there were not sufficient warships to enact this. So he tried to get the United Nations to do so and they did.

He deployed forces into Korea but again because of the cuts, they were underequipped and undermanned. General Douglas MacArthur wanted to attack the Chinese supply bases, but Truman rejected his plan, so he went to the Republican House leader Joseph Martin.

It got leaked to the press that the Soviets were supplying weapons to Korea. So Truman not only fired Louis A. Johnson but also MacArthur. Because of all this, there were calls for his impeachment. Then there was an assassination attempt on Truman by two Puerto Ricans.[178] They were hoping this would help them in their independence.

The Central Intelligence Agency, National Security Council, Council of Economic Advisers, and National Security Resources Board were either created or established during Truman's administration.

For economic purposes, Truman formed the Council of Economic Advisers. He made sure that it was staffed with conservatives and liberals. This I feel was a very smart move because he wanted different points of view. They were treated as presidential advisers instead of an independent body.

The war was over in August of 1945 so he concentrated on the liberal New Deal and conversion of the war-time economy to peace-time. This entailed putting the federal government in charge of managing the nation's economy and welfare for the needy. During the war, they did price and wage controls, rationing resources, and other controls. Now he had to redefine the government's role in the country's economy. Many of the programs went nowhere.

Then he had the scandals among senior administration

---

178   Harry S. Truman Library and Museum, http://www. trumanlibrary.org/trivia/assassin.htm

officials receiving bribes for favors. Well, that is nothing new, is it? The IRS was involved and was charged with tax-fixing and bribery charges.

Truman's approval rating was 22 percent in 1952. What is Obama's right now? Even Nixon's was not that low.

Dwight D. Eisenhower was a five star general and a Republican. He did not end the New Deal, and he enlarged Social Security. The Agricultural Act put farm operators and farm workers under Social Security coverage. He then signed the Social Security Amendments Act, which put professionals as well as clergymen into Social Security coverage. On the other hand, he opposed health care under Social Security.

Despite this, Congress passed a health care program for dependents of servicemen, payments to doctors for recipients of welfare, and money to study problems of the elderly.

They formed a new Senate investigation subcommittee. This later formed a full-fledge special committee. As you can see now, we have Medicare, which our administration of today is taking money from to form this other health program, which we do not need. There are state and federal programs in place to help people that cannot afford health care.

What about these politicians who say they want to help? How is forcing people to buy health insurance going to help them? This just takes from the money they need to pay bills like heat during the winter, food, rent, gas for the car to get back and forth to work, and so on. This makes it harder for them to live.

Eisenhower signed a bill that authorized an interstate highway system. He gave permission for the CIA to help Iran to overthrow the prime minister and put the shah back into power. It was to stop the spread of Communism. This became known as the Eisenhower Doctrine.

The French asked for help in Indochina. Later when South Vietnam asked for help, he offered military and economic aid. We got into the war by explaining that if we were giving aid and someone fired at us with a rifle, that was a declaration of war.

Now let's examine this. When Japan bombed Pearl Harbor, it was a declaration of war. When someone with a rifle fired at an aircraft carrier, it was a declaration of war. So when Clinton fired at Osama bin Laden, who was acting government in Afghanistan, it had to be seen as a declaration of war! So who really started the Afghanistan war? Are we in a declared war? Considering what we have stipulated as a declaration of war, Bill Clinton declared war on Afghanistan.

The attack on the Twin Towers was probable retaliation for what Clinton did! Now this does not mean I do not see them as a threat, but you have to question things. You cannot take it off and on like a coat when it is convenient to you, which is what Democrats are doing. Our government has declared war without our permission on Afghanistan and bin Laden. Afghanistan is not the only country Clinton fired upon either, and you want Hillary Clinton as president? People have short memories.

Truman passed the Civil Rights Act of 1957. He is the one that took over Arkansas's National Guard and had federal troops escort black children to Little Rock High School.

During the Korean War, Truman tried to take over the steel mills but failed, unlike previous presidents that took over railroads, coal mines, trucking, telegraph lines, and the Smith & Wesson Company during World War I and World War II.

The owners went to court; it became known as *Youngstown Sheet & Tube Co. et al. v. Sawyer*. The court found the president's actions unconstitutional. However, the government can exercise what is known as de facto emergency powers. Robert Higgs gave a very interesting view that since presidents had gotten away with it in the past, he would not have any problems doing it. Even though he could have used the Taft-Hartley Act, an eight-day waiting period, he used the national emergency grounds. Truman seized twenty-eight other industrial properties in labor disputes.[179]

It was under Truman that the amendment was passed limiting presidents to two terms; Eisenhower was the first president it affected. He was fully behind Nixon.

When Kennedy became president, I was almost ten years old. He went against everything a Democrat is for today. He believed that families should be self-sufficient. Remember his quote, "Ask not what your country can do for you, but what you can do for your country."

This is a far cry from that guy saying we are your little children and what are you going to do to help us or something like that during the Clinton campaign. I am no child that needs the government telling me what to do with my life, like I am too dumb to know what to do or like the British called us, "the little people." We can think for ourselves, but that is how we are viewed by the Democrats. I would not be surprised if this guy had been a plant.

My mom liked John F. Kennedy, but then most people did. He was a Democrat that defeated Nixon and the first Catholic president. I am not going to hash over his assassination because it has been done so much, but I have my own theory about that.

He had run against Humphrey and Morse. He did great expansions on social programs.[180] He included health insurance in Social Security, extended benefits, and people could retire at age sixty-two. He asked (did not tell) Congress for programs that included food stamps, extended benefits for the unemployed, and welfare payments for their children. He emphasized family rehabilitation and training instead of dependency. Some succeeded; however, Medicare and

179   Higgs, Robert, http://www.independent.org/publications/article.asp?id=1394

180   http://en.wikipedia.org/wiki/New_Frontier

Medicaid did not come in until Johnson because President Kennedy was assassinated.

The administration before him was planning to overthrow Fidel Castro. Kennedy told them to proceed but said not to use US air troops, which even I know is a big mistake. He ended up having to negotiate the release of 1,189 survivors of this attack. This of course led to not trusting the United States, and this later led to the Cuban Missile Crisis. Kennedy promised to not invade China and remove missiles from Turkey in exchange for the USSR removing their nuclear weapons from Cuba. Now we have a similar thing happening in South America where Russia is again setting them up. What is the Obama administration doing? Nothing!

Kennedy knew the importance of keeping them as far as he could from putting missiles in Cuba or near this continent.

The Vietnam crisis grew. Kennedy increased troops in South Vietnam. He then later decided to withdraw 1,000 troops but that order was canceled when Johnson took office. He limited testing of nuclear weapons but did not ban testing underground.

JFK got rid of the mandatory death penalty in the District of Columbia.

J. Edgar Hoover, head of the FBI, did not like Martin Luther King. Hoover thought King was a troublemaker and alleged that king's close advisors were Communists. They ended up wire tapping King's phones. Now we condemned Nixon for tapping the Democrats' campaign office, but I do not remember anyone getting after Hoover for his actions against blacks and tapping their phones.

Now this is something I came across when trying to find information about Martin Luther King. There was an article about Hoover saying that he possibly had black in his background. The article stated that there were discussions about it among the FBI agents. It continued to say that some young black girl's grandfather said that he was his second cousin. Now just because someone is someone's cousin does not mean they have black in them. It depends on who married who in the line. Now Hoover could be on that side and was ashamed that someone in his family had married a black. It really does not matter either way. Look up "the Mysterious Origins of J. Edgar Hoover."

Lyndon B. Johnson was the thirty-sixth president. Before he got into politics, he was a teacher. In 1930, he finally got his BA. He had been on the debate team in 1931 and was good at it. His team managed to win the district championship in Texas.

Richard Kleberg brought in Johnson to become his secretary in Washington. Johnson did the job for over three years. Later he became speaker of the "Little Congress."[181]

Johnson took over when Kennedy was assassinated. He continued to push the progressive agenda, like the new civil rights bill and a tax cut to stimulate growth. He urged the people to build a great society only to have his very party to tear it down. He won the election to be president. There were programs to help education, attack diseases, improve Medicare and conservation, fight against poverty, and control crime and delinquency. Many of the elderly got help with Medicare in 1965.

Unfortunately, even with these programs and the exploration in space, there was still unrest in the ghettos and segregation in schools.

Then there was the Vietnam War to haunt him. He had sent in additional troops to Vietnam. He sent planes to bomb

---

181   "Little Congress" is an organization that was established in 1986 for secretaries and staff of representatives and senators to have debates and invite politicians and the media. There are about 500 members, comprised of legislative directors, assistants, and correspondents, press secretaries, schedulers, staff assistants, and committee staff, representing congressional offices in every state in the United States. The first meeting was actually in December 1919.

Vietnam in hopes of forcing North Vietnam to the tables. However, North Vietnam was getting help from China and the USSR. We were not only fighting North Vietnamese but Chinese soldiers. Because Vietnam was becoming unpopular and people had no concept of what was really going on, his moves lowered his popularity. These moves did nothing to end the war at all.

In 1966, the Republicans gained seats in Congress, which ended Johnson's chance to get anything he wanted done. He told the nation that he would stop most of the bombing in North Vietnam and seek negotiations to end the war. Then he announced he would not seek reelection. He died five days before the United States surrendered. Yes, a withdrawal is considered a surrender. We give up too easy nowadays.

Since we are on the subject of the Vietnam War, let's get into a little depth on it. I watched documentary after documentary of the war while it was happening. I married a man who was in the Navy during the Vietnam War.

The war started in March of 1959. I was not quite eight years old at the time. The death toll was over 5 million: 3 million Vietnamese, 2 million Cambodians and Laotians. There were 58,159 US military Armed Forces deaths.[182]

Dwight D. Eisenhower was president at the time and Richard Nixon was vice president. However, Vietnam had sought independence from France during Woodrow Wilson's time. Wilson ignored the petition for help by the Vietnamese. The French wanted assistance but were declined by Roosevelt, but in 1945 Japan overthrew the French and declared an independent Vietnam. They set up a puppet state.

The first American to die in Vietnam was Lieutenant Colonel A. Peter Dewey, who was trying to release Americans the Japanese had captured. He was killed because they thought he was a Frenchman. He had arrived in Saigon on September

---

182   When Guide, http://www.whenguide.com/when-did-the-vietnam-war-start.html

4, 1945. The British armed French POWs to protect the city from Viet Minh attack. The French beat or shot Vietnamese who resisted.

Dewey complained. His flight was late so he went to lunch. When he was near, he got abused by Viet Minh troops and got shot in the head. Later they claimed that he was mistaken for a Frenchman.[183]

The British moved into South Vietnam. They freed French soldiers that had been imprisoned. The French made an agreement with China. They drove the French from the border with weapons they got from the Soviet Union and China.

President Truman sent in assistance when Hainan Island was captured. It was an anti-Communist move. These were military advisory groups to help them learn how to use equipment and for supplies.

Then came the Korean War, which took his time. Of course we backed out of that war, but Vietnam began to take more turns. The Geneva Conference in 1954 called for a temporary division of Vietnam until elections were held. This did not stop North Vietnam from forming a group to gain control of Laos and Cambodia. President Eisenhower sent in advisors to train the South Vietnamese. The French finally left Vietnam. Many Vietnamese fled to South Vietnam. The invasion of Laos began. Two advisors ended up dying.

Kennedy sent in 400 Army Special Forces to train the South Vietnamese. Kennedy met with Nikita Khrushchev to let him think about Laos being a neutral place. He passed the Foreign Assistance Act, which gave assistance to countries that were under attack by Communist forces. By the time of his death, he had increased the amount of soldiers from 900 to about 16,000. Kennedy was committed to stop the expansion of Communism.

Johnson saw that the marches, sit-ins, draft-card burnings,

---

183   http://en.wikipedia.org/wiki/A._Peter_Dewey

teach-ins,[184] and so on were from Communist influence. Supposedly the protests started when he increased bombing. Some people started to say he was going to use the atomic bomb, another way our enemies used to get people against the war. Why? Because they wanted the whole world under Communism.

When Leonard Marks told Johnson to declare victory and withdraw, he told Marks to get out.

Teachers were encouraging students to protest the war and helped with these teach-ins. Not having been taught the truth about Communism and what it is really like under that kind of regime, our young students protested.

Our troops were being spit on, having dung thrown at them, and other disgusting things. By the way, even today those that were in the Navy are not given the recognition they should on their part in the war. Because they did not step foot on the soil, they are not considered Vietnam Vets. Yet they would drop off supplies and other things as well as troops.

Now South Vietnam is under Communist rule and so many had fled North Vietnam to get away from it. We had forgotten how the French had helped us when we were trying to get our freedom from the injustices being done to us.

You had Jane Fonda posing on an enemy antiaircraft gun, slant of the news media, the Mai Lai Massacre, all making people believe that one is fighting a corrupt dictatorship as well as not showing what the North Vietnam, Chinese, and Soviet Union were doing. It was all one sided to influence the people. The only one who tried to show some of the things going on

---

184 Teach-ins were started by the Students for a Democratic Society at the University of Michigan. There is no real organized forum at these teach-ins. It is a good place to say whatever you wanted to say and push people's buttons to get them to believe what you say. Also, get them so hot under the collar they would demonstrate. Young people do not do research and if it sounds logical to them, they act on it. They are using this today to teach homosexuality.

was John Wayne when he did the movie *The Green Beret*. But people did not pay attention.

People asked if South Vietnam could be worse under Communism. This told me that the schools are not teaching the philosophies of Communism. So let's talk a little about Communism. During World War II, they would skin war prisoners alive and make lamp shades with their skins. They have no respect for life, which we are on the road to through abortion. Communists murdered Jews, gypsies, Poles, the disabled, and so on.[185] They dictate where you go, what your job will be, who you can talk to, and what you can or cannot say; they decide who is to live and who is to die, what you can or cannot believe, and where you live; shall I go on? Is this better than the freedom that our forefathers believed in and set up for us? I felt sorry for the people in Hong Kong when the British handed them back to China.

Lyndon Johnson imposed a chicken tax in response to the tax France and West Germany put on chickens being imported from the United States. Even today this tax on light trucks remains.

Johnson got the Voting Rights Act passed. This allowed a lot of blacks to vote for the first time. He condemned the KKK after the murder of Viola Liuzzo. He also passed the Immigration Act of 1965. Ted Kennedy assured people that the country would not be swamped with immigrants. He claimed that Americans would not lose their jobs.[186] So did people lose jobs? In 1970, 60 percent of foreign born were of European descent; in 2000, they only counted for 15 percent. Immigration doubled between 1965 and 1970. Then it doubled again between 1970 and 1990. Immigration had quadrupled in the number of first generation immigrants.

---

185   http://www.wermodandwermod.com/newsitems/
      news050120111253.html

186   Johnson, Ben, "The 1965 Immigration Act: Anatomy of a
      Disaster," FrontPageMagazine.com, December 10, 2002, http://
      archive.frontpagemag.com/readArticle.aspx?ARTID=20777

Read about the Great Society. Here is where more social programs came about, including Medicare, Medicaid, and environmental protection. How does the old saying go? "Give someone a fish and they eat for one day, but teach him to fish and he eats for a lifetime." Presidents from this point on brought up more social programs and environmental control programs and so-called saving nature.

Nixon became president in 1969. I remember my mom being mad when the Democrats tried to remove him by saying he bugged their office. What happened when they bugged Newt Gingrich's phone? Not one thing. No one put up a fuss about the Democratic Party tapping his phone. You cannot tell me that the news media is not one sided. My mom said, "How dare they replace my crook for their crook!" I had to laugh because she knew that all politicians were out for themselves. When my grandpa was asked if he would run for governor of Louisiana, he said that even if you go in honest, you will not stay honest. He said that he could do more help outside than inside.

My mom worked up in Washington DC and saw all the wheeling and dealing that goes on there. If you do not go along with them, they try and find something to turn the people against you so you would not get reelected. Nowadays all it seems you can do is vote for the candidate who is less crooked than the other.

When Richard Nixon took over, there was unrest within the nation and the Vietnam War was still going on. He ended the war and improved relationships with China and the USSR. On top of that, he ended the draft. He met with Soviet leader Leonid Brezhnev and made a treaty to reduce nuclear weapons.

However, I want to look at what they called his New Federalism, since that seems to be the real reason why the Democrats wanted to get rid of him. Remember they want power over us, and they think we are stupid. Now at the beginning of our government, the majority of power was to rest within the states, because they are a government within themselves. Our federal government started to go away from this and started socialistic programs. Nixon was into giving back some of the power and autonomy that the federal government had taken away during Franklin Roosevelt's New Deal. This included 1960's civil rights laws.

His economic policies were called wage and price controls. Of course they claimed that it makes for shortages. However, I do agree that price controls do not usually work.

I have argued with people who want to raise the minimum wage; this is useless. The reason is that the price of things goes up and the ratio ends up the same. My economics teacher agreed and said that it just makes people feel good. Well, I say forget about feeling good, do something that really helps. Then people will feel good when their bellies are filled.

When Nixon took office, there were 500,000 soldiers stationed in Vietnam. There were about 1,200 Americans dying a month. He approved a bombing campaign instead of withdrawing troops from Vietnam. It was considered a success, and he withdrew 25,000 soldiers; by 1972, 405,000 soldiers had returned home. He slowly replaced our troops with South Vietnamese troops.

When he announced that our troops were entering Cambodia, it led to protests by students. The reason probably was because at this point we had made mush of their brains with all this liberal philosophy. We had Socialists and Communists teaching our students and drugs were clogging their brains. After all, they were not inhaling any more than Clinton was, right?

Nixon looked into the draft that Johnson had brought in. After the report, the draft was ended in June 1973. The war steadily declined under his administration. After we withdrew all our troops, South Vietnam fell to the Communist North Vietnamese. All our blood that was spilt was for nothing and in vain. When we pull out of a war, we spit on the bodies of those who not only died in that war but all those who sacrificed and fought in that war.[187]

The economy grew. Federal payments to individual citizens grew by 6.3 percent, GNP grew to 8.9 percent, and public assistance grew from $6.6 billion to $9.1 billion; defense spending decreased. Nixon's program gave $80 billion to states and municipalities The Democratic Congress passed the Economic Stabilization Bill, hoping that Nixon would look indecisive to the American people. This bill was a bailout of the US financial system which was a response to the mortgage crisis.

Sound familiar? Democrats are doing bailouts today. They even tried to expand it into an amendment but it was rejected by the House of Representatives. In 2008, George Bush signed something similar called the Emergency Economic Stabilization Act, creating the Troubled Asset Relief Program to purchase assets from failing banks.

Nixon pointed out problems with Social Security and created Supplemental Security Income. He presented a balanced budget but then later gave in and presented a budget with deficit spending, declaring; "Now I am a Keynesian."

He was referring to British economist John Maynard Keynes, who believed in increasing government spending to keep unemployment low. So now we know where the Democrats get government spending from!

Spending does not work, because the money has to come from somewhere, and it is us: through higher taxes and borrowing, just like raising the minimum wage does not work.

Nixon started to print money with no gold backing, which reduced the value of the dollar. Obama thinks it is okay to print money without gold backing, and again the value of the dollar

---

187   Digital History, http://www.digitalhistory.uh.edu/database/article_display.cfm?HHID=619 : *Encyclopedia Britannica*.

is going down and buying power is lower for the American people, in the world economy as well as in the United States.

Nixon used his office to pass bills we would consider liberal. He passed the National Environmental Policy Act, the Clean Air Act, and the Federal Water Pollution Control Act of 1972. Nixon also established a lot of government agencies and declared war on drugs.

During his time, schools were integrated on a large scale. He fought for the law to be colored blind. He campaigned to have the Equal Rights Amendment ratified by the states. He was pro choice. This was something I did not know.

After his reelection, Nixon set price freezes because interest rates were going up. Price controls led to food shortages, and farmers started drowning their chickens rather than sell them at a loss. The stock market fell. Again we had another president wanting to make health insurance mandatory. Ted Kennedy opposed the plan because it did not go as far as he wanted.

Economist Paul Krugman's thoughts on the gold standard: "The current world monetary system assigns no special role to gold; indeed, the Federal Reserve is not obliged to tie the dollar to anything."

He continued to say that you can print as much money as you want and that there are advantages to this system. Something comes up, just print money. However, he did say that there are risks in doing this; he used as an example the uncertainties that international traders and investors would have.

Krugman talked about how the dollar has been worth anywhere from 120 yen to 80 yen. That I do know well because when my husband was stationed in Yokosuka, Japan, when the yen rate was high, we would trade our dollars for yen to buy things. When I got there in 1981, if my memory serves me right, the yen was 206 to the dollar. By December 1985, the yen rate was 202 to the dollar. Now it is about 83 yen to the dollar. So you can now see that our dollar is not as good as it used to be. So what year was it that we left the gold standard?

Well, in 1932 it went from $20 an ounce to $35 an ounce, which decreased the value of the dollar. When President Nixon officially took the gold standard away in 1971, the dollar lost a lot of its value. He did this in hopes to try and equalize trade.

Because the United States constantly prints money every time they need it, today it has lost 90 percent of its value, according to wiki.answers.com. So our buying power is less and continues as the Obama administration continues to print more money. Printing money with no backing devalues the dollar!

Krugman does say that even though it leaves monetary managers free to do good, there is a risk that they will be irresponsible.[188] However, I have pointed out that when we had gold as a backing, our economy was stable. So are we to believe some economist or history?

I remember this story: A young man was looking for a job and came across an old farmer. He asked him if there was anything he could do. The old man looked at his nice suit and then asked him what he had to offer. The young man told him about his PhD and all the clubs he had been a member of in school. The old man looked him straight in the eye and said, "Yes, that is nice but do you have common sense? Without common sense, that PhD means nothing."

Krugman stated that there was no real conclusion on whether to use gold as a standard or not. However, in the past, our economy grew when we used the gold standard. I feel the reason is because people put a great deal of value in gold, but he is right: it is just a metal (just like a diamond is just a rock). People determine the significance of these metals and stones.

President Nixon sent a letter to the Senate and asked for an

---

188   http://www.pkarchive.org/cranks/goldbug.html

amendment so lunches would be supplied to needy children, either free or at reduced prices.

Then Watergate came, referring to the Watergate Hotel. Nixon had been reelected in 1973. Watergate erupted in 1974. John Dean said that Nixon was doing his best to be up front to the American people. It was not until June of 1971 when a security leak happened about Vietnam that he started to become paranoid. Dean also stated that no one sat around and said how do we cover up what had been done.[189]

The break-in was realized when a security guard noticed tape over the door locks. He had taken them off only to see them back on the locks again. Five men, Virgilio González, Bernard Barker, James W. McCord, Jr., Eugenio Martinez, and Frank Sturgis, were arrested inside the Democratic National Committee's office in the Watergate Hotel.

After the trial and conviction, the investigation turned up that they were linked to the Committee to Reelect the President. Other members of Nixon's administration were imprisoned for the break-in and cover-up.

There were several theories as to the reason for the break-in. Some believe they were there to find out the Democrats' campaign strategies. The one most people think the reason is because Nixon thought that the Democrats had something on him. Meier told Richard Nixon's brother that O'Brien had information and documents. Of course this was not true. The information was supposed to have been some illegal contribution from Hughes to Nixon's campaign. If this is so, Nixon could have been set up.

The thing is, Nixon should never have refused to hand over the tapes, but most of all, he should not have covered up the break-in. Dean talks about Howard Hunt blackmailing the White House. The agreement to pay blackmail gave Congress the means to go for impeachment, because it was a sign of obstruction of justice.[(23)]

---

189 http://www.history.com/topics/watergate

Nixon fired people right and left to find someone who would fire special prosecutor, Archibald Cox. He finally found Raymond Bork, who dismissed him. Later Nixon resigned from office because criminal charges could still be brought against him. Gerald Ford gave him full pardon. Even upon his deathbed, Nixon claimed to be innocent.

Gerald Ford took over after Nixon resigned. Ford had been appointed vice president when Vice President Spiro Agnew resigned after pleading guilty to tax evasion, accepting bribes, and money laundering. When Ford took office from Nixon, he stated:

> My fellow Americans, our long national nightmare is over. Our Constitution *works*. Our great republic is a government of laws and not of men. Here, the people rule. But there is a higher power, by whatever name we honor Him. Who ordains not only righteousness but love, not only justice, but mercy... Let us restore the golden rule to our political process and let brotherly love purge our hearts of suspicion and hate.[190]

Well, even today there is suspicion of our politicians and with good reason. They are passing socialistic programs, trying to distribute everyone's wealth but theirs, taking away rights of citizens, and caring more about illegal aliens than the US citizens that voted for them; they are supposed to do what they want and not what other countries want them to do, like taking our sovereignty and handing it over to the UN, ignoring our Constitution, changing it, not to mention raising taxes after taxes, and shall I go on? Did you know that our forefathers said that no laws were to be passed where Congress, the president, or our judges could exempt themselves, and yet they have. The reason is because they would pass grievous laws.

---

190   http://en.wikipedia.org/wiki/Gerald_Ford

This starts to become a dictatorship. The health care program is unconstitutional!

Ford is the one who started the amnesty program for people who dodged the draft, but they give all the credit to Jimmy Carter.

Inflation was going up, but he never came up with a plan to reduce it. Even though he constantly ran a deficit, he still signed the Education for All Handicapped Children Act.

Jimmy Carter was a Baptist and deep in his faith. Yes, he is one of the Democrats I voted for. He owned a peanut farm, and I remember some of the jokes that went around about it.

He was against discrimination and put many people of color in statewide boards and offices when he was governor of Georgia.

He opposed abortion until *Roe vs. Wade*. He would not go for funding abortions though. The thing I did not know at the time that I voted for Carter was that he supported Lieutenant William Calley and was against the death penalty.

Who was William Calley? Remember what I said about how dehumanizing someone makes it easy to kill them? Well, that is just pretty much what happened in Vietnam. Calley was the only one convicted in the My Lai Massacre. Dennis Bunning said, "I would say most people in our company considered the Vietnamese human."

In order to explain what our troops were against, I am going to give you some insight. A company of soldiers was traveling and a pregnant woman on the side line suddenly pulled a weapon out and started shooting at them. There you had a hard time knowing who was your enemy. There were children with bombs and so on.

Calley saw what he thought was a suspected enemy position and started shooting; others in his company joined in. Some tried to stop it. So why out of all those men was only Calley convicted? Your guess is as good as mine. Some got off by testifying against him, but there were twenty-six officers and soldiers. The men that tried to stop it were harassed by people. There are still too many holes in this; I would like to know the truth.

In 2009, Calley said at a Kiwanis Club, "There is not a day that goes by that I do not feel remorse for what happened that day in My Lai. I feel remorse for the Vietnamese who were killed, for their families, for the American soldiers involved and their families. I am very sorry... If you are asking why I did not stand up to them when I was given the orders, I will have to say that I was a second lieutenant getting orders from my commander and I followed them—foolishly, I guess."

That is how it is with our military. They are given orders, and when they follow them to the letter and it goes bad, they become the scapegoat for the higher officers that gave the orders in the first place.

Thompson, one of the helicopter crew that tried to stop the killing, threw away the citation given him because of the fabrication of the events that happened. Rivers stated that Thompson should be the one in prison because he fired at American troops; Rivers started to get hate mail. In 1998, he and Colbum returned to that spot and received the Soldier's Medal.

China at that time was in charge of the UN. We were giving our enemies our battle plans. This is why we did not win. This is one of the reasons why I do not believe in the UN. The Soviet Union and China were supplying weapons to North Vietnam. This is why you do not let news media and other people know what you are doing!

Obama's administration is not the only administration to bail out the car industry. The problem is that the government no longer understands how a capitalistic economy works. If a company goes under because of the greed or stupidity of the CEO, another company will take its place. We do not need to bail out companies! Carter bailed out Chrysler.

One thing President Carter believes, if he has not changed

his mind, was not to tear down the military like Bill Clinton and President Obama believe, because it helps preserve the peace.[32]

He believed diplomacy should be tried first. How does that old saying go, that Roosevelt said, "Speak softly but carry a big stick"?

On August 31, 1979 Soviet troops were again reported in Cuba. A number of Soviet troops were stationed in Cuba and many Cuban troops were in Africa. Senator Richard Stone (D-FL) was trying to get an investigation to look into the matter but was being ignored. They said that he was up for reelection and denied the existence of a Soviet brigade there. But because of his insistence, Carter said he would look into it. The CIA took a lot of photos of the area. The CIA was more concerned about Cuban troops being in Africa and what they were doing there.

Intelligence did not know when they formed, how many, and what the purpose was. Frank Church said he believed that Cuba had them there in case the United States did something because of what they were doing in Africa.

Senator Stone said, "The president should invoke the Monroe Doctrine and oppose the establishment of what constitutes a Soviet military base in our hemisphere."[65]

It was told that it was the biggest base they had in the world. The United States deployed troops bordering the USSR.

The SALT hearings were postponed one day. This was to put attention on what was going on in Cuba.

Church and Stone were the most outspoken. *Time* magazine suggested that the reason Stone was outspoken was because of all the Cubans in his state, or because of his stand on the Panama Canal treaty and putting limits on intelligence activity. On top of that, not long before he had called Fidel Castro his friend.

President Carter's senior aide said that they did not want to turn it into another missile crisis. Many thought that if we let the Soviets keep the combatant troops in there, we were letting them thumb their noses at us. Some believed it was a test on the Carter's administration and related to SALT II.

Carter's National Security Advisor, Zbigniew Brzezinski, told *Time* magazine that the best way was for Congress to ratify SALT II, that we should increase defense and be ready to compete with the Soviets. Sound advice, I would say. Carter's aide also claimed that if they were not concern about us, we should not be concerned about them. This included the eighty Soviet advisors that were in Afghanistan.

I want you to know at this point that Carter wanted to get rid of nuclear weapons completely from the earth. Well, that is not going to happen because of man's lust for power. You are seeing it today as well as the past.

Carter claimed that since we did not know the whole situation of the bases, we should step back and look at the situation in a calm and diplomatic way. He continued to say that we should refrain from making the situation worse.[65]

The Soviets invaded Afghanistan in December of the same year. Walter Mondale could not believe all these things that the Soviets were doing. Well, believe it. That is the way Communists are. Russia has not changed since the wall fell down. The cold war is not over. Just look at today and the wars in the Muslim countries.

The United States started giving limited aid to Islamist factions. I will not go into the theories of why each group did what. The United States terminated the wheat deal with the Soviets and refused to let our athletes go to Moscow for the 1980 Olympics, which was probably a smart move even though it was not popular. Their lives most likely would have been in danger.

Then President Carter reinstated the draft. He cut off financial aid to Pakistan because of the military dictatorship that took over the country had burnt our embassy there. We all know that we trained people in Pakistan and Afghanistan to fight the Soviets. The United States offered $400 million to help with the anti-Communist Mujahideen in Afghanistan but General Zia said it was insufficient and refused it. So we paid more.

Well, if I was president I would have said okay and would have not given him anything. Critics can sit there and blame Carter and Reagan for what is going on today but there was never any real rest in all those countries.

Let's talk about the Iran hostage crisis. The Shah of Iran, Mohammad Rezahlavi, was a strong ally with the United States. Now get this, because I did not even know this. The Eisenhower administration along with the shah formed a coup to remove Iran's elected prime minister, Mohammed Mossadegh. (Wikipedia).

Why are we deciding that we will remove other countries' officials? Especially one the people elected. Let them take care of him and decide if he is not doing right. Their own culture is different from ours. Our nation is different and unlike any other nation because it was based on Biblical principles. This is why we are hated by the world. They want us destroyed. We have shown that the government does not have to dictate people's lives. We can have liberty and not liberties. Of course, I hope, you know this is not the only time our country has done this.

When Iran took fifty-two Americans hostage, they had these demands (Wikipedia):

- The return of the shah to Iran for trial
- The return of the shah's wealth to the Iranian people
- An apology and admission of past actions in Iran by the United States
- A promise that they would not interfere in Iran's affairs in the future

Carter could not end the crisis even though the shah

left and died in Egypt from cancer. One of the attempts was called Operation Eagle Claw, where eight helicopters went in. However, the sand made it a failure. My husband said that they should have known better. There were other ways that they could have done it successfully. He did not go into any details, and I can understand why. Carter froze the accounts that were in US banks to see if it would work.

The economy was weak because of less gold backing. Inflation and unemployment were high. The effort to reduce them caused a short recession.[191] Inflation and interest rates reached 18 percent.

I found a very interesting comment from the UNC Press. They stated:

> For every loser in inflation there has to be a winner. Creditors are hurt, but debtors are helped as their indebtedness is reduced when adjusted for price changes. It is difficult to determine precisely who loses and who gains, but we know enough to suggest that widespread perceptions are probably incorrect. We tend to think of lower income families as the most vulnerable, but one careful study, published while inflation was raging in 1980, found that it was not the poor but the upper income classes that were hurt more by the inflation due to a drop in the value of their assets.[192]

They claimed that the two major things affecting the inflation rate were the tight money policy that the Federal Reserve had to control inflation and the revision in the budget that started a panic on the financial side of the economy. Even though the increase was small and reasonable, according to the article, the market was looking at an overspending by

---

191   James Carter/White House.
192   UNC Press, http://uncpress.unc.edu/browse/page/218

the government. I wonder what they think now with all the spending our government is doing today.

Carter said, "The federal government simply must accept discipline on itself as an example for others to follow." He said that it would take time for his plan to take effect.

Reagan said that the government is the one that causes inflation. Now get this. He said that the government needed to cut out deficits and stop printing money![46] Thank you, Ronald Reagan; at least someone up there in Washington had common sense.

Any economist worth a grain of salt would tell you that! Ted Kennedy wanted controls on wages and prices. He also tried to become president during the election because he was not happy with President Carter. Well, I was pretty happy with him and I do believe that the Federal Reserve was part of the problem with the economy during his time.

Carter's simulative macroeconomics lowered unemployment but only by 2 percent. However, the inflation rate was high. Carter decided to try and get full employment and restrictive monetary and fiscal policies. This was to try and cut the inflation rate. However, he did it too late, and it was during the election year. He lost that election to Reagan.[193]

Let's talk about Ronald Reagan and his economy. I have been waiting to talk about him because of all the lies that were said by the other party. They went around and said that he hurt the economy because of tax cuts to the rich. I remember a liberal at work constantly cutting down Reaganomics, saying how it hurt the economy.

Reagan said, "Entrepreneurs and their small enterprises are responsible for almost all the economic growth in the United States."[21, 74] You cannot build yourself up by tearing businesses down.

You cannot build a country on class hatred. It does not

---

193   http://www.csulb.edu/~astevens/posc420/files/hibbs.html

work. This is what Socialists do to turn people against their government.

Reagan had specific goals in mind when he ran, and you could see it in his campaign. Just like you can see specific goals Herman Cain has in mind. People want specifics, not worthless information and lies. You know the old saying, "You can fool some of the people some of the time but you cannot fool all the people all of the time." Well, you can see it in the nation today. There are some people still fooled about what is going on, but a lot of people have woken up to what is going on.

Reagan's goals were to build up the economy, reduce taxes, balance the budget, and reduce government. He wanted to build up the military and confront the Soviets, which you cannot do if you do not have that big stick! Even Steve Moore of the *Wall Street Journal* agreed with Reagan. He talked about how Reagan's policies helped the economy.

After the assassination attempt, most of his economic packages passed. However, Congress did not cut spending as much as was advised for them to do. Things did get shaky and his party wanted to get rid of Paul Volcker (Carter's appointee to the Federal Reserve) but Reagan refused to do so.

He concentrated on the recession. Inflation subsided even though unemployment had gone up. However, the economy turned around in 1983 and there was growth the rest of his term!

Let's look closely at Reaganomics and what it did, since a lot of people think the economy went down because of the untruths going around. Now it is true that he lowered the tax on oil profits. Result: oil prices stayed low and ended the oil crisis. Benefit to us. Domestic oil was $6 a barrel while world price was $30 a barrel. He had lowered or eliminated price controls not only on oil and gas but on cable, telephone long-distance, bus service, and overseas shipping.

Now let's look at this today. We have our gas going up

more and more. When I was in my twenties, gas was 50 cents a gallon (1973). Today in 2010, it is about $3 a gallon. In 2008, it even peaked to about $4. I heard that they want it to be even with the prices overseas, which are about $7 a gallon.

Are you seeing what I mean, that they are trying to make us like those overseas? Broke, fending for food, gas, and whatever else we need. This is telling me they are either deliberately hiking the prices to make more money or the government is wanting to hike it in order to force us to what they want us to drive with this phony green thing they got going. In the past thirty-four years, gas has gone up an average 493.39 percent.[194]

Now I am not sure when the government capped all those wells but you see we are being forced to depend on the most expensive oil. By the way, did you know that the oil companies might be the ones that have the patent on a car that can get 100 miles to the gallon? I got that in my economics class. They are holding out to sell more gas.

Also, there are enough wells already drilled to supply this country for about a hundred years. I got that when I had tried to major in petroleum engineering but was told by the oil company that I could be nothing but a secretary. I know Mr. B wonders why I dropped the major but I could not see why I should be an overeducated secretary after spending all that money for my education.

Under Reagan, the federal spending decreased from 4 to 2.5 percent. There were no real changes in domestic programs, which included Social Security. The growth was small, and the defense spending was higher than he wanted. The changes on the tax code brought individual income tax from 70 to 28 percent and corporate tax from 48 to 34 percent. Most of the poor were exempt. There was a slight increase in Social Security tax in 1977, but like the health care, it was not to take

---

194   United States Department of Labor, Bureau of Labor Statistics, http://data.bls.gov/pdq/SurveyOutputServlet

effect until later. Deductions were reduced and excise tax rates were increased slightly.

There were investment incentives and reduction of tax bias of the deferent investments and new ones. This was for individuals as well as businesses. This reduced the federal revenue share from 20.2 to 19.2 percent in eight years. How can the liberals say there was no growth and that it was bad?

The deregulation that Carter had started continued under Reagan and approved the reduction of money growth by the Federal Reserve. He did not intervene in the markets for foreign exchange.

The results of his policies; Economic growth of 2.8 percent, GDP per working adults went from 0.8 to 1.8 percent, productivity went from 1.4 to 3.8 percent, unemployment declined from 7 to 5.4 percent, inflation declined from 10.4 to 4.2 percent, and import taxes increased from 12 to 23 percent.

He failed to get the cuts he wanted to lower the deficit because of Congress, and later the debt went from 22.3 to 38.1 percent. They claimed that the slow response to the savings and loan problem led to the increased debt.[195]

The Libertarian 1996 study showed eight of the ten main economic elements under Reagan performed better than any other president so far. Family income grew by $4,000 and lost $1,500 in post-Reagan years. I had gotten an $11 an hour job in 1985.

They said that interest rates, inflation, and unemployment fell faster under him than any other president. The only thing that got worse was the savings rate. I know that it was not as low as it is today. Productivity went up but not as high as in post-Reagan years. It was higher than pre-Reagan years.[74]

Reagan had an average growth of 3.2 percent during his years. Carter had a 2.8 percent growth, and Bush along with Clinton had only 2.1 percent economic growth. The

---

195 *The Concise Encyclopedia of Economics.*

productivity rate was higher in pre-Reagan years and lower in post-Reagan years.[196]

The economy grew to almost one third larger than at the beginning of Reagan's administration. There were 17 million new jobs from 1981 to 1989. When Reagan took office, the unemployment rate was 7.6 percent. It did peak in his first year of office to 9.7 percent but fell continuously, and when he left office, it was 5.5 percent. Liberals want you to think that things were bad during his time, but it was not bad. Why can't people remember the truth and how good it was during his time?

This is how the Average Annual Real Growth Rate went: Eisenhower 2.3%, Kennedy/Johnson 4.9%, Nixon/Ford 3%, Carter 2.5%, Reagan 3.2%, Bush 1.3%, and Clinton was 2.6%. So you see the growth was not that high for Clinton or Carter. Kennedy and Johnson had the highest growth rate.

Unemployment was going up before Reagan took office but it started to go down and so on. So you liberals, quit telling those lies about Reagan. Read *Supply Side Tax Cuts* by William A. Niskanen and Stephen Moore. These men cut the fable that the rich took from the poor in the Reagan years.

Then he turned his attention to foreign matters. He got reelected because of the turn in the economy. Well, at least that is why some of my friends reelected him. He seemed to know what he was doing and was a strong leader.

Even though arms were sold to Iran and the money diverted to the Contra rebels, there has never been any evidence that President Reagan knew anything about it. I think in my time of voting, he was the best president so far.

Ronald Reagan said, "Freedom is never more than one generation away from extinction" (Quote). He continued to say that it was not passed to our children through inheritance. That we must continue to fight for it, protect it, and hand it down for them to do the same, otherwise we will be telling not

---

196   http://www.doge.us/govecon/SupplySideTaxCuts.pdf

only our children but children's children what it was like long ago when the United States was free.

D. H. Lawrence said, "Men fight for liberty and win it with hard knocks. Their children, brought up easy, let it slip away again, poor fools. And their grandchildren are once more slaves" (Classical American Literature, 1922).

George Bush Sr. was elected after President Reagan. He had a degree in economics from Yale University. Reagan had appointed him ambassador to the United Nations. He also was the last World War II veteran to be president. When he was on a mission, his aircraft was hit but despite his engine being on fire, he completed his mission. He ended up in a raft until rescued.

In 1976, he was appointed director of the Central Intelligence Agency until January 20, 1977. He became vice president with Reagan. Then he became president in 1989.

Let's look at his economy. I had already showed that the growth rate was not as good as Reagan's. His economic growth was only 1.3 percent.

I have to talk about NAFTA because it is not working. Neither side is stopping and doing business with the United States. Canada is going straight to Mexico and Mexico is going straight to Canada. The United States is losing business. It actually went through during Clinton's time, even though Bush started it.

So what is NAFTA exactly? It eliminates tariffs and is supposed to encourage trade among the three countries. However, one country is being left out: ours. They claim that our economy has grown 54 percent since NAFTA, but I do not see it. The cattlemen here in Colorado complain that they have been losing because Mexico now is the chief supplier to Canada. They go straight through to Canada with the cattle. Mexico is cheaper because they pay no tariffs and we have a minimum wage. Therefore, things cost more here.

It also claimed that it created 25 million new jobs. So how

many jobs has it destroyed? John J. Sweeney says that the trade deficit with Canada and Mexico has gone up to twelve times the size before NAFTA; in 2004, it reached $111 billion.

I want to talk about the raising of taxes during Bush's administration. Congress was controlled by the Democrats just like they were when Obama took office. The Republicans wanted to cut spending but the Democrats wanted to raise taxes. Bush wanted to curb the deficit badly.

Republicans felt betrayed because Bush had promised "no new taxes." So the Republicans in Congress did what they could to defeat Bush's proposal on spending cuts and tax increases, which I say shame on them. They should have gone ahead and did what they could on spending cuts.

So Bush accepted the demands for higher taxes by the Democrats. Of course the Democrats blamed it all on Bush when it was they that really raised the taxes. Bush was forced into going along with them because, guess what? It is Congress that makes the decision on whether to raise taxes or not.[197]

The Republicans, even though it was a type of revenge, gave the Democrats what they wanted. However, the Democrats were able to turn it around and blame it on the Republicans and Bush. It was they that voted to have taxes raised. They had the majority to not get it passed if they did not want higher taxes.

Let's talk about good old Bill Clinton and his wife Hillary, since she told the press that she would have to talk to him when there seemed to be a contradiction between what she said and he said. I did not vote for him because I knew he was not the right person for this country, and he proved me right. Hillary Clinton is no better than Obama because she is going to the UN to surpass our Constitution just like Obama.

During this time, I lost an $11-per-hour job and got unemployment for about three months. It may have been a little longer but I started taking temporary jobs. We could not

---

197   101st United States Congress, http://en.wikipedia.org/wiki/101st_
United_States_Congress

get any assistance. They said that my husband made too much on his military retirement. He was bringing home a little over $800 a month. Our mortgage was about $889 a month.

We put our home up for sale because neither I nor my husband was making the money. I would get phone calls from creditors. I was still looking for a permanent job after a year. The phone company was about to shut off the phone but I told them what was going on and said that I need the phone to find a job. Also, companies could call me in if there was a temporary job available. They disconnected the phone but then put it in my name. The house was going down in value and we were not getting enough in to pay for food. We would go to the flea market and take food that was being thrown out.

I could go on how we lived on 6.1 acres of land with no running water for ten years and so on. I could tell you we did not have the money for a big solar system so we did not have electricity for the appliances that all these nice politicians do not have to worry about losing while they make all these plans on how they can take our money and spend it wildly.

Clinton took office in 1993, and right off the bat he cut defense spending. He closed our bases on the coastline, which is a big mistake, but I already talked about that. Did the Clintons do this country any favors with the economy? No! The Democrats have been pointing the finger at Bush Jr. but the economy started going down during the Clinton administration. Are you getting the point about all that finger pointing? So lets look at the things that went on during his administration and see what Bush had to deal with when he got into office.

Between 1993 and 1994, 154 firms announced that there will be layoffs. In April, May, and June 1996, there were 2,816 layoff events that brought about 266,205 people claiming unemployment insurance. The second quarter was 1,247, which there were 139,390 unemployment claimants. In September of 1996 there were 498 mass layoffs, which was measured by employers' new filings for unemployment insurance during that month. It totaled 40,964 workers. The states that claimed the most filing were California (12,184); Pennsylvania (3,699); Illinois (2,845); South Carolina (1,948); and Texas (1,904). Manufacturing held 52 percent of these initial layoff claims and 46 percent of all mass layoffs in September. The total initial claimants in 1996 were 936,591. In 1995 from July through December, you had 739,799 initial claimants.[198]

Then in 1997, you had a total of 1,124,945, not counting October through December. In 1998, there were 1,747,338 initial layoffs. In 1999, there were 1,404,779 initial layoffs, and in the year 2000, there were 1,835,592 initial claimants for unemployment insurance. Of course this does not include people that quit looking or extended their claim. So you see that things were not looking good during the Clinton administration, and yet people have forgotten. They voted for Hillary Clinton anyway.[199]

However, I would not be fair if I did not put how many were employed these years. For the year 2000, only 34,161 got jobs; in 1996 only 32,343 got jobs, in 1997 only 33,341 jobs, in 1998 only 34,298 jobs, and in 1999, it was about the same. So you see more jobs were lost than gained. That is how it is today. So why do people that lived during that time not remember?

Clinton also went for a stimulus package but the Republicans filibustered and it fell through. Clinton on his own accord dropped the tax cuts for middle-class people. The main thing that he passed was NAFTA, which cut the United States out. I already went through that. We did not need Hillary or Obama for president!

On October 22, 2000, Kim Weissman reported that when Clinton was in office and the Democrats controlled Congress, the Dow Jones Industrial Average was 7.8 percent

---

198   http://www.bls.gov/news.release/history/mmls_112096.txt
199   http://www.bls.gov/news.release/history/mmls_02012001.txt

and NASDAQ was 4.1 percent. When Congress was mostly Republicans and under their control, Dow Jones was 25 percent and NASDAQ was 35 percent.[200]

Clinton opposed any constitutional amendment that would force a balanced budget. Obama is doing the same thing. The Democratic Congress raised taxes and the Republican Congress cut them. So even though the stock market looked great on the average from the beginning to the end, no one tells you that it did not start doing well until it was under a Republican-controlled Congress. Do you not remember at the beginning that the news kept saying how the stock market would go down and it would only go up a little until close to the end of Clinton's presidency?

The new taxes that they raised did not go to the deficit; they went to new pork barrel projects of the Democrats! Then we became more dependent on foreign oil because of Clinton's policy, which stopped us from using the fuel we already have here in the United States. We have a lot of wells already capped off. Yet our government refuses to let us use it. I do agree with Weissman that the Clinton-Gore energy policy is really an environmental policy.

Now the government we have today wants us to be paying $7 a gallon for gas in order to force us into dropping our cars and traveling by other means, which is hard to do if you live out in the country. Oh that is right, we are to move to the city, where they can keep an eye on us and our land goes to the frogs, the bogs, and the logs. They do not want us living out here in the country. So if we do what they dictate, we can use bicycles. I am glad someone was not brainwashed by all these lies.

At the end of Clinton's term, he used his executive orders to create seventeen new national monuments and expand four more. This made up 4.6 million acres in forty-eight states.

---

200   Weissman, Kim, Stock Market Bull Clinton, October 22, 2000,
       http://www.tysknews.com/Depts/Taxes/bull_clinton.htm

None of this went before Congress for approval. Do you want to continue to tell me that the government is not into herding us up like cattle in small areas? You want to continue to tell me that liberals do not put animals and land above people? Do you want to tell me that nature (excluding people) is not their god and religion?

If you do not think you have been brainwashed, then why is it people signed a petition to ban water when the scientific description (H_2O) was used? People sign things without checking them out.[201]

We cannot forget those six missiles that Clinton fired in Afghanistan. They claimed that they had evidence that bin Laden, sheltered by the Islamic rulers, had been involved in the bombings of the embassies in East Africa. Clinton claimed that they were planning additional terrorist attacks on our citizens and others.

Lets look at what he was saying. In February 1993, a car blew up in a parking garage under the World Trade Center; six people died and about 1,000 were injured. In November of 1995, a van parked in front of an American-run military training center in Saudi Arabia exploded, killing five Americans and two Indians. In August 1998, cars exploded at United States embassies in Nairobi, Kenya, and Dares Salaam, Tanzania, which killed 224 and injured 5,000 people. The news claimed that these attacks were tied to Osama bin Laden, and the suspects were convicted in the United States federal court. At this point, President Clinton shot missiles into Afghanistan to hit Osama bin Laden, who was only linked to the bombings in Africa. Was he trying to draw attention away from the scandal with Monica Lewinsky? Whether he was or not, he had declared war on Afghanistan by firing those missiles.[202]

---

201   Lazaroff, Cat, "Sun Sets on President Clinton's Environmental Legacy," http://www.ens-newswire.com/ens/jan2001/2001-01-19-06.asp

202   Dead on Tracks, http://www.snopes.com/rumors/clinton.asp

Then the relationship between the United States and Cuba got bad during his administration. Cuba shot down two supposedly civilian planes from the United States because they violated Cuban air space. Although it seems that no one has put it on the Internet (or the Clinton administration managed to get rid of it) I do remember Clinton sent aircraft to Cuba to kill Castro. Colin Powell was in Cuba trying to negotiate at the time. So was Clinton going to kill a US citizen along with Castro? Congress got onto him, and he called the planes back. Does anyone remember that? Maybe because Colin Powell was black, it did not matter that he got killed.

How about Clinton trying to suppress the website that was leaking unflattering information about him?[203] He lied about Monica Lewinsky yet he got away with it. He should have resigned because he was only to stay in office as long as he was in good standing and moral.

Many talked about Sarah Palin because she had never been in Washington and had only been a governor of a state. Was that not the same with Bill Clinton? Obama was a freshman congressman. People soaked it up instead of thinking.

I do not want to leave with all negative things. What about Americorps that he worked on, which helps students with their college?

Clinton's administration did get things in to clean up the water and smog. His administration did strengthen the Safe Drinking Water Act, requiring water utilities to provide reports to their customers; however, some places did not conform to that and ended up with salmonella in their water.

I am not going to go through Bush Jr. but I hope you see the progression. We have had problems with Cuba since Kennedy's administration. That 9/11 was not just because of one administration, but Clinton being trigger happy did not help matters. There were other ways of doing things than what Clinton did.

---

203 The Clinton Legacy, http://www.zpub.com/un/bclegacy.html

Edmund Burke[204] said that people only give up their liberties under some delusion.

Now I am going to get both sides mad at me. Obama said, "We are no longer a Christian nation," and then he changed it quickly to "We are no longer *just* a Christian nation."

First, we were never a Christian nation. We never declared Christianity a state religion. We let all religions into this Union. It is a nation built upon Christian principles and the Bible, and they stated that it was the best book to build a nation upon.

Keith Ellison was a Catholic that turned to Islam while attending one of our colleges. He was sworn into Congress on the Koran.[205]

I have heard some say we are a Christian nation because we are built upon the principles of the Bible. Be very careful of what you are saying remember the atrocities done to our forefathers. So think about what was said.

> *A boss creates fear, a leader confidence. A boss fixes*
> *blame, a leader corrects mistakes. A boss knows*
> *all, a leader asks questions. A boss makes work*
> *drudgery, a leader makes it interesting.*
> —Russell H. Euing (a British journalist)

Louis D. Brandeis the first Jewish Supreme Court Judge said, "The greatest dangers to liberty lurk in insidious encroachment by men of zeal, well-meaning but without understanding."

---

204 Edmund Burke served in the House of Commons of Great Britain. He was of the Whig party. He supported the cause of the American Revolutionaries but opposed the French Revolution. He was an Anglo-Irish statesman, author, orator, political theorist, and philosopher. One of his books was *Reflections on the Revolution in France.*

205 http://www.associatedcontent.com/article/217462/the_koran_used_by_keith_ellison_has.html

No Heroes, Welcome

I scurry through the brush,
As bullets buzz by my head.
The limbs grab at my fatigues.
My palms are full of sweat.
As I cling to my weapon tightly,
The enemy I confront.
With every heavy heart beat,
I watch my friends and comrades die,
Only to realize it was all an illusion.
There were no bands that played
And no hero's welcome home, just only me with one leg
And four old dusty walls where I lie.

Notation

All truths are easy to understand once they are discovered; the point is to discover them.
—Galileo (1564–1642)

As I was picking up my grandchildren the other day, I thought about the things I was writing. I knew what they, as well as other children, would be taught in school. I asked God if there is any hope.

Then something came to mind: "Where there are embers there is a fire." So there is still hope. It is up to the American people to see the truth and act upon it, just like our forefathers. We need not let fear consume us.

People must stop looking at things that have been tried and have failed. Albert Einstein once said, "Insanity is defined as doing the same thing over and over again and EXPECTING different results."

Who had deceived thee so often as thyself?
—Benjamin Franklin

"Semper fidelis."

References

1. Junto Society Presidential Inaugural Speech, http://www. juntosociety.com/inaugural/gcleveland1st.html

2. *199 Things Every American Should Know*, American Heritage, a division of Forbes, New York, 1997.

3. John Covode, *Abraham Lincoln's White House*, http://www. mrlincolnswhitehouse.org/inside.asp?ID=702&subjectID=2

4. John Adams, *Thoughts on Government,* http://www.liberty. org/thoughts.htm . For the American Revolution and HTML project.

5. *An Outline of American History,* Chapter 4, http://odur.let. rug.nl/~usa/H/1990/ch4_p7.htm

6. G. Zorn, *Karl Marx's 10 Point Program of Communism and the Democrat Agenda*, October 1, 2010, http://www. sodahead.com/united-states/compare-and-contrast-karl-marx-10-point-program-of-communism-and-the-democrat-agenda/question-1260795/

7. Antitrust Laws, Cornell University Law School, http://www. law.cornell.edu/uscode/15/usc_sec_15_00000012----000-. html

8. Sir Ernest Baker, *The Political Thought of Plato and Aristotle,* Dover Publications, New York, 1959.

9. Gerald L. Baliles, *A Life in Brief; Ronald Wilson Reagan,* University of Virginia, 2010; http://millercenter.org/academic/americanpresident/reagan/essays/biography/1

10. David Barton, *Celebrate Liberty! (Famous Patriotic Speeches & Sermons)*, Wallbuilder Press, Aledo, Texas, 2003.

11. David Barton, *Education and the Founding Fathers* (video), Wallbuilders, Aledo, Texas, 1991.

12. W. Carl Biven, *Jimmy Carter's Economy*, University of North Carolina, UNC Press, 2002, http://uncpress.unc.edu/browse/page/218

13. Black Americans in Congress, http://baic.house.gov/member-profiles/profile.html?intID=14 , http://baic.house.gov/historical-essays/essay.html?intID=1&intSectionID=10 , Created and maintained by the Office of the Clerk, US Capitol, Room H154, Washington, DC.

14. Brainy Quote, http://www.brainyquote.com/quotes/quotes/t/thomasjeff157216.html

15. Fred Burks, *Best JFK Assassination* (video), August 22, 2009, http://video.google.com/videoplay?docid=-9137354720737304741#

16. George W. Cary, *Republic (government)* http://www.mmisi.org/ir/39_01_2/carey.pdf

17. Checks & Balance*s within United State*s Government, FreeOnlineResearchPapers.com, http://www.freeonlineresearchpapers.com/checks-and-balance

18. Raven Clabough, *The New American*, November 24, 2010, http://www.thenewamerican.com/index.php/culture/family/5266-president-clevelands-words-ring-true-in-texas

19. Digital History, "Andrew Jackson," http://www.digitalhistory.uh.edu/database/article_display.cfm?HHID=637

20. Documents from Magna Carta to George W. Bush's 2001 address to State of the Union 2008, http://odur.let.rug.nl/~usa/D/index.htm#b1400

21. *Encyclopedia Britannica*, 15th edition, 1982.

22. Steve Farrell, *John Adams: Party of One*, June 21, 2005, http://www.americandaily.com/s-farrell-6-21-05.htm

23. Watergate.info, http://watergate.info/chronology/brief.shtml

24. For my Family, God, Nation, Culture, and Freedom, http://www.youtube.com/user/Goodfightlads?blend=23&ob=5

25. Franklin D. Roosevelt, http://www.whitehouse.gov/about/presidents/franklindroosevelt

26. *Gale Encyclopedia of US History*, "Advice to the Unemployed in the Great Depression," June 11, 1932, by Henry Ford, http://www.answers.com/topic/a-pub-caret1-dvice-to-the-unemployed-in-the-great-depression-11-june-1932-by-henry-ford

27. Edward Gibbon, *The History of the Decline and Fall of the Roman Empire,* Vol. I, London, The Folio Society, 1998.

28. Guttmaster Institute, http://www.guttmacher.org/pubs/USTPtrends.pdf Jan. 2010

29. Verno M. Hall, Joseph A. Montgomery, *The Christian History of the Constitution of the United States of America*, Foundation for American Christian Education, San Francisco, Ca 1975.

30. Historycentral.com, "Treaty of Washington," http://www.historycentral.com/rec/TreatyofWash.html

31. First State Recognized Slave, http://current.com/groups/learn/92619535_first-state-recognized-slave-was-owned-by-anthony-johnson-a-black-man.htm

32. "Jimmy Carter" (video), History.com, http://www.history.com/topics/jimmy-carter/videos?paidlink=1&vid=HIS_SEM_Search&keywords=jimmy%2Bcarter%2Bpresident&utm_source=google&utm_medium=cpc&utm_campaign=presidents&utm_term=jimmy%20carter%20president#jimmy-carter-on-defense

33. Jeffery Rosen, "Justice John Paul Stevens," New York Magazine, September 23, 2007, http://www.nytimes.com/2007/09/23/magazine/23stevens-t.html?pagewanted=1&_r=1

34. Richard Lacayo, *The Making of America: Theodore Roosevelt,* http://www.time.com/time/magazine/article/0,9171,1207820-1,00.html

35. MassResistance, "The Fistgate Tapes: Part I," http://www.massresistance.org/docs/issues/fistgate/tape01.html

36. Isaac M. McPhee, *The Rutherford B. Hayes Presidency*, May 5, 2008, http://www.suite101.com/content/the-rutherford-b-hayes-presidency-a52957

37. Morning Coffee, October 6, 2006, http://morningcoffee.wordpress.com/2006/10/06/who-funds-the-aclu/

38. William Munro, Thomas Kennelly, Christopher McCarthy, *Social Civics,* The American School, Chicago, 1985

39. William A. Nikanen, *The Concise Encyclopedia of Economics,* http://www.econlib.org/library/Enc1/Reaganomics.html

40. George F. Parker, *Recollections of Grover Cleveland*, The Century Co., New York, 1909, Ebook and Texts Archive, http://www.archive.org/details/cu31924030932499

41. Nathaniel Phibrick, *Mayflower*, Penguin Group, New York, 2006.

42. Marvin Pinkert, Lee Ann Potter, *Letters from President Millard Fillmore to the Emperor of Japan*, March 1, 2004, http://www.highbeam.com/doc/1G1-115345005.html

43. Presidential Pet Museum, President James Madison, 2002–2010, http://www.presidentialpetmuseum.com/presidents/04JM.htm

44. J. Rank, "James Monroe: Economic Policy," http://www.presidentprofiles.com/Washington-Johnson/James-Monroe-Economic-policy.html

45. J. Rank, "George Washington: First Term," http://www.presidentprofiles.com/Washington-Johnson/George-Washington-First-term.html

46. "Reaganomics," Wikipedia free encyclopedia, http://en.wikipedia.org/wiki/Reaganomics

47. Rosalie J. Salter, *Noah Webster's First Edition of an American Dictionary of the English Language* (reprint of the 1828 dictionary), Foundation for American Christians.

48. Joseph Silver, *The Debate over an Economic Interpretation of the Constitution: Where has Beard Taken Us and Where Are We after McGuire's "New" Interpretation?* IIT, Kent College of Law, Chicago, http://works.bepress.com/joseph_silvia/2/

49. Rosalie J. Slater, *Teaching and Learning America's Christian History, American Revolution, Bicentennial Edition,* Iversen-Norman Associates, New York, 1975.

50. Spartacus Educational, http://www.spartacus.schoolnet. co.uk/USArooseveltF.htm

51. Statutes at Large, 1789–1875, http://memory.loc.gov/ammem/amlaw/lwsl.html

52. Stead Networks, Progressive Era, September 16, 2010, eNotes.com, http://www.enotes.com/public-health-encyclopedia/national-health-insurance

53. Susanne A. Stoiber, "National Health Insurance," 2010, eNotes.com, http://www.enotes.com/public-health-encyclopedia/national-health-insurance

54. Frances Symes, "How Congress Set Its Own Pay," http://www.congress.org/news/2010/08/23/how_congress_sets_its_own_pay

55. Rev. B. F. Tefft, *The Speeches of Daniel Webster,* Chesterfield Society, London, New York, 1930.

56. The Capitalist Conservative Republican, "Is Welfare Unconstitutional?" 1999, http://gopcapitalist.tripod.com/constitution.html

57. The Constitution Online, Library of Congress, http://www.usconstitution.net/jeffwall.html

58. "The Great Deceit: Socialists as 'Social Scientists,'" TeachingAmericanHistory.org, http://teachingamericanhistory.org/library/index.asp?document=2324

59. "The New Deal," USHistory.com, http://www.u-s-history.com/pages/h1851.html

60. *The O'Reilly Factor*, "Where Does the ACLU Get Its Money?" Fox News, http://www.foxnews.com/story/0,2933,74843,00.html

61. The Social Security Act, http://www.u-s-history.com/pages/h1609.html

62. "The Truth about Marxism," http://www.youtube.com/watch?v=LMrFsdgrv1Y

63. Bill W. Tillery, Eldon D. Enger, Frederick C. Ross, *Integrated Science*, 2nd Edition, McGraw-Hill, New York, 2004.

64. *Time*, "Jimmy Carter vs. Inflation," http://www.time.com/time/magazine/article/0,9171,921854-2,00.html#ixzz12Bwb2LZK

65. *Time*, Storm over Cuba, http://www.time.com/time/magazine/article/0,9171,920639-9,00.html#ixzz125t2lvso , http://www.time.com/time/magazine/article/0,9171,920639-4,00.html#ixzz124Tq8QlU , http://www.time.com/time/magazine/article/0,9171,920639-1,00.html

66. Timothy Tregarthen, Libby Rittenberg, *Macroeconomics*, 2nd Edition, Worth Publishers, New York, 2000.

67. United States Senate, "Millard Fillmore, 12th Vice President (1849–1850)," http://www.senate.gov/artandhistory/history/common/generic/VP_Millard_Fillmore.htm

68. Veritas Foundation, "The Great Deceit, Social Pseudo-Sciences," *Christian American History*, Chapter 5, http://www.alexanderhamiltoninstitute.org/lp/Contact.htm

69. Virtual American Biographies, *Appletons Encyclopedia*, 2001, Virtualology, http://www.famousamericans.net/davidramsay/

70. Mortimer Adler, *We Hold These Truths,* New York, Ny: Macmillan, 1987, Reprints of the Federalist and Anti-Federalist Papers, Short Biographical Sketch, http://www.ditext.com/adler/adler.html

71. "White House Presidents," http://www.whitehouse.gov/about/presidents

72. *The O'Reilly Factor*, "Who Funds the ACLU," Fox News, http://www.tangle.com/view_video?viewkey=c22c3c8d938e bc8366de

73. Walter E. Williams, "Charity Not a Proper Function of the American Government," The Liberal Institute, http://www.liberalinstitute.com/CharityNotProperGovernmentFunction.html

74. Wikipedia, http://en.wikipedia.org/wiki/Ronald_Reagan

75. "Wilson Ensures Enactment of Federal Reserve Act," http://www.xtimeline.com/evt/view.aspx?id=73070

76. WorldWarI.com, Woodrow Wilson, http://www.worldwar1-history.com/Woodrow-Wilson-.aspx

77. "We, the People," The United States Capitol Historical Society, Washington, DC, 1976.

78. "Gay Lobby Admits," http://publicadvocateusa.org/news/article.php?article=7048 , Queerty, http://www.queerty.com/can-we-please-just-start-admitting-that-we-do-actually-want-to-indoctrinate-kids-20110512/ ; Public Advocate of the United States, Press Releases, http://publicadvocateusa.org/news/

79. Church of England, http://www.churchofengland.org/about-us/history.aspx

80. The Patriot Post, Mark Alexander, June 9, 2011, http://patriotpost.us/alexander/2011/06/09/obama-proclaims-june-gender-confusion-month/

81. Joseph Story, Supreme Court Justice, On Marriage, http://founderswisdom.wordpress.com/category/joseph-story/